The Bash Programmer's Guide: Writing Efficient Shell Scripts

Shoichi Eiko

Shoichi Eiko is a seasoned software engineer and a passionate advocate for open-source technologies, with over a decade of experience in system automation, DevOps, and Linux-based environments. Specializing in Bash scripting and shell programming, Shoichi has been crafting efficient, reliable, and scalable solutions for both startups and large enterprises.

Throughout his career, Shoichi has developed a deep understanding of the power of the command line and how shell scripting can streamline complex workflows. His expertise spans from optimizing scripts for high-performance computing to automating infrastructure management in cloud-native environments. As a frequent contributor to open-source projects, Shoichi is dedicated to sharing knowledge and fostering a community of programmers who can harness the full potential of Bash.

A firm believer in practical learning, Shoichi's approach to teaching focuses on real-world applications and hands-on examples. His goal is to empower programmers of all skill levels to write clean, efficient, and secure shell scripts. The Bash Programmer's Guide: Writing Efficient Shell Scripts reflects his years of experience and is designed to be an accessible resource for anyone looking to master Bash scripting.

When he's not scripting or contributing to open-source projects, Shoichi enjoys exploring cutting-edge technologies, contributing to Linux communities, and mentoring aspiring developers.

Welcome to **The Bash Programmer's Guide: Writing Efficient Shell Scripts**. Whether you are a beginner looking to dip your toes into shell scripting or an experienced programmer seeking to optimize your Bash skills, this book is designed to help you master the art of writing efficient, readable, and powerful shell scripts.

Bash is one of the most versatile and widely-used scripting languages in the world, powering everything from simple file management to complex system automation. Its efficiency and flexibility make it an essential tool for system administrators, DevOps engineers, software developers, and anyone who works in a Linux or Unix environment. Yet, despite its ubiquity, many overlook Bash's potential to automate tasks, streamline workflows, and save time.

This book takes a structured, hands-on approach, breaking down complex concepts into manageable chapters. You'll start with the basics and work your way through to advanced techniques that can be applied in real-world scenarios. Along the way, you'll learn best practices for writing scripts that are not only functional but also optimized for performance and maintainability.

Chapter 1: Introduction to Shell Scripting

We begin by laying the foundation. You'll learn what shell scripting is, why Bash is such a powerful tool, and how it differs from other scripting languages. This chapter also covers how to set up your Bash environment across various operating systems, so you're ready to script right away.

Chapter 2: Bash Basics: Getting Started

In this chapter, we introduce the essential Bash commands, syntax, and file system navigation. You'll explore how to work with files, directories, and understand input/output redirection. By the end of this chapter, you will be comfortable with the basic building blocks of Bash scripting.

Chapter 3: Writing Your First Script

Here, we'll walk you through writing your very first Bash script, starting from the shebang (#!/bin/bash) to running and debugging it. You'll learn about script permissions and best practices for making your scripts readable and maintainable.

Chapter 4: Conditional Statements and Loops

Learn how to introduce decision-making into your scripts using if statements, case constructs, and loops (for, while, and until). These control structures are essential for automating repetitive tasks and creating dynamic scripts that can adapt to different inputs.

Chapter 5: Functions: Modularizing Your Scripts

Functions are a powerful way to organize and reuse code. This chapter covers how to define and call functions, manage scope, and modularize your scripts for better readability and maintainability. You'll also learn best practices for writing clean, modular code.

Chapter 6: Command-line Arguments and User Input

Scripts often need to process user inputs or command-line arguments. This chapter shows you how to handle these inputs with positional parameters, getopts for parsing options, and reading user input interactively.

Chapter 7: Working with Strings and Text Processing

Master string manipulation and text processing in Bash. From simple string operations to advanced text filtering using powerful tools like grep, sed, and awk, this chapter teaches you how to efficiently handle and process data within your scripts.

Chapter 8: File Operations: Efficient File Handling

Managing files is one of Bash's core strengths. This chapter covers file reading, writing, and searching, as well as working with compressed files and managing file permissions. You'll learn how to automate common file operations to save time and avoid errors.

Chapter 9: Process Management in Bash

Understand how to manage system processes directly from your scripts. You'll learn how to run background jobs, monitor processes, use pipelines, and even terminate processes when necessary. This chapter equips you with tools for automating system-level tasks.

Chapter 10: Error Handling and Debugging

No script is complete without proper error handling. This chapter focuses on writing robust scripts that can handle errors gracefully and are easy to debug. You'll learn about exit codes, signals, and using tools like set -x and trap to track down issues in your scripts.

Chapter 11: Performance Optimization

Writing efficient scripts is crucial in larger or more resource-intensive environments. This chapter teaches you how to optimize loops, minimize memory usage, and parallelize tasks for faster execution. You'll also learn how to benchmark your scripts for performance improvements.

Chapter 12: Working with External Tools

Bash scripts often interact with other tools and services. Here, you'll learn how to integrate Bash with external commands like curl, wget, and APIs, as well as automate tasks using cron jobs. We'll also explore how Bash can interact with cloud services like AWS or GCP.

Chapter 13: Advanced Scripting Techniques

This chapter dives into more advanced topics, including arrays, subshells, and dynamic execution with eval. You'll also learn how to write more secure scripts by following best practices and using static analysis tools like shellcheck to improve script quality.

Chapter 14: Version Control for Shell Scripts

Using Git to version-control your scripts is a must for tracking changes and collaborating. In this chapter, you'll learn how to set up a Git repository for your scripts, manage versions, and automate script deployments using Git hooks.

Chapter 15: Case Studies and Real-world Examples

This chapter brings everything together through real-world examples and case studies. From automating backups to writing system monitoring scripts, you'll see how the techniques you've learned are applied in practical scenarios, complete with sample scripts.

Chapter 16: Appendix: Useful Bash Shortcuts and Resources

As a bonus, the appendix contains a handy collection of Bash one-liners, best practices, and a cheat sheet for quick reference. You'll also find recommended resources for further learning, including books, online courses, and community resources.

By the end of The Bash Programmer's Guide, you will have gained a deep understanding of Bash scripting, equipped with the tools and techniques needed to write efficient, reliable, and maintainable scripts. Whether you are automating routine tasks, managing systems, or developing applications, this book will serve as your go-to resource for all things Bash. Let's get started!

1. Introduction to Shell Scripting

In this chapter, we'll explore the fundamentals of shell scripting and its importance in the world of programming and system automation. You'll learn what a shell script is, why Bash is one of the most widely used shells, and how it compares to other shells like Zsh and Fish. We'll also cover how Bash scripts can simplify complex tasks, automate repetitive processes, and help you manage your system more efficiently. By the end of this chapter, you'll understand the key benefits of using Bash, and how to set up your environment to start scripting.

1.1 What is a Shell Script?

A shell script is a text file containing a sequence of commands that are executed by the Unix shell. Shells are command-line interpreters that provide a user interface for accessing the services of the operating system. Common shells include Bash (Bourne Again SHell), Zsh (Z Shell), and Ksh (Korn Shell), among others. Shell scripts automate tasks that would otherwise require manual input in the command line, enabling users to execute complex sequences of commands, manage system resources, and streamline repetitive processes. Understanding what shell scripts are and how they function is essential for anyone looking to harness the power of the command line.

The Basics of Shell Scripting

At its core, a shell script is a simple text file that contains commands typically executed in a command-line interface (CLI). These commands can include anything from simple file manipulation tasks to complex system administration commands. The ability to write and execute shell scripts transforms the way users interact with the operating system, allowing for automation and efficiency.

Structure of a Shell Script

A shell script generally starts with a shebang (#!) followed by the path to the interpreter. For instance, the line #!/bin/bash at the top of a script indicates that the script should be executed using the Bash shell. This line is crucial as it tells the system how to execute the script.

Here's a simple example of a shell script:

```
#!/bin/bash
echo "Hello, World!"
```

When executed, this script prints "Hello, World!" to the terminal. The simplicity of shell scripts makes them accessible, even for those with minimal programming experience.

Why Use Shell Scripts?

Shell scripts provide several advantages that make them a popular choice for automation and system management:

Automation of Repetitive Tasks: Shell scripts can automate tasks that would otherwise require manual effort. For instance, a script can be written to back up files, clean temporary directories, or process data. Automating these tasks saves time and reduces the likelihood of human error.

Efficiency and Speed: Running a shell script can be significantly faster than executing commands manually. A well-written script can perform complex sequences of tasks in seconds, which would take much longer if done by hand.

Batch Processing: Shell scripts can process multiple files or inputs in a single execution. For example, a script can be designed to convert all files in a directory from one format to another in one go, rather than converting each file individually.

Scheduling and Cron Jobs: Shell scripts can be scheduled to run at specific times using tools like cron, allowing for regular maintenance tasks without user intervention. For example, you could schedule a script to back up a database every night at midnight.

System Administration: Many system administration tasks are repetitive and can be tedious. Shell scripts can automate these tasks, such as user account creation, file management, and system updates, making system administration more efficient.

Portability: Shell scripts can often be executed on any Unix-like operating system without modification. This portability makes them an excellent choice for system administrators and developers working across different environments.

Key Components of Shell Scripts

Understanding the components of a shell script is crucial for writing effective scripts. Here are some key elements:

Variables: Variables are used to store data that can be reused throughout the script. In Bash, you can define a variable by using the following syntax:

variable_name=value

For example:

greeting="Hello, World!"
echo $greeting

This script defines a variable called greeting and then prints its value.

Control Structures: Shell scripts can include control structures such as conditional statements (if, else, case) and loops (for, while, until). These structures allow you to control the flow of the script based on specific conditions.

Example of an if statement:

```
if [ "$user" == "admin" ]; then
    echo "Welcome, Admin!"
else
    echo "Access denied."
fi
```

Functions: Functions allow you to encapsulate reusable code within your script. You can define a function once and call it multiple times, which promotes code reuse and improves readability.

Example of a function:

```
greet() {
    echo "Hello, $1!"
}

greet "Alice"
```

Comments: Adding comments to your script is essential for documentation. Comments in shell scripts are preceded by the # symbol and are ignored during execution. Comments help you and others understand the purpose of specific sections of code.

Example of a comment:

This is a comment explaining what the script does
echo "Executing my script"

Error Handling: Robust shell scripts include error handling to deal with potential issues gracefully. You can check the exit status of commands using $? to determine if a command was successful or failed, allowing you to take appropriate action.

Example of error handling:

cp file.txt backup.txt
if [$? -ne 0]; then
    echo "Error: File copy failed."
fi

Common Use Cases for Shell Scripts

Shell scripts are versatile and can be used in various scenarios. Some common use cases include:

File Management: Automating tasks like copying, moving, renaming, and deleting files.

System Monitoring: Writing scripts to check system performance, disk usage, or process activity, and sending alerts if thresholds are exceeded.

Backup and Recovery: Creating scripts to back up databases, application data, or entire file systems, and restoring them when needed.

Environment Setup: Automating the installation of software, libraries, and dependencies for development or production environments.

Deployment: Writing scripts to deploy applications, run migrations, or configure servers automatically.

Data Processing: Processing and analyzing large datasets using command-line tools within a script to generate reports or transform data formats.

Best Practices for Writing Shell Scripts

To write effective and maintainable shell scripts, consider the following best practices:

Use Meaningful Names: Name your scripts and variables descriptively to clarify their purpose. This helps others (and yourself) understand the code more easily.

Comment Generously: Use comments to explain complex logic and document the purpose of functions and variables. This improves readability and maintainability.

Test Thoroughly: Always test your scripts in a safe environment before deploying them in production. This helps catch errors and ensure functionality.

Handle Errors Gracefully: Implement error handling to manage failures and provide informative feedback to the user. This makes your scripts more robust.

Follow Consistent Formatting: Consistent indentation, spacing, and line breaks enhance readability and make it easier to follow the script's logic.

Use Version Control: Store your scripts in a version control system like Git to track changes, collaborate with others, and maintain a history of modifications.

In summary, shell scripts are powerful tools for automating tasks, managing systems, and enhancing productivity. They allow users to execute sequences of commands efficiently, transforming complex processes into simple, repeatable tasks. By understanding the fundamentals of shell scripting, including its components, use cases, and best practices, you can unlock the full potential of the command line and significantly improve your workflow. Whether you are a system administrator, developer, or data analyst, mastering shell scripting will empower you to work more efficiently and effectively in any Unix-like environment.

1.2 History of Bash

The Bourne Again SHell, commonly known as Bash, is one of the most widely used command-line shells in the Unix/Linux environment. Its development is rooted in the history of earlier Unix shells, particularly the original Bourne Shell (sh). Understanding the evolution of Bash provides insight into its design, features, and the reasons behind its popularity. This section outlines the history of Bash, tracing its origins, key developments, and its impact on the Unix/Linux ecosystem.

Early Beginnings: The Bourne Shell

The journey of Bash begins in the late 1970s with the creation of the original Bourne Shell, developed by Stephen Bourne at AT&T's Bell Labs. Released in 1979 as part of Version 7 Unix, the Bourne Shell (sh) provided a command-line interface for users to interact with the operating system. It introduced many fundamental features that are still in use today, such as:

- **Command-Line Editing**: Users could type commands directly into the shell prompt.
- **Scripting Capabilities**: The Bourne Shell supported scripting, allowing users to automate tasks through command sequences stored in text files.
- **Control Structures**: It provided basic control flow constructs like conditionals (if, case) and loops (for, while).

While the Bourne Shell was functional, it had limitations, particularly in user interface features and ease of use.

The Need for Improvement

As Unix systems evolved, so did the need for enhanced shells that could offer better usability and additional features. Various alternatives emerged, each aiming to improve upon the Bourne Shell. Notable among them were:

C Shell (csh): Developed by Bill Joy in the late 1970s, the C Shell introduced a C-like syntax, history features, and job control, making it more user-friendly compared to the Bourne Shell.

Korn Shell (ksh): Developed by David Korn in the early 1980s, ksh combined features of the Bourne Shell and C Shell, adding enhancements such as associative arrays and improved command-line editing.

Despite the advancements offered by these shells, there was still a need for a shell that combined the best features of these predecessors while remaining open source.

Birth of Bash

Bash was developed by Brian Fox in 1987 as a free and open-source shell for the GNU Project. The primary goals of Bash were to be compatible with the Bourne Shell while incorporating useful features from other shells like the C Shell and Korn Shell. Here are some key features introduced with Bash:

Command-Line Editing: Bash introduced interactive command-line editing using the GNU Readline library, allowing users to edit commands conveniently.

Enhanced Scripting Features: Bash expanded upon the scripting capabilities of the Bourne Shell, introducing features such as arrays, arithmetic evaluation, and improved input/output redirection.

Job Control: Bash implemented advanced job control, allowing users to manage multiple processes easily.

History Mechanism: Bash introduced a command history feature, enabling users to recall and reuse previous commands.

The first version of Bash, Bash 1.0, was released in 1989, and it quickly gained popularity among developers and system administrators due to its rich feature set and GNU licensing, which encouraged its use and distribution.

Continued Evolution

Bash continued to evolve through the years, with several significant versions released that introduced new features and improvements:

Bash 2.0 (1996): This version introduced many enhancements, including better support for arrays, new syntax for conditional expressions, and additional built-in commands.

Bash 3.0 (2004): Bash 3.0 brought significant performance improvements and new features such as associative arrays, the compopt command for programmable completion, and improvements in quoting and escaping.

Bash 4.0 (2009): This version introduced several new features, including support for anonymous arrays, enhanced pattern matching, and the printf command for formatted output. Bash 4.0 also added support for the new coproc command, allowing for easier interaction with subprocesses.

Bash 5.0 (2019): Bash 5.0 added new features, such as the ability to associate variable attributes with variables, improvements to the read command, and better control over shell options.

Bash in the Modern Era

Today, Bash is the default shell for many Linux distributions and is commonly used in macOS as well. Its widespread adoption can be attributed to several factors:

Standardization: Bash became the default shell for many Unix-like systems, contributing to its standardization. Many scripts written for Bash can be executed on different systems without modification.

Compatibility: Bash maintains compatibility with the Bourne Shell, ensuring that existing scripts can run without issues, making it easier for users to transition from older systems.

Extensive Documentation: A wealth of resources, documentation, and community support is available for Bash, enabling users to learn and troubleshoot effectively.

Active Development: Bash continues to be actively developed, with regular updates that introduce new features, enhancements, and bug fixes.

Impact on the Unix/Linux Ecosystem

The influence of Bash extends beyond just being a command-line shell. It has become an integral part of the Unix/Linux ecosystem, providing a foundation for:

System Administration: System administrators rely on Bash scripts to automate tasks such as backups, user management, and system monitoring.

DevOps and CI/CD: Bash is commonly used in DevOps practices and continuous integration/continuous deployment (CI/CD) pipelines for automating deployment processes and system configurations.

Education and Learning: Bash has become a standard teaching tool for understanding the command line, scripting, and operating systems. Its widespread use in educational settings has contributed to its ongoing popularity.

Bash's history is a testament to the evolution of shell scripting and the ongoing need for efficient, user-friendly command-line interfaces. From its origins in the Bourne Shell to its status as the de facto standard for many Unix-like systems, Bash has continuously adapted to meet the needs of users while maintaining compatibility with its predecessors. Its rich feature set, ease of use, and active community support ensure that Bash remains a vital tool for system administrators, developers, and users alike, solidifying its place in the annals of computing history. As technology continues to evolve, Bash is likely to remain an essential part of the Unix/Linux landscape for years to come.

1.3 Comparing Shells: Bash vs Zsh, Fish, etc.

Shells are critical components of the Unix/Linux ecosystem, serving as command-line interpreters that enable users to interact with the operating system. Among the various shells available, Bash (Bourne Again SHell) is perhaps the most widely used. However, alternatives like Zsh (Z Shell), Fish (Friendly Interactive SHell), and others offer unique features and improvements. This section provides a comprehensive comparison of these shells, examining their key features, strengths, weaknesses, and suitable use cases.

1. Bash (Bourne Again SHell)

Overview:

Bash is the default shell for many Linux distributions and macOS. It was developed as a free replacement for the Bourne Shell and incorporates features from other shells, such as C Shell and Korn Shell.

Key Features:

- **Scripting Compatibility**: Bash is highly compatible with existing Bourne Shell scripts, making it easy for users to transition from older systems.
- **Command-Line Editing**: Offers basic command-line editing with history features.
- **Job Control**: Allows users to manage multiple processes easily.
- **Extensive Documentation**: A wealth of resources and community support is available for Bash.

Strengths:

- **Portability**: Bash scripts can run on any Unix-like system without modification.
- **Stability**: Being the default shell for many systems, it is well-tested and stable.

- **Scripting Power**: Bash provides powerful scripting capabilities, making it suitable for automation and system administration tasks.

Weaknesses:

- **User-Friendliness**: While functional, the command-line experience can be less user-friendly compared to other modern shells.
- **Limited Features**: Lacks some advanced features found in newer shells like Zsh and Fish.

2. Zsh (Z Shell)

Overview:

Zsh is an extended version of the Bourne Shell with many enhancements. It is highly customizable and is favored by many developers for its advanced features.

Key Features:

- **Improved Command-Line Editing**: Zsh provides advanced command-line editing features and allows for custom keybindings.
- **Auto-Completion**: Offers intelligent tab completion that can provide suggestions based on context, making it easier to use.
- **Plugin Support**: Zsh supports plugins and themes, especially through frameworks like Oh My Zsh, enhancing user experience and productivity.
- **Globbing and Aliasing**: Improved file globbing and aliasing capabilities for better handling of command shortcuts.

Strengths:

- **Customization**: Highly customizable, allowing users to tailor the shell to their preferences.
- **Powerful Features**: Includes powerful features like shared history, better globbing, and enhanced script compatibility.
- **User-Friendly**: The intelligent completion and customization options make it more user-friendly.

Weaknesses:

- **Learning Curve**: New users may face a steeper learning curve due to its many features and customization options.
- **Performance**: Can be slower than Bash in some scenarios, particularly with many plugins loaded.

3. Fish (Friendly Interactive SHell)

Overview:

Fish is designed to be user-friendly and interactive, focusing on ease of use and accessibility without sacrificing power. It aims to offer an improved command-line experience for users of all levels.

Key Features:

- **Smart Auto-Completion**: Fish provides sophisticated auto-completion that suggests commands and options as you type.
- **Syntax Highlighting**: Commands are color-coded for clarity, making it easier to identify errors before executing commands.
- **Web-Based Configuration**: Fish offers a web-based configuration interface for customization.
- **No Configuration Files Required**: Unlike other shells, Fish works well out of the box without requiring extensive configuration.

Strengths:

- **User-Friendly**: Designed with the end-user in mind, making it very approachable for beginners.
- **Interactive Features**: The combination of syntax highlighting and smart completion enhances productivity and reduces errors.
- **Modern Design**: Uses modern conventions and provides a clean and intuitive interface.

Weaknesses:

- **Compatibility**: Fish is not fully compatible with Bash scripts, which may require rewriting scripts to work in Fish.
- **Less Popularity**: Fish is less widely adopted than Bash and Zsh, meaning there may be fewer resources and community support.

4. Ksh (Korn Shell)

Overview:

The Korn Shell is another powerful shell that incorporates features from both the Bourne Shell and C Shell. Developed by David Korn in the early 1980s, it is known for its scripting capabilities.

Key Features:

- **Performance**: Ksh is designed for high performance, particularly in scripting.
- **Array Support**: Provides support for arrays, allowing for more complex data handling.
- **Job Control**: Offers advanced job control features for managing processes.

Strengths:

- **Scripting Capabilities**: Strong scripting features make it suitable for complex automation tasks.
- **Compatibility**: Compatible with both Bourne and C Shell scripts, making it versatile for users.

Weaknesses:

- **Less User-Friendly**: The command-line interface may not be as intuitive as those of more modern shells.
- **Niche Use**: While powerful, it has a smaller user base compared to Bash and Zsh.

Choosing the right shell depends on your specific needs, preferences, and level of experience. Bash remains the most popular shell due to its stability, compatibility, and extensive documentation. Zsh offers advanced features and customization, making it ideal for users who want more control and flexibility. Fish excels in user-friendliness and modern design, making it a great choice for beginners who prioritize an interactive experience. Ksh is suited for users who require powerful scripting capabilities and performance.

Ultimately, understanding the strengths and weaknesses of these shells will help you make an informed decision about which one aligns best with your workflow and requirements, enhancing your productivity and command-line experience. Whether you're a seasoned developer, a system administrator, or a newcomer to the command line, the choice of shell can significantly impact your efficiency and effectiveness in using Unix/Linux systems.

1.4 Bash Use Cases: Why Shell Scripting Matters

Bash scripting is an essential skill in the realm of software development and system administration. It allows users to automate tasks, streamline workflows, and efficiently manage systems. This section explores the various use cases of Bash, illustrating its importance and the practical benefits it offers to developers, system administrators, and everyday users.

1. Automation of Routine Tasks

One of the primary reasons Bash scripting is valuable is its ability to automate repetitive tasks. For instance:

File Management: Users can create scripts to automate file backup, organization, and archiving. A simple Bash script can automate the process of moving files from one directory to another based on criteria such as date or file type, reducing the need for manual intervention.

Data Processing: Scripts can be written to process large datasets, automate data transformation, and generate reports. For example, parsing log files for specific patterns or generating summary statistics can be done with a few lines of Bash code.

Example: A script can automatically archive logs older than a certain number of days, freeing up space and keeping the directory organized.

2. System Administration

System administrators frequently rely on Bash scripting to manage and maintain systems efficiently. Use cases in this area include:

User Management: Scripts can automate user account creation, modification, and deletion, helping admins manage user permissions more effectively.

System Monitoring: Bash scripts can monitor system performance and resource usage, sending alerts when thresholds are exceeded. This allows administrators to proactively manage system health.

Example: A script can check disk usage daily and send an email alert if usage exceeds 90%, allowing for timely intervention.

3. Deployment and Configuration Management

In software development and DevOps, Bash scripting plays a crucial role in deployment and configuration management:

Continuous Integration/Continuous Deployment (CI/CD): Bash scripts are often used in CI/CD pipelines to automate testing, building, and deploying applications. They can execute build commands, run tests, and deploy artifacts to production environments.

Configuration Management: Tools like Ansible and Puppet often use Bash scripts to execute commands on remote servers, manage configurations, and ensure consistency across environments.

Example: A script can be triggered to deploy a new version of an application after passing unit tests, streamlining the deployment process.

4. Data Extraction and Reporting

Bash scripts excel at data extraction from various sources, enabling users to generate reports and insights:

Log Analysis: Administrators can write scripts to analyze logs, extract useful information, and generate reports. This can include tracking user activity, error rates, and performance metrics.

Web Scraping: While more complex than traditional scripting, Bash can be used in conjunction with tools like curl and grep to extract data from websites, making it possible to automate data collection tasks.

Example: A script can run nightly to extract relevant metrics from web server logs, aggregating data into a CSV file for further analysis.

5. Process Automation

Bash scripting allows for the automation of processes across various applications and tools:

Batch Processing: Scripts can automate batch jobs, such as processing a list of images or files. Users can create scripts that take a set of input files, process them, and output the results in a specified format.

Integration with Other Tools: Bash scripts can interface with other command-line tools, allowing users to combine functionalities for greater efficiency. This includes piping output from one command to another, creating complex workflows.

Example: A script can be written to resize a batch of images using ImageMagick, automating the process without the need for manual adjustments.

6. Backup and Recovery

Automating backup processes is another vital use case for Bash scripting:

Scheduled Backups: Users can create scripts that automate the backup of important files and directories at regular intervals, ensuring data is preserved without manual effort.

Disaster Recovery: Scripts can facilitate the restoration of systems and data in the event of a failure, allowing for quick recovery and minimizing downtime.

Example: A script can be scheduled to run daily, compressing and archiving important directories, and transferring them to a remote server for safekeeping.

7. Development Environment Setup

For developers, setting up development environments can be time-consuming. Bash scripts can streamline this process:

Environment Configuration: Scripts can automate the installation of dependencies, configuration of tools, and setup of development environments, reducing setup time.

Project Initialization: Scripts can scaffold new projects, creating necessary directories, files, and configuration settings according to best practices.

Example: A script can initialize a new project by creating a directory structure, setting up version control, and installing required packages.

8. Educational and Training Purposes

Bash scripting is not just practical; it is also an excellent educational tool:

Learning Programming Concepts: For beginners, writing Bash scripts introduces essential programming concepts such as loops, conditionals, and functions in a straightforward environment.

System Interaction: Students can learn how to interact with the operating system, understand file systems, and grasp the importance of command-line tools.

Example: Educational institutions often use Bash scripting in their curricula to teach students about programming logic and operating system concepts.

Bash scripting is a powerful tool that plays a crucial role in automating tasks, managing systems, and enhancing productivity in various fields. Its versatility allows users to handle everything from simple file management to complex deployment processes. Understanding and utilizing Bash scripting not only improves efficiency but also empowers users to take control of their environments, making it an invaluable skill for developers, system administrators, and tech enthusiasts alike.

Whether you're automating routine tasks, managing system resources, or facilitating software deployment, mastering Bash scripting will significantly enhance your capabilities and open doors to new efficiencies in your workflow. The importance of shell scripting cannot be overstated, as it serves as the backbone of many automation processes in today's technology-driven world.

1.5 Preparing Your Environment: Bash on Linux, macOS, and Windows

Bash (Bourne Again SHell) is a powerful command-line interface widely used in Unix-like operating systems, including Linux and macOS. While Bash is readily available on these systems, Windows users may require additional steps to access it. This section will guide you through setting up a Bash environment on Linux, macOS, and Windows, ensuring you can take full advantage of Bash scripting regardless of your operating system.

1. Bash on Linux

Most Linux distributions come with Bash pre-installed as the default shell. Here's how to verify and prepare your Bash environment on a Linux system:

Step 1: Check for Bash Installation

To check if Bash is installed and which version you have, open a terminal and run:

bash --version

If Bash is installed, this command will display the version information.

Step 2: Update Your Package Manager

While most systems come with Bash installed, it's essential to keep your package manager and Bash updated. You can use the following commands depending on your distribution:

For Ubuntu/Debian-based systems:

sudo apt update
sudo apt upgrade

For Red Hat/CentOS-based systems:

sudo yum update

For Fedora:

sudo dnf update

Step 3: Configuring Your Bash Environment

You can customize your Bash environment by editing the ~/.bashrc file. This file is executed every time you open a new terminal session. Common customizations include:

Setting Environment Variables: You can set variables that define the behavior of your shell. For example:

export PATH="$PATH:/path/to/your/directory"

Custom Aliases: Create shortcuts for commonly used commands. For example:

alias ll='ls -la'

Prompt Customization: Customize your shell prompt by modifying the PS1 variable:

export PS1='\u@\h:\w\$ '

After making changes to ~/.bashrc, run source ~/.bashrc to apply them.

2. Bash on macOS

Bash is also pre-installed on macOS, but the version may not be the latest due to licensing changes. You can set up Bash on macOS as follows:

Step 1: Verify Bash Installation

Open the Terminal application and run:

bash --version

Step 2: Install Homebrew (Optional)

Homebrew is a package manager for macOS that makes it easy to install software. If you want the latest version of Bash, you can install it via Homebrew. First, install Homebrew if you haven't already:

/bin/bash -c "$(curl -fsSL https://raw.githubusercontent.com/Homebrew/install/HEAD/install.sh)"

Step 3: Install the Latest Bash

Once Homebrew is installed, you can install the latest version of Bash:

brew install bash

Step 4: Change Default Shell (Optional)

If you want to use the newly installed Bash as your default shell, you can change it by adding it to the list of allowed shells and then changing the default shell:

Add the new Bash to the list of allowed shells:

echo "/usr/local/bin/bash" | sudo tee -a /etc/shells

Change your default shell:

chsh -s /usr/local/bin/bash

Step 5: Configuring Your Bash Environment

Similar to Linux, you can customize your Bash environment in ~/.bash_profile or ~/.bashrc. You can add the same configurations mentioned earlier.

3. Bash on Windows

Windows does not come with Bash pre-installed, but you can access it through several methods, including Windows Subsystem for Linux (WSL), Git Bash, or Cygwin. Each method provides a different level of integration with Windows.

Option 1: Windows Subsystem for Linux (WSL)

WSL allows you to run a Linux distribution alongside your Windows environment, providing access to Bash. Here's how to set it up:

Step 1: Enable WSL

Open PowerShell as Administrator and run:

wsl --install

Restart your computer when prompted.

Step 2: Install a Linux Distribution

After enabling WSL, you can install a Linux distribution from the Microsoft Store. Popular options include Ubuntu, Debian, and Kali Linux.

Step 3: Accessing Bash

After installation, open the installed distribution from the Start menu to access Bash.

Option 2: Git Bash

Git Bash is a lightweight application that provides a Bash emulation environment on Windows. It is primarily used for Git version control but also provides a Bash command line.

Step 1: Download and Install Git

Visit the Git for Windows website.

Download the installer and follow the installation prompts. During installation, select "Use Git from the Windows Command Prompt" and check "Git Bash Here" options.

Step 2: Open Git Bash

Once installed, you can open Git Bash from the Start menu or by right-clicking in any folder and selecting "Git Bash Here."

Option 3: Cygwin

Cygwin provides a large collection of GNU and Open Source tools that provide functionality similar to a Linux distribution on Windows.

Step 1: Download Cygwin

Visit the Cygwin website.

Download the setup executable.

Step 2: Install Cygwin

Run the installer and select the packages you want, including Bash and any other tools you may need.

Step 3: Open Cygwin Terminal

After installation, you can open the Cygwin terminal to access Bash.

Setting up Bash in your environment is a straightforward process, whether you're using Linux, macOS, or Windows. By preparing your Bash environment correctly, you can take full advantage of its powerful features for scripting and automation.

Linux and macOS provide native support for Bash, making installation and configuration simple. Windows users have multiple options, including WSL, Git Bash, and Cygwin, allowing for a seamless Bash experience. Whichever method you choose, ensuring your Bash environment is properly configured will enhance your productivity and set the stage for effective shell scripting.

With Bash up and running, you can dive into scripting, automate tasks, and improve your command-line proficiency, paving the way for more efficient workflows and greater mastery of your system.

2. Bash Basics: Getting Started

In this chapter, you'll dive into the core concepts of Bash and the command line. You'll learn how to navigate the file system using essential commands like cd, ls, and pwd, and work with files and directories using cp, mv, and rm. We'll also introduce key concepts like input/output redirection and piping, which allow you to combine commands and manage data flow efficiently. By mastering these foundational commands and syntax, you'll gain the skills needed to start writing basic Bash scripts and managing your system with confidence.

2.1 Navigating the File System: cd, ls, pwd

Navigating the file system is a fundamental skill for any user working with Bash. The ability to move through directories, list files, and determine your current location in the file system is essential for efficient command-line usage. This chapter introduces three key commands: cd, ls, and pwd, which are indispensable for file system navigation in Bash.

1. The cd Command

The cd (change directory) command is used to navigate between directories in the file system. Understanding how to use cd effectively is crucial for accessing files and executing scripts located in different directories.

Basic Usage:

Changing to a Specific Directory: To change to a specific directory, use the following syntax:

cd /path/to/directory

For example, to change to the Documents directory in your home folder:

cd ~/Documents

The ~ symbol represents your home directory, making it a convenient shorthand.

Moving Up the Directory Tree: To move up one level in the directory hierarchy, use:

cd ..

This command takes you to the parent directory of your current location. To move up multiple levels, you can chain ..:

cd ../../

Changing to the Home Directory: Simply typing cd without any arguments will take you back to your home directory:

cd

Using Relative Paths: You can also navigate using relative paths. For instance, if you are in the Documents folder and want to access a subfolder named Projects, you can use:

cd Projects

2. The ls Command

The ls (list) command is used to display the contents of a directory. It provides a quick way to see which files and subdirectories are present in the current directory.

Basic Usage:

Listing Files and Directories: Simply type ls to list the files and directories in your current location:

ls

Detailed Listing: To see more information about each file, such as permissions, owner, size, and modification date, use the -l (long) option:

ls -l

This command will display a detailed list, including:

Permissions (e.g., drwxr-xr-x)

Number of links

Owner and group

File size

Last modification date

File or directory name

Including Hidden Files: Files and directories that start with a dot (.) are hidden by default. To include hidden files in the listing, use the -a option:

ls -a

Combining Options: You can combine options to customize the output further. For example, to list all files (including hidden ones) in a detailed format, use:

ls -la

3. The pwd Command

The pwd (print working directory) command displays the current working directory. This is especially useful when navigating complex directory structures, as it helps you keep track of your location.

Basic Usage:

To see your current directory, simply type:

pwd

The output will be the full path of your current working directory, for example:

/home/username/Documents

4. Combining Commands for Navigation

Using these commands in conjunction can enhance your navigation efficiency. For example, you can use pwd to check your current location, then cd to move to a new directory, and finally ls to see its contents. Here's an example workflow:

Check your current directory:

pwd

Change to the Downloads directory:

cd ~/Downloads

List the contents of the Downloads directory:

ls

Navigating the file system with Bash is an essential skill for users and administrators alike. Mastering the cd, ls, and pwd commands will enhance your ability to interact with files and directories efficiently. As you progress in your Bash scripting journey, these commands will serve as the foundation for more advanced file and directory management tasks.

With a firm grasp of these fundamental commands, you can confidently explore your file system, locate necessary files, and navigate complex directory structures, making your command-line experience more productive and enjoyable.

2.2 Basic File Operations: cp, mv, rm, touch

In Bash, performing basic file operations is essential for managing files and directories effectively. This section introduces four fundamental commands: cp, mv, rm, and touch. Each command serves a specific purpose, allowing users to copy, move, delete, and create files easily. Understanding these commands is crucial for efficient file management in any Bash environment.

1. The cp Command: Copying Files and Directories

The cp (copy) command is used to create copies of files and directories. It allows you to duplicate files, enabling you to keep backups or make modifications without affecting the original.

Basic Usage:

Copying a File: The simplest use of the cp command is to copy a single file. The syntax is as follows:

cp source_file destination_file

For example, to copy a file named report.txt to a new file called report_backup.txt, you would use:

cp report.txt report_backup.txt

Copying to a Different Directory: You can also copy a file to a different directory. For example, to copy report.txt to the Documents directory:

cp report.txt ~/Documents/

Copying Multiple Files: To copy multiple files into a directory, specify the files followed by the destination directory:

cp file1.txt file2.txt ~/Documents/

Copying Directories: To copy an entire directory and its contents, use the -r (recursive) option:

cp -r source_directory destination_directory

This command copies the source directory and all its subdirectories and files.

2. The mv Command: Moving and Renaming Files

The mv (move) command is used to move files and directories from one location to another. Additionally, it can rename files or directories.

Basic Usage:

Moving a File: To move a file from one location to another, use the following syntax:

mv source_file destination_directory/

For example, to move report.txt to the Documents directory, you would execute:

mv report.txt ~/Documents/

Renaming a File: You can also rename a file using the mv command. For example, to rename report.txt to summary.txt, use:

mv report.txt summary.txt

Moving Multiple Files: To move multiple files into a directory, specify the files followed by the destination directory:

mv file1.txt file2.txt ~/Documents/

3. The rm Command: Removing Files and Directories

The rm (remove) command is used to delete files and directories. It is a powerful command that should be used with caution, as it permanently removes files without sending them to a trash or recycle bin.

Basic Usage:

Removing a File: To remove a single file, use:

rm file_to_remove.txt

For example, to delete report.txt, you would execute:

rm report.txt

Removing Multiple Files: To delete multiple files, specify the files you want to remove:

rm file1.txt file2.txt

Removing Directories: To remove an empty directory, use the rmdir command:

rmdir empty_directory

To remove a directory and its contents (including subdirectories and files), use the -r (recursive) option with rm:

rm -r directory_to_remove/

Warning: Be very cautious when using rm -r as it will delete everything in the specified directory without confirmation.

4. The touch Command: Creating and Updating Files

The touch command is primarily used to create empty files or update the timestamps of existing files. This command is useful for quickly creating files without needing to open a text editor.

Basic Usage:

Creating a New File: To create a new, empty file, simply type:

touch newfile.txt

If newfile.txt does not already exist, it will be created. If it does exist, the command will update its access and modification timestamps to the current time.

Creating Multiple Files: You can create multiple empty files in one command:

touch file1.txt file2.txt file3.txt

Understanding how to perform basic file operations with cp, mv, rm, and touch is essential for efficient file management in Bash. These commands provide the necessary tools for copying, moving, renaming, deleting, and creating files and directories.

As you become more familiar with these commands, you'll find that they significantly enhance your productivity when working in the command line environment. Being adept at file operations enables you to manage your files and directories effectively, paving the way for more complex tasks and scripting in the future.

With this knowledge, you're well-equipped to handle everyday file management tasks in Bash, making your command-line experience smoother and more efficient.

2.3 Understanding Input/Output: Redirection and Piping

In Bash, understanding how to manage input and output is crucial for effective command-line usage and scripting. This section explores two essential concepts: redirection and piping. These features allow you to control where your data comes from and where it goes, enabling more complex and powerful command-line operations.

1. Redirection

Redirection is the process of changing the default input and output sources for commands in Bash. By default, commands read from standard input (stdin) and write to standard output (stdout). Redirection allows you to redirect these streams to files or other commands.

Basic Redirection Operations:

Standard Output Redirection: To redirect the output of a command to a file, you use the > operator. For example, to write the output of the ls command to a file named file_list.txt, you would execute:

ls > file_list.txt

This command creates file_list.txt (or overwrites it if it already exists) and writes the output of the ls command into it.

Appending Output: If you want to append the output to a file instead of overwriting it, use the >> operator:

echo "New file entry" >> file_list.txt

This command adds the text "New file entry" to the end of file_list.txt without deleting its existing content.

Standard Error Redirection: By default, error messages are sent to standard error (stderr). To redirect error messages to a file, you use 2>. For example:

ls nonexistentfile 2> error_log.txt

This command tries to list a nonexistent file and redirects the error message to error_log.txt.

Redirecting Both Standard Output and Error: You can redirect both stdout and stderr to the same file using:

command > output.txt 2>&1

This command combines both output streams and directs them to output.txt.

Using Input Redirection: Input redirection allows you to take input from a file instead of the keyboard. The < operator is used for this purpose. For example:

sort < unsorted_list.txt

This command takes input from unsorted_list.txt and sorts the contents.

2. Piping

Piping is a powerful feature that allows you to use the output of one command as the input to another command. This enables you to chain commands together, creating complex command sequences that can perform multiple operations in one line.

Basic Usage of Pipes:

Using the Pipe Operator (|): To pipe the output of one command into another, use the | operator. For example, to list files in a directory and then count how many files there are, you can combine ls and wc (word count) like this:

ls | wc -l

This command lists the files in the current directory and pipes the output to wc -l, which counts the number of lines, effectively giving you the number of files.

Combining Multiple Commands: You can combine several commands using pipes. For example, to find the number of .txt files in a directory, sort them, and then display the result:

*ls *.txt | sort | wc -l*

Here, ls *.txt lists all .txt files, sort organizes them alphabetically, and wc -l counts the total number of .txt files.

3. Practical Examples of Redirection and Piping

Redirecting Command Output to a File:

echo "Hello, World!" > greeting.txt

This command creates a file called greeting.txt containing the text "Hello, World!".

Appending Data:

date >> greeting.txt

This appends the current date and time to the end of greeting.txt.

Filtering Output with Pipes:

To filter processes running on your system that include the word "bash":

ps aux | grep bash

In this command, ps aux lists all running processes, and grep bash filters that list to show only processes that contain "bash".

4. Combining Redirection and Piping

You can also combine redirection and piping to enhance data manipulation. For example, if you want to save the output of a command that includes error messages to a file:

find /path/to/directory -name ".txt" 2> error_log.txt | sort > sorted_files.txt*

In this command, find searches for .txt files and directs any error messages to error_log.txt, while the sorted list of found files is saved to sorted_files.txt.

Mastering input/output redirection and piping in Bash is essential for effective command-line usage. Redirection allows you to control where your output goes and where your input comes from, while piping enables you to chain commands together to create powerful command sequences.

By using these features, you can efficiently manage data, filter results, and perform complex operations with minimal effort. As you become more comfortable with redirection and piping, you will find that your productivity and ability to handle data in Bash will significantly increase, making it a powerful tool in your command-line toolkit.

2.4 Basic Shell Syntax: Variables, Command Substitution

Understanding the basic shell syntax in Bash is crucial for writing effective scripts and executing commands. This section covers two essential components of Bash syntax: variables and command substitution. Mastering these concepts will enhance your ability to manipulate data and automate tasks efficiently.

1. Variables in Bash

Variables are a fundamental aspect of any programming or scripting language, including Bash. They allow you to store data that can be used and manipulated throughout your script. Bash variables can hold various types of data, including strings, integers, and file paths.

Creating and Using Variables:

Defining Variables: To create a variable in Bash, you simply assign a value to a name without any spaces around the equal sign (=). For example:

my_variable="Hello, World!"

In this case, my_variable holds the string "Hello, World!".

Accessing Variable Values: To use the value of a variable, prefix its name with a dollar sign ($). For instance:

echo $my_variable

This command prints the value of my_variable, which would output:

Hello, World!

Variable Naming Conventions: Bash variable names must start with a letter or an underscore, followed by letters, numbers, or underscores. They are case-sensitive, meaning myVariable and myvariable are treated as different variables.

Exporting Variables: To make a variable available to child processes (such as scripts executed from the current script), use the export command:

export my_variable

This command ensures that my_variable can be accessed by any subprocess or script invoked after the export.

Read-only Variables: If you want to create a variable that cannot be modified later in the script, you can declare it as read-only using the readonly keyword:

readonly pi=3.14159

Attempting to change pi later in the script will result in an error.

2. Command Substitution

Command substitution is a powerful feature that allows you to execute a command and use its output as part of another command. This functionality enables dynamic script execution, where commands can be nested and their results utilized immediately.

Using Command Substitution:

Syntax for Command Substitution: There are two ways to perform command substitution:

Using backticks (`):

current_date=`date`

Using the $(...) syntax, which is generally preferred for readability and allows for nested commands:

current_date=$(date)

Both methods assign the current date and time to the variable current_date.

Using Command Substitution in Commands: You can directly use command substitution within commands. For example, to list the files in the current directory and store the output in a variable:

files=$(ls)
echo "Files in the directory: $files"

Example of Using Command Substitution: Suppose you want to create a backup of a directory and include the current date in the backup filename. You can do this using command substitution:

backup_file="backup_$(date +%Y%m%d).tar.gz"
tar -czf $backup_file /path/to/directory

In this example, $(date +%Y%m%d) generates the current date in the format YYYYMMDD, which is then used to create a uniquely named backup file.

Mastering variables and command substitution in Bash is crucial for effective scripting and command-line usage. Variables allow you to store and manipulate data dynamically, while command substitution provides a way to execute commands and use their output in other commands.

As you continue to develop your skills in Bash, you'll find that these concepts enable you to create more complex scripts, automate repetitive tasks, and manage data efficiently. With a solid understanding of basic shell syntax, you're well on your way to becoming proficient in Bash programming, paving the way for more advanced scripting techniques in the future.

2.5 Introduction to Aliases and Shell Customization

Customizing your shell environment can significantly enhance your productivity and streamline your workflow. Two important aspects of this customization in Bash are aliases and various shell settings. This section introduces you to the concept of aliases and provides an overview of shell customization techniques that can improve your command-line experience.

1. Understanding Aliases

Aliases are shortcuts or abbreviations for longer commands. They allow you to create simplified versions of commands that you use frequently, helping to reduce typing and minimize the chance of errors. This feature is particularly useful for commands that require complex arguments or that you execute regularly.

Creating and Using Aliases:

Defining an Alias: You can create an alias using the alias command. The syntax is as follows:

alias name='command'

For example, to create an alias called ll for ls -l, you would use:

alias ll='ls -l'

Now, whenever you type ll in the terminal, it will execute ls -l, displaying a detailed list of files and directories.

Viewing Existing Aliases: To see all currently defined aliases, simply type:

alias

Removing an Alias: If you no longer need an alias, you can remove it using the unalias command:

unalias ll

Making Aliases Persistent: By default, aliases are available only for the duration of the current session. To make them permanent, you can add your alias definitions to your shell's configuration file, typically ~/.bashrc or ~/.bash_profile. For example:

echo "alias ll='ls -l'" >> ~/.bashrc

After adding this line, you will need to either restart your terminal or run source ~/.bashrc for the changes to take effect.

2. Shell Customization Techniques

In addition to using aliases, you can customize your Bash environment in several other ways to improve usability and enhance your workflow.

Common Customization Options:

Prompt Customization: The Bash prompt can be customized to display useful information, such as the current working directory or the username. The prompt variable is PS1, which you can set in your .bashrc file. For example:

export PS1="\u@\h:\w$ "

This sets the prompt to show the username (\u), hostname (\h), and current working directory (\w).

Environment Variables: Environment variables can be customized to change the behavior of various commands and programs. For example, setting the EDITOR variable to specify your preferred text editor:

export EDITOR=nano

Shell Options: You can modify shell behavior using the shopt command to enable or disable specific options. For example, to enable "ignore both case" when using tab completion, you can add:

shopt -s nocaseglob

Custom Functions: In addition to aliases, you can create custom functions in your .bashrc file. Functions are more powerful than aliases, allowing you to execute multiple commands or accept arguments. For example:

function greet() {
*   echo "Hello, $1!"*
}

You can call this function with:

greet Alice

This would output:

Hello, Alice!

Aliases and shell customization are powerful features that can significantly enhance your Bash experience. By defining aliases, you can streamline repetitive tasks and make your command-line workflow more efficient. Additionally, customizing your prompt, environment variables, and shell options allows you to tailor the shell to your specific needs, improving usability and productivity.

As you explore these customization options, you'll discover that creating a personalized Bash environment not only makes your work easier but also fosters a deeper understanding of how the shell operates. With these tools at your disposal, you can develop a command-line environment that suits your preferences and enhances your overall productivity in Bash scripting and system administration.

3. Writing Your First Script

In this chapter, you'll take the exciting step of writing your very first Bash script. We'll walk through the process of creating a script file, adding the shebang (#!/bin/bash), and setting executable permissions. You'll learn how to run your script and debug any errors along the way. We'll also cover essential scripting practices like using comments to make your code readable and structuring your script for clarity. By the end of this chapter, you'll have created simple, functional Bash scripts and gained the foundational skills to build more complex ones.

3.1 Creating a Bash Script: From Text File to Executable

Creating a Bash script is a fundamental skill for automating tasks and managing systems effectively. A Bash script is essentially a text file containing a series of commands that the Bash shell can execute. This section will guide you through the steps to create a simple Bash script, from writing the script in a text file to making it executable.

1. Understanding the Basics of Bash Scripts

A Bash script is a plain text file that contains a sequence of commands that can be executed by the Bash shell. The primary purpose of a Bash script is to automate repetitive tasks, simplify command sequences, and enhance productivity.

File Extension: While it is not mandatory to use a specific file extension for Bash scripts, it is a common practice to use the .sh extension. This helps users identify the file as a shell script easily.

2. Writing Your First Bash Script

To create a Bash script, you can use any text editor of your choice, such as nano, vi, or gedit. Here's a step-by-step guide to writing a basic Bash script:

Step 1: Open Your Text Editor

Open a terminal and use your preferred text editor to create a new file. For example, to create a script called hello_world.sh using nano, you would type:

nano hello_world.sh

Step 2: Add the Shebang

At the very top of your script, include the shebang line (#!/bin/bash). This line tells the system that the script should be run using the Bash shell:

#!/bin/bash

Step 3: Write Your Commands

Below the shebang, write the commands you want the script to execute. For example, a simple script that prints "Hello, World!" might look like this:

#!/bin/bash

echo "Hello, World!"

Step 4: Save and Exit

If you are using nano, press CTRL + X, then Y to confirm saving, and Enter to exit. If you are using vi, press Esc, type :wq, and then hit Enter.

3. Making the Script Executable

Once your script is written and saved, you need to make it executable so that you can run it. This is done using the chmod command:

chmod +x hello_world.sh

This command changes the file permissions to make it executable for the user.

4. Running the Bash Script

Now that your script is executable, you can run it from the terminal. There are two primary ways to execute the script:

Using the Relative Path: If you are in the same directory as the script, you can execute it with:

./hello_world.sh

Using the Absolute Path: If you are in a different directory, specify the full path to the script:

/path/to/your/script/hello_world.sh

When you run the script, it should output:

Hello, World!

5. Additional Considerations for Bash Scripts

Comments: You can add comments in your script using the # symbol. Comments are ignored by the Bash interpreter and are useful for documenting your code:

This is a comment
echo "Hello, World!" # This prints a greeting

Script Parameters: You can pass arguments to your Bash script, allowing for more flexible and dynamic behavior. For example, you could modify your script to greet a user by name:

#!/bin/bash

echo "Hello, $1!"

When running this script, you can provide a name as an argument:

./hello_world.sh Alice

This would output:

Hello, Alice!

Exit Status: Every command in Bash returns an exit status. The exit status of the last executed command can be accessed using $?. A status of 0 typically indicates success, while any non-zero value indicates an error.

Creating a Bash script is a straightforward process that can significantly enhance your ability to automate tasks and manage systems. By following the steps outlined above, you can write simple scripts that execute commands, take input parameters, and include helpful comments for documentation.

As you become more comfortable with Bash scripting, you can explore more advanced features, such as loops, conditional statements, and functions, to create complex scripts that meet your specific needs. With practice, Bash scripting can become an invaluable tool in your software development and system administration toolkit.

3.2 Adding the Shebang (#!/bin/bash)

The shebang (#!) is a crucial component of Bash scripts that specifies the interpreter to be used when executing the script. This section will explain the importance of the shebang, how to use it effectively, and its role in the execution of Bash scripts.

1. What is a Shebang?

The shebang is a character sequence that appears at the very beginning of a script file, indicated by the characters #!. This sequence is followed by the path to the interpreter that should execute the script. In the case of Bash scripts, the shebang is typically written as:

#!/bin/bash

The line indicates that the script should be run using the Bash shell located at /bin/bash.

2. Why is the Shebang Important?

The shebang serves several critical purposes:

Interpreter Specification: The shebang specifies which interpreter should execute the script. This is particularly important in environments where multiple interpreters may be available (e.g., Python, Ruby, Perl). Without the shebang, the operating system may not know how to execute the script.

Portability: By explicitly stating the interpreter in the script, you make it portable across different systems. Regardless of the user's default shell, the specified interpreter will execute the script correctly.

Ease of Use: The shebang allows users to run scripts directly from the command line without needing to explicitly call the interpreter. This means you can execute the script as a command rather than typing bash script.sh.

3. How to Add the Shebang to Your Script

Adding the shebang to your Bash script is simple. Here are the steps to follow:

Step 1: Open Your Script in a Text Editor

If you have an existing Bash script (for example, example_script.sh), open it in a text editor:

nano example_script.sh

Step 2: Add the Shebang Line

At the very top of your script, add the shebang line:

#!/bin/bash

The beginning of your script should look like this:

#!/bin/bash

echo "This is my first Bash script!"

Step 3: Save and Exit

After adding the shebang, save your changes and exit the text editor. In nano, this would involve pressing CTRL + X, then Y, and Enter.

4. Running a Script with Shebang

After adding the shebang, you can run the script directly from the terminal without needing to specify the Bash interpreter:

./example_script.sh

If the shebang is correctly specified and the script is executable, this command will execute the script, displaying the output.

5. Alternative Shebangs

While #!/bin/bash is the most common shebang for Bash scripts, there are other variations you might encounter, depending on the environment and the shell you want to use:

Bash in Different Locations: On some systems, the Bash interpreter might be located in a different directory, such as /usr/bin/bash. In such cases, you would use:

#!/usr/bin/bash

Using env for Portability: To enhance portability, you can use the env command to find the interpreter in the user's PATH. This is particularly useful when you're unsure of where Bash is installed:

#!/usr/bin/env bash

This approach allows the script to locate and use the Bash interpreter regardless of its location on the system.

6. Common Mistakes to Avoid

Missing Shebang: Forgetting to include the shebang can lead to confusion when trying to execute the script. If you run a script without a shebang, it may fail or run in the current shell, which might not be what you intended.

Incorrect Path: Ensure the path to the Bash interpreter is correct. Running which bash in the terminal can help you verify the location of the Bash interpreter on your system.

Omitting Execution Permissions: After adding the shebang, remember to make your script executable using the chmod command:

chmod +x example_script.sh

The shebang (#!/bin/bash) is an essential feature in Bash scripting that dictates how the script is executed. By including the shebang, you ensure that the script runs with the intended interpreter, enhancing portability and usability.

Whether you are creating simple scripts or more complex automation tools, properly utilizing the shebang will help streamline your workflow and ensure your scripts run smoothly across different environments. As you continue to explore Bash scripting, understanding the shebang and its implications will be a key factor in developing robust and efficient scripts.

3.3 Running Scripts: chmod +x, Direct Execution

Once you've created a Bash script, the next step is to run it. This involves making the script executable and then executing it in the terminal. This section will cover the process of setting execution permissions using the chmod +x command and the various methods to directly execute your script.

1. Making a Script Executable with chmod +x

Before you can run a Bash script, you need to ensure it has the appropriate permissions. By default, new files are not executable. To change this, you use the chmod command with the +x option, which grants execute permission.

How to Use chmod +x:

Open Your Terminal: Navigate to the directory where your script is located.

Use the chmod Command: Run the following command, replacing script_name.sh with the name of your script:

chmod +x script_name.sh

For example, to make a script called hello_world.sh executable, you would use:

chmod +x hello_world.sh

Verify Permissions: You can check if the script is executable by using the ls -l command, which lists file permissions. Look for an x in the permission string:

ls -l hello_world.sh

The output will look something like this:

-rwxr-xr-x 1 user user 123 Oct 16 12:00 hello_world.sh

The rwx indicates that the user has read, write, and execute permissions.

2. Running the Script Directly

After making your script executable, you can run it directly from the terminal. There are two primary methods for executing a Bash script: using a relative path and an absolute path.

Method 1: Using Relative Path

If you are currently in the directory where the script is located, you can execute it using the ./ prefix, which signifies the current directory:

./hello_world.sh

This command runs the script named hello_world.sh located in the current directory.

Method 2: Using Absolute Path

If your script is located in a different directory, you can run it by specifying the full path. For example, if your script is in /home/user/scripts, you would execute it like this:

/home/user/scripts/hello_world.sh

3. Running Scripts with bash Command

You can also execute a Bash script without making it executable by using the bash command followed by the script name. This method does not require you to change the file permissions:

bash hello_world.sh

This command explicitly tells the Bash shell to execute the script, regardless of whether it has execute permissions.

4. Handling Script Output

When you run a Bash script, any output generated by the commands within the script will be displayed in the terminal. For example, if your hello_world.sh script contains the line:

echo "Hello, World!"

When you execute the script, you will see the following output:

Hello, World!

5. Common Errors and Troubleshooting

Permission Denied Error: If you try to run a script and receive a "Permission denied" error, it indicates that the script does not have execute permissions. To resolve this, ensure you use chmod +x on your script.

Command Not Found Error: If you receive a "command not found" error when trying to run your script, make sure you are using the correct path and that the script exists in that location.

Incorrect Shebang: If your script is not running as expected, verify that you have included the correct shebang line at the top of your script (e.g., #!/bin/bash). An incorrect shebang can cause the script to run with the wrong interpreter.

Running Bash scripts is a straightforward process once you understand how to set the appropriate permissions and execute the script correctly. Using chmod +x to make your script executable is a necessary step before running it directly, either with a relative or absolute path.

Understanding how to execute scripts and troubleshoot common errors will empower you to create and run more complex scripts efficiently. As you delve deeper into Bash scripting, these foundational skills will serve you well in automating tasks and enhancing your command-line proficiency.

3.4 Using Comments for Readability and Documentation

In Bash scripting, comments are an essential tool for enhancing the readability and maintainability of your code. Comments allow you to explain the purpose of your code, document your thought process, and make it easier for others (or yourself in the future) to understand the logic behind your scripts. This section will delve into the importance of comments, how to use them effectively, and best practices for maintaining clarity in your scripts.

1. What are Comments?

Comments are non-executable lines in a script that the Bash interpreter ignores when running the code. They are used solely for documentation purposes, helping to clarify the script's functionality, structure, and usage. In Bash, comments start with the # symbol.

Example:

 # This is a comment in a Bash script
echo "Hello, World!" # This prints a greeting

2. Why Use Comments?

Using comments in your Bash scripts serves several important purposes:

Enhance Readability: Comments help others (or your future self) understand the intent and functionality of the code, making it easier to read and comprehend.

Documentation: Comments can provide a high-level overview of what the script does, including its inputs, outputs, and any dependencies.

Debugging Aid: When debugging scripts, comments can help you isolate sections of code or provide context for why certain choices were made.

Maintenance: Well-commented code is easier to maintain and update, especially if the script is revisited after some time or passed on to another developer.

3. How to Write Comments

There are a few different styles and best practices for writing comments in Bash scripts:

Single-line Comments: Use the # symbol for single-line comments. Place the comment on its own line or at the end of a command line.

 # This script greets the user

echo "Hello, World!" # Print a greeting

Multi-line Comments: Bash does not have a native multi-line comment syntax. However, you can achieve this using consecutive single-line comments or by using a here-document approach:

Consecutive Single-line Comments:

 # This script performs several tasks:
 # 1. Greets the user
 # 2. Shows the current date and time

Using Here-Document (Less common for comments, but possible):

: << 'END'
This is a multi-line comment
that spans several lines.
END

4. Best Practices for Using Comments

To make the most of comments in your Bash scripts, consider the following best practices:

Be Clear and Concise: Write comments that are straightforward and to the point. Avoid overly verbose explanations; instead, aim for clarity.

Explain Why, Not Just What: While it's important to explain what a piece of code does, it's often more beneficial to explain why you chose a particular approach. This context can be invaluable for future maintenance.

Keep Comments Updated: As you modify your code, make sure to update your comments accordingly. Outdated comments can be misleading and counterproductive.

Use Consistent Formatting: If you choose to use a specific format for comments (e.g., marking sections of code), stick to it throughout your script for consistency.

Document Functionality: At the beginning of your script, include a comment block that describes the script's purpose, usage, and any input/output parameters.

Example:

```bash
#!/bin/bash

# Script Name: greet_user.sh
# Purpose: This script greets the user based on the provided name.
# Usage: ./greet_user.sh [name]
# Example: ./greet_user.sh Alice

# Check if a name was provided
if [ -z "$1" ]; then
    echo "Usage: $0 [name]"
    exit 1
fi

# Greet the user
echo "Hello, $1!"
```

Comments are a vital part of writing effective Bash scripts, contributing to their readability, maintainability, and overall quality. By clearly documenting your code, you not only help others understand your work but also make it easier for yourself when revisiting your scripts in the future.

Adopting best practices for commenting, such as being concise, explaining the rationale behind your code, and keeping comments updated, will enhance your scripting skills and improve collaboration with others in coding projects. As you continue to write Bash scripts, remember that well-commented code is a hallmark of a thoughtful and professional programmer.

3.5 Simple Script Examples: Hello World, Date, and User Info

In this section, we will explore a few simple Bash scripts that illustrate fundamental scripting concepts. These examples include a "Hello World" script, a script that displays the current date and time, and another that provides user information. Each script will demonstrate basic syntax, usage of commands, and how to execute the scripts effectively.

1. Hello World Script

The classic "Hello World" program is often the first program written when learning a new programming language or scripting language. This simple script demonstrates how to output text to the terminal.

Script Example: hello_world.sh

#!/bin/bash

 # This script prints "Hello, World!" to the terminal.
echo "Hello, World!"

How to Create and Run the Script:

Create the Script: Open a terminal and use a text editor (like nano or vim) to create the script file:

nano hello_world.sh

Add the Script Content: Copy and paste the code above into the file.

Make the Script Executable:

chmod +x hello_world.sh

Run the Script:

./hello_world.sh

Output:

Hello, World!

2. Date Script

This script retrieves and displays the current date and time. It demonstrates the use of the date command and shows how to format the output.

Script Example: current_date.sh

#!/bin/bash

```
# This script displays the current date and time.
echo "Current date and time: $(date '+%Y-%m-%d %H:%M:%S')"
```

How to Create and Run the Script:

Create the Script:

```
nano current_date.sh
```

Add the Script Content: Copy and paste the code above into the file.

Make the Script Executable:

```
chmod +x current_date.sh
```

Run the Script:

```
./current_date.sh
```

Output (the actual date and time will vary):

```
Current date and time: 2024-10-16 15:45:22
```

3. User Info Script

This script retrieves and displays information about the current user, such as the username and the home directory. It uses the whoami and echo commands.

Script Example: user_info.sh

```
#!/bin/bash

# This script provides information about the current user.
echo "User Information:"
echo "Username: $(whoami)"
echo "Home Directory: $HOME"
```

How to Create and Run the Script:

Create the Script:

nano user_info.sh

Add the Script Content: Copy and paste the code above into the file.

Make the Script Executable:

chmod +x user_info.sh

Run the Script:

./user_info.sh

Output:

User Information:
Username: shoichi
Home Directory: /home/shoichi

4. Summary

These simple Bash script examples demonstrate the basic components of scripting, including:

- **Outputting Text**: Using the echo command to display messages to the terminal.
- **Executing Commands**: Utilizing built-in commands like date and whoami to retrieve system information.
- **Script Structure**: Including a shebang at the beginning of the script and comments to enhance readability.

By practicing these simple examples, you will become more familiar with Bash syntax and how to create scripts that automate basic tasks. As you continue to explore Bash scripting, you can build upon these foundations to create more complex scripts tailored to your needs.

4. Conditional Statements and Loops

In this chapter, you'll learn how to bring logic and decision-making into your Bash scripts using conditional statements and loops. We'll explore if, elif, and else constructs for evaluating conditions, along with case statements for handling multiple choices. You'll also discover how to automate repetitive tasks with loops, including for, while, and until, allowing your scripts to iterate over data or execute commands until certain conditions are met. By mastering these control structures, you'll be able to write dynamic and flexible scripts that adapt to different inputs and scenarios.

4.1 Conditional Logic with if Statements

Conditional statements are a fundamental concept in programming and scripting, allowing you to execute specific blocks of code based on certain conditions. In Bash scripting, the if statement is the primary means of implementing conditional logic. This section will cover the syntax and usage of if statements, along with practical examples to illustrate how to use them effectively.

1. Understanding the if Statement Syntax

The basic syntax for an if statement in Bash is as follows:

if [condition]; then
    # commands to execute if condition is true
elif [another_condition]; then
    # commands to execute if the previous condition is false and this condition is true
else
    # commands to execute if all conditions are false
fi

- **if**: This keyword begins the conditional statement.
- **[condition]:** The condition to evaluate. This is usually enclosed in square brackets. It can involve comparisons, string evaluations, or file tests.
- **then**: Marks the start of the block of commands that will run if the condition is true.
- **elif**: Stands for "else if," allowing for multiple conditions to be evaluated.
- **else**: Optional; defines a block of commands to execute if none of the conditions are true.

- **fi**: Marks the end of the if statement (it is if spelled backward).

2. Example: Simple if Statement

Let's create a simple Bash script that checks if a number is positive, negative, or zero.

Script Example: check_number.sh

```bash
#!/bin/bash

# Prompt user for a number
echo "Enter a number: "
read number

# Check if the number is positive, negative, or zero
if [ "$number" -gt 0 ]; then
    echo "The number is positive."
elif [ "$number" -lt 0 ]; then
    echo "The number is negative."
else
    echo "The number is zero."
fi
```

How to Create and Run the Script:

Create the Script:

nano check_number.sh

Add the Script Content: Copy and paste the code above into the file.

Make the Script Executable:

chmod +x check_number.sh

Run the Script:

./check_number.sh

Output Example:

Enter a number:
5
The number is positive.

3. Example: Checking File Existence

You can also use if statements to check for the existence of files or directories. This is especially useful for scripts that depend on certain files being present.

Script Example: check_file.sh

```bash
#!/bin/bash

# Prompt user for a filename
echo "Enter the filename to check: "
read filename

# Check if the file exists
if [ -e "$filename" ]; then
    echo "The file '$filename' exists."
else
    echo "The file '$filename' does not exist."
fi
```

How to Create and Run the Script:

Create the Script:

nano check_file.sh

Add the Script Content: Copy and paste the code above into the file.

Make the Script Executable:

chmod +x check_file.sh

Run the Script:

./check_file.sh

Output Example:

Enter the filename to check:
test.txt
The file 'test.txt' does not exist.

4. Using Logical Operators

You can combine multiple conditions using logical operators such as -a (and) and -o (or). These allow you to evaluate more complex conditions.

Example: Checking Multiple Conditions

```bash
#!/bin/bash

# Prompt user for two numbers
echo "Enter first number: "
read num1
echo "Enter second number: "
read num2

# Check if both numbers are positive
if [ "$num1" -gt 0 ] && [ "$num2" -gt 0 ]; then
    echo "Both numbers are positive."
else
    echo "At least one number is not positive."
fi
```

In this example, the script checks if both numbers entered by the user are greater than zero.

The if statement is a powerful tool in Bash scripting that allows you to implement conditional logic, enabling your scripts to respond to different situations dynamically. By understanding the syntax and structure of if statements, you can create scripts that can make decisions based on user input, file existence, and other conditions.

In this section, we covered:

- The basic syntax of if statements in Bash.

- How to use elif and else for additional conditional logic.
- Practical examples to demonstrate the use of if statements, including checking for positive/negative numbers and file existence.
- How to use logical operators to combine multiple conditions.

By incorporating conditional logic into your scripts, you can enhance their functionality and adaptability, making them more useful for various tasks and automation scenarios. As you continue your journey in Bash scripting, mastering if statements will provide a solid foundation for writing more complex and capable scripts.

4.2 elif and else: Handling Multiple Conditions

In Bash scripting, controlling the flow of execution based on different conditions is crucial for creating flexible and responsive scripts. While the if statement allows for basic condition checks, the elif (short for "else if") and else constructs enable you to handle multiple conditions effectively. This section will explore how to use elif and else statements, including their syntax, examples, and best practices.

1. Understanding elif and else Syntax

The elif and else keywords work in conjunction with the if statement to provide additional pathways for conditional execution. The structure for using these constructs is as follows:

if [condition1]; then
   # Commands to execute if condition1 is true
elif [condition2]; then
   # Commands to execute if condition1 is false and condition2 is true
else
   # Commands to execute if both conditions are false
fi

- **elif**: Allows you to check another condition if the previous if statement is false.
- **else**: Specifies a block of commands that will execute if none of the preceding conditions are true.

2. Example: Grade Evaluation Script

Let's create a Bash script that evaluates a student's grade based on their score and provides feedback based on multiple conditions.

Script Example: grade_evaluation.sh

```bash
#!/bin/bash

# Prompt user for a score
echo "Enter your score (0-100): "
read score

# Evaluate the score and provide feedback
if [ "$score" -ge 90 ]; then
    echo "Grade: A"
elif [ "$score" -ge 80 ]; then
    echo "Grade: B"
elif [ "$score" -ge 70 ]; then
    echo "Grade: C"
elif [ "$score" -ge 60 ]; then
    echo "Grade: D"
else
    echo "Grade: F"
fi
```

How to Create and Run the Script:

Create the Script:

nano grade_evaluation.sh

Add the Script Content: Copy and paste the code above into the file.

Make the Script Executable:

chmod +x grade_evaluation.sh

Run the Script:

./grade_evaluation.sh

Output Example:

Enter your score (0-100):
85
Grade: B

3. Example: Weather Condition Script

Let's consider a weather application that recommends attire based on temperature conditions using elif and else.

Script Example: weather_advice.sh

```bash
#!/bin/bash

# Prompt user for the current temperature
echo "Enter the current temperature in Celsius: "
read temperature

# Provide clothing advice based on the temperature
if [ "$temperature" -ge 30 ]; then
    echo "It's hot outside. Wear light clothing."
elif [ "$temperature" -ge 20 ]; then
    echo "The weather is nice. A t-shirt and shorts are fine."
elif [ "$temperature" -ge 10 ]; then
    echo "It's a bit chilly. Consider wearing a sweater."
else
    echo "It's cold! Wear a coat and stay warm."
fi
```

How to Create and Run the Script:

Create the Script:

nano weather_advice.sh

Add the Script Content: Copy and paste the code above into the file.

Make the Script Executable:

```
chmod +x weather_advice.sh
```

Run the Script:

```
./weather_advice.sh
```

Output Example:

Enter the current temperature in Celsius:
15
It's a bit chilly. Consider wearing a sweater.

4. Chaining Conditions with elif

The elif statement allows you to evaluate additional conditions without nesting if statements, which can make your scripts more readable and organized. You can use as many elif statements as necessary to cover different scenarios.

Example: Checking for Multiple Day Types

```bash
#!/bin/bash

# Prompt user for a day of the week
echo "Enter a day of the week: "
read day

# Provide activity suggestion based on the day
if [ "$day" == "Saturday" ] || [ "$day" == "Sunday" ]; then
    echo "It's the weekend! Time to relax."
elif [ "$day" == "Monday" ]; then
    echo "Start of the work week. Let's get productive!"
elif [ "$day" == "Friday" ]; then
    echo "It's almost the weekend! Finish strong!"
else
    echo "It's a regular weekday. Keep pushing through!"
fi
```

How to Create and Run the Script:

Create the Script:

nano day_activity.sh

Add the Script Content: Copy and paste the code above into the file.

Make the Script Executable:

chmod +x day_activity.sh

Run the Script:

./day_activity.sh

Output Example:

Enter a day of the week:
Friday
It's almost the weekend! Finish strong!

The elif and else statements in Bash scripting allow you to handle multiple conditions efficiently. This enhances the logic of your scripts, making them capable of responding to various inputs and scenarios.

In this section, we covered:

- The syntax of elif and else statements.
- Practical examples demonstrating how to evaluate multiple conditions, including grading systems and weather advice.
- How to chain conditions to create clear and organized logic flows without excessive nesting.

By mastering elif and else, you can build more complex and responsive scripts that effectively handle a wide range of conditions and user inputs, enhancing the utility and functionality of your Bash scripts. As you continue to develop your scripting skills, practice creating scripts that incorporate multiple conditions to reinforce these concepts.

4.3 Using case for Multi-way Branching

In Bash scripting, the case statement provides a powerful and efficient way to handle multi-way branching. It is particularly useful when you need to evaluate a single variable against multiple patterns, allowing for cleaner and more readable code compared to a series of if, elif, and else statements. This section will explore the syntax and usage of the case statement, along with practical examples to illustrate its application.

1. Understanding the case Statement Syntax

The basic syntax of a case statement in Bash is as follows:

```
case variable in
    pattern1)
        # Commands to execute if variable matches pattern1
        ;;
    pattern2)
        # Commands to execute if variable matches pattern2
        ;;
    *)
        # Commands to execute if none of the above patterns match
        ;;
esac
```

- case variable in: Starts the case statement and specifies the variable to be evaluated.
- pattern): Defines a pattern to match against the variable. If it matches, the associated commands will be executed.
- ;;: Indicates the end of commands for that particular pattern.
- *): This is the default case, executed if none of the specified patterns match. It acts like an else statement.
- esac: Ends the case statement (it is case spelled backward).

2. Example: Day of the Week Script

Let's create a Bash script that provides a message based on the day of the week using the case statement.

Script Example: day_message.sh

#!/bin/bash

```bash
# Prompt user for a day of the week
echo "Enter a day of the week: "
read day

# Use case to determine the message for the day
case $day in
    Monday)
        echo "Start of the work week!"
        ;;
    Tuesday | Wednesday | Thursday)
        echo "Midweek hustle!"
        ;;
    Friday)
        echo "Almost the weekend!"
        ;;
    Saturday | Sunday)
        echo "Enjoy your weekend!"
        ;;
    *)
        echo "That's not a valid day!"
        ;;
esac
```

How to Create and Run the Script:

Create the Script:

nano day_message.sh

Add the Script Content: Copy and paste the code above into the file.

Make the Script Executable:

chmod +x day_message.sh

Run the Script:

./day_message.sh

Output Example:

Enter a day of the week:
Friday
Almost the weekend!

3. Example: Menu Selection Script

Another common use case for the case statement is implementing a menu selection system where the user can choose from several options.

Script Example: menu_selection.sh

```bash
#!/bin/bash

# Display menu options
echo "Please select an option:"
echo "1) List files"
echo "2) Display current date"
echo "3) Show system uptime"
echo "4) Exit"
read -p "Enter your choice: " choice

# Use case to handle menu selection
case $choice in
    1)
        echo "Listing files in the current directory:"
        ls
        ;;
    2)
        echo "Current date and time: $(date)"
        ;;
    3)
        echo "System uptime:"
        uptime
        ;;
    4)
        echo "Exiting the program. Goodbye!"
        ;;
    *)
        echo "Invalid choice. Please select a valid option."
```

        ;;
esac

How to Create and Run the Script:

Create the Script:

nano menu_selection.sh

Add the Script Content: Copy and paste the code above into the file.

Make the Script Executable:

chmod +x menu_selection.sh

Run the Script:

./menu_selection.sh

Output Example:

Please select an option:
1) List files
2) Display current date
3) Show system uptime
4) Exit
Enter your choice: 2
Current date and time: Wed Oct 16 15:45:22 UTC 2024

4. Advantages of Using case

Readability: The case statement makes the script easier to read, especially when dealing with multiple conditions. It eliminates the need for nested if statements and makes the logic straightforward.

Simplicity: The case statement simplifies the handling of multiple conditions. Instead of repeating the variable name for each condition as you would with multiple if statements, you define it once and specify the patterns.

Grouping Patterns: You can group multiple patterns that lead to the same outcome. For example, in the day message script, both Saturday and Sunday share the same message.

The case statement in Bash scripting is a powerful construct for handling multi-way branching based on pattern matching. It enhances the clarity and maintainability of your scripts when dealing with multiple potential values for a single variable.

In this section, we covered:

- The syntax of the case statement and how to use it for multi-way branching.
- Practical examples, including determining messages based on the day of the week and creating a menu selection system.
- The advantages of using case for improving readability and simplifying condition handling.

By incorporating the case statement into your Bash scripts, you can streamline your code and handle complex conditional logic more effectively. As you continue to develop your scripting skills, practice using case in various scenarios to reinforce your understanding and enhance the functionality of your scripts.

4.4 for Loops: Iterating Over Lists and Ranges

In Bash scripting, for loops are a fundamental construct that allow you to iterate over a series of items, whether they be elements in a list, files in a directory, or a range of numbers. This capability makes for loops a powerful tool for automating repetitive tasks and processing data efficiently. In this section, we will explore the syntax and usage of for loops in Bash, along with practical examples to illustrate their application.

1. Basic Syntax of for Loops

The syntax of a for loop in Bash can take two main forms, depending on whether you are iterating over a list of items or a range of numbers:

1.1 Iterating Over a List

for item in list; do
    # Commands to execute for each item
done

- **item**: A variable that takes on the value of each element in the list during each iteration.
- **list**: A space-separated list of items to iterate over.
- **do**: Indicates the beginning of the loop body.
- **done**: Marks the end of the loop.

1.2 Iterating Over a Range of Numbers

```
for ((i=start; i<=end; i++)); do
    # Commands to execute for each value of i
done
```

- **i**: A variable that increments with each iteration, starting from start and continuing until end.
- **start**: The initial value for i.
- **end**: The final value for i.

2. Example: Iterating Over a List

Let's create a simple Bash script that iterates over a list of fruits and prints each one.

Script Example: fruit_list.sh

```bash
#!/bin/bash

# Define a list of fruits
fruits=("Apple" "Banana" "Cherry" "Date" "Elderberry")

# Use for loop to iterate over the list of fruits
for fruit in "${fruits[@]}"; do
    echo "I like $fruit."
done
```

How to Create and Run the Script:

Create the Script:

```
nano fruit_list.sh
```

Add the Script Content: Copy and paste the code above into the file.

Make the Script Executable:

chmod +x fruit_list.sh

Run the Script:

./fruit_list.sh

Output Example:

I like Apple.
I like Banana.
I like Cherry.
I like Date.
I like Elderberry.

3. Example: Iterating Over a Range of Numbers

Now let's create a script that uses a for loop to print numbers from 1 to 10.

Script Example: number_range.sh

#!/bin/bash

 # Use for loop to iterate from 1 to 10
for ((i=1; i<=10; i++)); do
*   echo "Number: $i"*
done

How to Create and Run the Script:

Create the Script:

nano number_range.sh

Add the Script Content: Copy and paste the code above into the file.

Make the Script Executable:

chmod +x number_range.sh

Run the Script:

./number_range.sh

Output Example:

Number: 1
Number: 2
Number: 3
Number: 4
Number: 5
Number: 6
Number: 7
Number: 8
Number: 9
Number: 10

4. Example: Iterating Over Files in a Directory

You can also use for loops to iterate over files in a directory. This is especially useful for batch processing files.

Script Example: process_files.sh

#!/bin/bash

 # Use for loop to iterate over all .txt files in the current directory
for file in *.txt; do
  echo "Processing $file..."
   # Add any commands to process the file here
done

How to Create and Run the Script:

Create the Script:

nano process_files.sh

Add the Script Content: Copy and paste the code above into the file.

Make the Script Executable:

chmod +x process_files.sh

Run the Script:

./process_files.sh

Output Example:

Processing file1.txt...
Processing file2.txt...
Processing file3.txt…

5. Using break and continue with for Loops

You can control the flow of a for loop using the break and continue statements:

- **break**: Exits the loop prematurely.
- **continue**: Skips the rest of the commands in the current iteration and moves to the next iteration.

Example: Using break and continue

```bash
#!/bin/bash

# Use for loop to iterate from 1 to 10
for ((i=1; i<=10; i++)); do
   if [ $i -eq 5 ]; then
      echo "Skipping number 5."
      continue
   fi

   if [ $i -eq 8 ]; then
      echo "Breaking the loop at number 8."
      break
   fi
```

```
    echo "Number: $i"
done
```

Output Example:

Number: 1
Number: 2
Number: 3
Number: 4
Skipping number 5.
Number: 6
Number: 7
Breaking the loop at number 8.

The for loop is a versatile and powerful feature in Bash scripting, allowing you to iterate over lists, ranges, and files effortlessly. By mastering for loops, you can automate repetitive tasks and process data efficiently.

In this section, we covered:

- The basic syntax of for loops for iterating over lists and ranges.
- Practical examples demonstrating how to use for loops to process data and files.
- How to use break and continue statements to control loop execution.

By incorporating for loops into your Bash scripts, you can enhance their functionality and make them more efficient. As you continue to develop your scripting skills, practice using for loops in various contexts to reinforce your understanding and improve your code's effectiveness.

4.5 while and until: Looping with Conditions

In Bash scripting, while and until loops provide powerful ways to execute commands repeatedly based on conditions. These loops allow you to create scripts that can run indefinitely or until a specific condition is met, making them ideal for tasks that require continuous checking of state or for processing data until certain criteria are fulfilled. In this section, we will explore the syntax and usage of both while and until loops, accompanied by practical examples to illustrate their application.

1. Basic Syntax of while and until Loops

1.1 while Loop

The while loop continues executing a block of code as long as a specified condition evaluates to true. The syntax is as follows:

while [condition]; do
    # Commands to execute while condition is true
done

condition: The expression to evaluate. The loop will run as long as this condition returns true.

1.2 until Loop

The until loop is the opposite of the while loop; it continues executing as long as the specified condition is false. The syntax is as follows:

until [condition]; do
    # Commands to execute until condition is true
done

condition: The expression to evaluate. The loop will run until this condition returns true.

2. Example: Using a while Loop to Count Down

Let's create a Bash script that counts down from a specified number to zero using a while loop.

Script Example: countdown.sh

```
#!/bin/bash

# Prompt user for a countdown start number
read -p "Enter a number to countdown from: " countdown

# Use while loop to count down to zero
while [ $countdown -gt 0 ]; do
    echo "$countdown"
```

    countdown=$((countdown - 1))
done

echo "Countdown complete!"

How to Create and Run the Script:

Create the Script:

nano countdown.sh

Add the Script Content: Copy and paste the code above into the file.

Make the Script Executable:

chmod +x countdown.sh

Run the Script:

./countdown.sh

Output Example:

Enter a number to countdown from: 5
5
4
3
2
1
Countdown complete!

3. Example: Using an until Loop to Wait for a Condition

Now, let's create a script that uses an until loop to wait for a specific condition. In this case, we will prompt the user to enter a valid password.

Script Example: password_prompt.sh

#!/bin/bash

```bash
# Initialize password variable
password="secret"
user_input=""

# Use until loop to prompt user for the correct password
until [ "$user_input" == "$password" ]; do
    read -sp "Enter the password: " user_input
    echo  # Print a new line after the input
    if [ "$user_input" != "$password" ]; then
        echo "Incorrect password. Try again."
    fi
done

echo "Access granted!"
```

How to Create and Run the Script:

Create the Script:

nano password_prompt.sh

Add the Script Content: Copy and paste the code above into the file.

Make the Script Executable:

chmod +x password_prompt.sh

Run the Script:

./password_prompt.sh

Output Example:

Enter the password: wrongpassword
Incorrect password. Try again.
Enter the password: secret
Access granted!

4. Common Use Cases for while and until Loops

Waiting for Conditions: You can use until loops to wait for a particular condition to be true before proceeding, such as waiting for a file to be created or for a service to become available.

Processing Data: Both while and until loops can be employed to process data from files or user input, especially in scenarios where you do not know the exact number of iterations in advance.

Polling: These loops are ideal for polling external processes or resources, continuously checking their state until a desired condition is met.

5. Using break and continue with while and until Loops

Just like with for loops, you can control the flow of while and until loops using the break and continue statements:

- **break**: Exits the loop prematurely, regardless of the loop condition.
- **continue**: Skips the remainder of the commands in the current iteration and proceeds to the next iteration.

Example: Using break and continue in a while Loop

```bash
#!/bin/bash

count=1

# Use while loop to iterate until count is less than or equal to 10
while [ $count -le 10 ]; do
    if [ $count -eq 5 ]; then
        echo "Skipping number 5."
        count=$((count + 1))
        continue
    fi

    if [ $count -eq 8 ]; then
        echo "Breaking the loop at number 8."
        break
    fi

    echo "Number: $count"
```

```
    count=$((count + 1))
done
```

Output Example:

Number: 1
Number: 2
Number: 3
Number: 4
Skipping number 5.
Number: 6
Number: 7
Breaking the loop at number 8.

while and until loops are essential constructs in Bash scripting that enable you to create dynamic and responsive scripts based on conditions. These loops are ideal for scenarios where the number of iterations is not predetermined, allowing for flexible execution based on user input or system state.

In this section, we covered:

- The basic syntax and usage of while and until loops.
- Practical examples, including a countdown script and a password prompt script.
- Common use cases for both loops, such as waiting for conditions and processing data.
- How to use break and continue statements to control loop execution.

By mastering while and until loops, you can enhance the functionality of your Bash scripts and create more interactive and adaptable solutions. As you continue to develop your scripting skills, practice implementing these loops in various contexts to reinforce your understanding and improve your scripts' effectiveness.

4.6 Breaking and Continuing Loops: Control Flow

In Bash scripting, control flow statements such as break and continue are essential tools that allow you to manage the execution of loops. These statements enable you to manipulate the flow of your scripts dynamically, providing greater flexibility and control over how iterations are processed. In this section, we will delve into the break and continue statements, explore their syntax, and illustrate their usage through practical examples.

1. Understanding break and continue Statements

1.1 The break Statement

The break statement is used to exit a loop prematurely, regardless of the loop's condition. When break is encountered, control is transferred to the first statement following the loop. This is particularly useful when you want to terminate a loop based on a specific condition or when a certain criterion has been met.

Syntax:

break

Example Use Case: Breaking out of a loop when a specific condition is met.

1.2 The continue Statement

The continue statement, on the other hand, skips the remaining commands in the current iteration and proceeds to the next iteration of the loop. This allows you to bypass certain conditions without terminating the entire loop.

Syntax:

continue

Example Use Case: Continuing to the next iteration when a specific condition is encountered.

2. Example: Using break in a Loop

Let's create a Bash script that uses the break statement to exit a loop when a specific number is encountered. In this example, we will sum numbers from 1 to 10, but we will exit the loop if we reach the number 5.

Script Example: sum_until_five.sh

#!/bin/bash

```bash
sum=0

# Use a for loop to iterate from 1 to 10
for ((i=1; i<=10; i++)); do
    if [ $i -eq 5 ]; then
        echo "Breaking the loop at number $i."
        break
    fi
    sum=$((sum + i))
done

echo "The sum is: $sum"
```

How to Create and Run the Script:

Create the Script:

nano sum_until_five.sh

Add the Script Content: Copy and paste the code above into the file.

Make the Script Executable:

chmod +x sum_until_five.sh

Run the Script:

./sum_until_five.sh

Output Example:

Breaking the loop at number 5.
The sum is: 10

In this script, the loop calculates the sum of numbers from 1 to 4 and exits before adding 5 to the total. The break statement effectively halts the loop's execution when the specified condition is met.

3. Example: Using continue in a Loop

Now let's create a script that uses the continue statement to skip over certain numbers while iterating through a list. In this case, we will print all numbers from 1 to 10, but we will skip the even numbers.

Script Example: print_odds.sh

```bash
#!/bin/bash

# Use a for loop to iterate from 1 to 10
for ((i=1; i<=10; i++)); do
   if [ $((i % 2)) -eq 0 ]; then
      continue  # Skip even numbers
   fi
   echo "Odd number: $i"
done
```

How to Create and Run the Script:

Create the Script:

nano print_odds.sh

Add the Script Content: Copy and paste the code above into the file.

Make the Script Executable:

chmod +x print_odds.sh

Run the Script:

./print_odds.sh

Output Example:

Odd number: 1
Odd number: 3
Odd number: 5
Odd number: 7
Odd number: 9

In this example, the continue statement allows the loop to skip any even numbers, thus only printing odd numbers from 1 to 10.

4. Combining break and continue in a Loop

You can combine both break and continue statements within the same loop to control the flow based on different conditions.

Example: This script prints numbers from 1 to 10, skips even numbers, and breaks the loop if it encounters the number 7.

```bash
#!/bin/bash

# Use a for loop to iterate from 1 to 10
for ((i=1; i<=10; i++)); do
   if [ $i -eq 7 ]; then
      echo "Breaking the loop at number $i."
      break
   fi

   if [ $((i % 2)) -eq 0 ]; then
      continue  # Skip even numbers
   fi

   echo "Number: $i"
done
```

How to Create and Run the Script:

Create the Script:

nano mix_control_flow.sh

Add the Script Content: Copy and paste the code above into the file.

Make the Script Executable:

chmod +x mix_control_flow.sh

Run the Script:

./mix_control_flow.sh

Output Example:

Number: 1
Number: 3
Number: 5
Breaking the loop at number 7.

In this combined example, the script skips even numbers while also breaking out of the loop when it reaches the number 7.

Understanding how to effectively use the break and continue statements in your Bash scripts can significantly enhance your ability to control loop execution. These statements give you the power to manage the flow of your scripts dynamically, allowing for more sophisticated logic and improved readability.

In this section, we covered:

- The purpose and syntax of the break statement for exiting loops prematurely.
- The purpose and syntax of the continue statement for skipping to the next iteration.
- Practical examples demonstrating how to implement these control flow statements in loops.
- Combined usage of break and continue within the same loop for complex conditions.

By incorporating break and continue into your Bash scripts, you can create more efficient and effective loops that respond appropriately to your specific conditions and requirements. As you continue to develop your scripting skills, experiment with these control flow statements to see how they can streamline your code and improve its functionality.

5. Functions: Modularizing Your Scripts

This chapter introduces the concept of functions, a powerful way to organize and modularize your Bash scripts. You'll learn how to define functions to group related commands, making your scripts more readable and reusable. We'll cover how to pass arguments to functions, return values, and manage variable scope within them. By breaking your script into smaller, manageable units, you'll improve maintainability and reduce redundancy. By the end of this chapter, you'll be able to write clean, modular scripts using functions, making complex tasks simpler to manage and troubleshoot.

5.1 Defining Functions in Bash

Functions in Bash scripting are essential for promoting code reuse, improving organization, and enhancing the readability of scripts. They allow you to encapsulate a block of code that performs a specific task, making it easy to call this code from different parts of your script without needing to rewrite it. In this section, we will explore how to define functions in Bash, including their syntax, best practices, and practical examples.

1. Understanding Functions in Bash

A function in Bash is a named block of code that can be executed when called upon. Functions can take arguments, return values, and help in structuring your script logically. By using functions, you can break your script into manageable sections, which makes it easier to maintain and debug.

2. Basic Syntax of Function Definition

The basic syntax for defining a function in Bash is as follows:

```
function_name() {
    # Commands to execute
}
```

Alternatively, you can also define a function using the function keyword:

```
function function_name {
    # Commands to execute
}
```

Both forms are valid, but the first one is more commonly used in Bash scripting.

3. Calling a Function

To execute the function, simply call it by its name followed by parentheses. However, parentheses are optional in Bash:

```
function_name    # Valid
function_name() # Valid but optional
```

4. Example: Defining and Using a Simple Function

Let's create a Bash script that defines a function to print a greeting message.

Script Example: greeting.sh

```bash
#!/bin/bash

# Define a function to print a greeting
greet() {
    echo "Hello, $1! Welcome to Bash scripting."
}

# Call the function with an argument
greet "Alice"
```

How to Create and Run the Script:

Create the Script:

```
nano greeting.sh
```

Add the Script Content: Copy and paste the code above into the file.

Make the Script Executable:

```
chmod +x greeting.sh
```

Run the Script:

./greeting.sh

Output Example:

Hello, Alice! Welcome to Bash scripting.

In this example, the greet function takes one argument (the name of the person) and prints a personalized greeting message.

5. Functions with Multiple Arguments

Functions can accept multiple arguments, making them even more versatile. You can access these arguments within the function using the special variables $1, $2, $3, etc., for the first, second, third arguments, respectively.

Example: A function that adds two numbers:

```bash
#!/bin/bash

# Define a function to add two numbers
add_numbers() {
   sum=$(( $1 + $2 ))
   echo "The sum of $1 and $2 is: $sum"
}

# Call the function with two arguments
add_numbers 5 7
```

How to Create and Run the Script:

Create the Script:

nano add_numbers.sh

Add the Script Content: Copy and paste the code above into the file.

Make the Script Executable:

chmod +x add_numbers.sh

Run the Script:

./add_numbers.sh

Output Example:

The sum of 5 and 7 is: 12

In this example, the add_numbers function takes two arguments and calculates their sum, which is then printed to the console.

6. Returning Values from Functions

Bash functions can also return values. While you cannot return a value like in some other programming languages, you can use the echo command to output the result and capture it when you call the function.

Example: A function that returns the square of a number:

```bash
#!/bin/bash

# Define a function to calculate the square of a number
square() {
    echo $(( $1 * $1 ))  # Return the square
}

# Call the function and capture the output
result=$(square 4)
echo "The square of 4 is: $result"
```

How to Create and Run the Script:

Create the Script:

nano square.sh

Add the Script Content: Copy and paste the code above into the file.

Make the Script Executable:

chmod +x square.sh

Run the Script:

./square.sh

Output Example:

The square of 4 is: 16

In this example, the square function calculates the square of the given number and echoes it back, allowing us to capture the value in the result variable.

7. Best Practices for Defining Functions in Bash

Use Descriptive Names: Choose meaningful names for your functions that indicate what the function does, making it easier for others (and yourself) to understand your script.

Keep Functions Focused: Each function should perform a single, specific task. This enhances readability and maintainability.

Use Comments: Document your functions with comments explaining their purpose, parameters, and return values.

Check for Required Arguments: You can implement error checking within your functions to ensure that the necessary arguments are provided.

```
check_arguments() {
   if [ $# -lt 2 ]; then
      echo "Error: Two arguments are required."
      return 1
   fi
}
```

Avoid Global Variables: Try to limit the use of global variables within functions. Instead, pass variables as arguments to keep your functions self-contained.

Defining functions in Bash is a powerful way to organize your scripts, enhance code reusability, and simplify complex tasks. In this section, we covered:

- The basic syntax for defining and calling functions in Bash.
- How to use functions with multiple arguments.
- The technique for returning values from functions using echo.
- Best practices for writing effective functions.

By leveraging functions in your Bash scripts, you can create more structured, modular, and maintainable code. As you continue to work with Bash scripting, practice defining functions to see how they can streamline your code and improve your scripting efficiency.

5.2 Passing Arguments to Functions

Passing arguments to functions in Bash allows you to customize their behavior and make them more versatile. Arguments enable functions to operate on different input values without needing to modify the function code itself. This section will explore how to pass arguments to functions in Bash, how to access them, and best practices for using arguments effectively.

1. Understanding Function Arguments

When you define a function in Bash, you can pass values to it when you call it. These values, known as arguments, are accessible within the function using special variables. The first argument is accessed with $1, the second with $2, and so on. Additionally, $# gives the number of arguments passed to the function, and $@ provides all the arguments as a list.

2. Defining a Function with Arguments

Here's how you can define a function that takes arguments:

function_name() {
   # Access arguments using $1, $2, etc.
}

You can call the function by providing arguments after its name:

function_name arg1 arg2

3. Example: Passing Arguments to a Function

Let's create a Bash script that demonstrates passing arguments to a function that calculates the area of a rectangle.

Script Example: area_rectangle.sh

```bash
#!/bin/bash

# Function to calculate the area of a rectangle
calculate_area() {
    local length=$1   # First argument
    local width=$2    # Second argument
    local area=$(( length * width ))  # Calculate area
    echo "The area of the rectangle is: $area"
}

# Call the function with arguments
calculate_area 10 5
```

How to Create and Run the Script:

Create the Script:

nano area_rectangle.sh

Add the Script Content: Copy and paste the code above into the file.

Make the Script Executable:

chmod +x area_rectangle.sh

Run the Script:

./area_rectangle.sh

Output Example:

The area of the rectangle is: 50

In this example, the calculate_area function takes two arguments, calculates the area of the rectangle, and prints the result.

4. Accessing Arguments in Functions

Arguments passed to a function can be accessed as follows:

- $1, $2, etc.: Represents the first, second, and subsequent arguments.
- $#: Represents the total number of arguments passed to the function.
- $@: Represents all arguments as individual words.
- $*: Represents all arguments as a single word.

Example: A script that demonstrates accessing and printing all arguments:

```bash
#!/bin/bash

# Function to print all arguments
print_arguments() {
    echo "Total arguments: $#"
    echo "All arguments: $@"
}

# Call the function with multiple arguments
print_arguments "apple" "banana" "cherry"
```

How to Create and Run the Script:

Create the Script:

nano print_arguments.sh

Add the Script Content: Copy and paste the code above into the file.

Make the Script Executable:

chmod +x print_arguments.sh

Run the Script:

./print_arguments.sh

Output Example:

Total arguments: 3
All arguments: apple banana cherry

In this example, the print_arguments function counts and prints all the arguments passed to it.

5. Default Values for Function Arguments

You can set default values for function arguments to ensure that the function behaves as expected even if no arguments are provided. This is done using parameter expansion.

Example: A function with a default value for the second argument:

```bash
#!/bin/bash

# Function to greet with a default name
greet() {
   local name=${1:-"Guest"}  # Default to "Guest" if no name is provided
   echo "Hello, $name!"
}

# Call the function without an argument
greet

# Call the function with an argument
greet "Alice"
```

How to Create and Run the Script:

Create the Script:

nano greet_default.sh

Add the Script Content: Copy and paste the code above into the file.

Make the Script Executable:

chmod +x greet_default.sh

Run the Script:

./greet_default.sh

Output Example:

Hello, Guest!
Hello, Alice!

In this example, the greet function uses a default value of "Guest" if no name is provided.

6. Handling a Variable Number of Arguments

Sometimes, you may want to handle a variable number of arguments in your functions. You can loop through all arguments using $@ or $*.

Example: A function that prints all provided arguments:

```bash
#!/bin/bash

# Function to print a variable number of arguments
print_all() {
   echo "Arguments provided:"
   for arg in "$@"; do
      echo "- $arg"
   done
}

# Call the function with multiple arguments
print_all "one" "two" "three" "four"
```

How to Create and Run the Script:

Create the Script:

nano print_all.sh

Add the Script Content: Copy and paste the code above into the file.

Make the Script Executable:

chmod +x print_all.sh

Run the Script:

./print_all.sh

Output Example:

Arguments provided:
- one
- two
- three
- four

In this example, the print_all function uses a loop to iterate through all the provided arguments and print them.

7. Best Practices for Passing Arguments to Functions

Use Meaningful Argument Names: Choose clear and descriptive names for your arguments to convey their purpose.

Validate Arguments: Check for the required number of arguments and validate their types within the function to prevent errors.

```
validate_arguments() {
    if [ $# -lt 1 ]; then
        echo "Error: At least one argument is required."
        return 1
    fi
}
```

Document Your Functions: Include comments that describe the purpose of the function and the expected arguments.

Limit the Number of Arguments: Aim to keep the number of arguments manageable to ensure that the function remains easy to understand and use.

Consider Using Associative Arrays: For complex data, consider using associative arrays to pass multiple named values.

Passing arguments to functions in Bash scripting enhances the flexibility and reusability of your code. In this section, we covered:

- How to define functions that accept arguments.
- How to access and manipulate arguments within functions.
- Techniques for handling default values and a variable number of arguments.
- Best practices for using arguments effectively.

By mastering the use of arguments in your Bash functions, you can create more dynamic and robust scripts that can adapt to different inputs and use cases, ultimately leading to more maintainable and efficient code.

5.3 Returning Values from Functions

Returning values from functions in Bash is a fundamental concept that allows scripts to produce output based on the input provided. While Bash does not have a return statement like many other programming languages, it can achieve similar functionality through the use of echo to output results and command substitution to capture those outputs. This section will explore how to effectively return values from Bash functions, including practical examples and best practices.

1. Understanding Value Returns in Bash

In Bash, functions can "return" values in two primary ways:

Using echo: You can print the desired value from the function using echo. The calling code can capture this output.

Using the return statement: The return statement in Bash only returns an exit status (an integer value between 0 and 255). This status indicates whether the function executed successfully (returning 0) or encountered an error (returning a non-zero value).

It's essential to understand that while you can use return for exit status, actual data transfer between functions is done using echo.

2. Returning a Value Using echo

To return a value from a function, you define the function, use echo to produce the value, and then capture it using command substitution when calling the function.

Example: A function that calculates the square of a number and returns the result.

```bash
#!/bin/bash

# Function to calculate the square of a number
calculate_square() {
   local number=$1     # First argument
   echo $(( number * number ))  # Return the square
}

# Capture the returned value
result=$(calculate_square 5)

# Print the result
echo "The square of 5 is: $result"
```

How to Create and Run the Script:

Create the Script:

nano square_function.sh

Add the Script Content: Copy and paste the code above into the file.

Make the Script Executable:

chmod +x square_function.sh

Run the Script:

./square_function.sh

Output Example:

The square of 5 is: 25

In this example, the calculate_square function uses echo to return the square of the provided number, which is captured in the result variable.

3. Using return for Exit Status

While you can use return to send a numeric value back to the caller, this is typically used to indicate the success or failure of a function rather than returning actual data.

Example: A function that checks if a number is even and returns an appropriate exit status.

```
#!/bin/bash

# Function to check if a number is even
is_even() {
   local number=$1
   if (( number % 2 == 0 )); then
      return 0  # Success (even)
   else
       return 1  # Failure (odd)
   fi
}

# Call the function
is_even 4

# Check the exit status
if [[ $? -eq 0 ]]; then
   echo "4 is an even number."
else
   echo "4 is an odd number."
fi
```

How to Create and Run the Script:

Create the Script:

nano even_check.sh

Add the Script Content: Copy and paste the code above into the file.

Make the Script Executable:

chmod +x even_check.sh

Run the Script:

./even_check.sh

Output Example:

4 is an even number.

In this example, the is_even function uses the return statement to communicate whether the input number is even or odd.

4. Capturing Output from Multiple Values

Sometimes, you might need to return multiple values from a function. One approach is to use echo to output multiple values separated by spaces or newlines and then capture them.

Example: A function that returns both the area and the perimeter of a rectangle.

```bash
#!/bin/bash

# Function to calculate area and perimeter
calculate_rectangle() {
    local length=$1
    local width=$2
    local area=$(( length * width ))
    local perimeter=$(( 2 * (length + width) ))
    echo "$area $perimeter"  # Return both values
```

}

Capture the returned values
read area perimeter < <(calculate_rectangle 10 5)

Print the results
echo "Area: $area, Perimeter: $perimeter"

How to Create and Run the Script:

Create the Script:

nano rectangle_calculation.sh

Add the Script Content: Copy and paste the code above into the file.

Make the Script Executable:

chmod +x rectangle_calculation.sh

Run the Script:

./rectangle_calculation.sh

Output Example:

Area: 50, Perimeter: 30

In this example, the calculate_rectangle function uses echo to return both the area and perimeter, which are captured using the read command.

5. Using Arrays to Return Multiple Values

Bash also supports arrays, which can be useful for returning multiple values from a function.

Example: A function that returns the first and last elements of an array.

#!/bin/bash

```bash
# Function to return first and last elements of an array
get_first_last() {
    local arr=("$@")  # Capture all arguments into an array
    echo "${arr[0]} ${arr[-1]}"  # Return first and last elements
}

# Call the function with multiple values
read first last < <(get_first_last "apple" "banana" "cherry" "date")

# Print the results
echo "First: $first, Last: $last"
```

How to Create and Run the Script:

Create the Script:

nano first_last.sh

Add the Script Content: Copy and paste the code above into the file.

Make the Script Executable:

chmod +x first_last.sh

Run the Script:

./first_last.sh

Output Example:

First: apple, Last: date

In this example, the get_first_last function captures an array of elements and returns the first and last elements.

6. Best Practices for Returning Values from Functions

Use echo for Data: Always use echo to return actual data from functions. Avoid using return for returning data as it only indicates success or failure.

Limit Use of return to Exit Status: Use return to indicate the success (0) or failure (non-zero) of the function rather than for data transmission.

Be Mindful of Output: If a function produces output that may conflict with other parts of your script, consider redirecting it or managing output carefully to avoid confusion.

Document Your Functions: Clearly state in comments what values your function is expected to return, both in terms of data (via echo) and exit status (via return).

Consider Readability: When returning multiple values, ensure your method of capturing these values is clear to anyone reading your code.

Returning values from functions in Bash scripting is an essential skill that enhances the reusability and clarity of your code. In this section, we covered:

- How to use echo to return values from functions.
- The use of the return statement for indicating exit status.
- Techniques for returning multiple values using spaces, newlines, or arrays.
- Best practices for effective function value returns.

By mastering these techniques, you can create more dynamic, flexible, and maintainable Bash scripts that respond to varying inputs and conditions, ultimately leading to higher-quality automation solutions.

5.4 Local vs Global Variables in Functions

In Bash scripting, understanding the distinction between local and global variables is crucial for writing efficient and error-free scripts. Variables play a significant role in controlling the flow of data within functions and across the script. This section will explore the differences between local and global variables, how to declare them, and the best practices for their usage.

1. Understanding Variables in Bash

Before diving into local and global variables, it's essential to understand what variables are in Bash:

- Variables are used to store data that can be used and manipulated within a script or a function.

- They can hold various data types, including strings, numbers, and arrays.

In Bash, variables are typically declared without specifying a type, and they can be accessed by their names. For example:

name="Shoichi"
echo $name # Outputs: Shoichi

2. Global Variables

Global Variables are accessible throughout the entire script, including all functions.

They are declared without any special keywords and can be used and modified anywhere in the script.

Example of Global Variables:

#!/bin/bash

 # Global variable
global_var="I am global"

function print_global() {
*   echo "$global_var"*
}

print_global # Outputs: I am global
echo "$global_var" # Outputs: I am global

How to Create and Run the Script:

Create the Script:

nano global_example.sh

Add the Script Content: Copy and paste the code above into the file.

Make the Script Executable:

chmod +x global_example.sh

Run the Script:

./global_example.sh

Output Example:

I am global
I am global

In this example, the global_var variable is accessible both in the print_global function and outside of it.

3. Local Variables

Local Variables are restricted in scope to the function in which they are defined.

They are declared using the local keyword within a function, ensuring they do not interfere with variables of the same name defined elsewhere in the script.

Example of Local Variables:

```bash
#!/bin/bash

# Global variable
global_var="I am global"

function print_local() {
    local local_var="I am local"
    echo "$local_var"
}

print_local  # Outputs: I am local
echo "$global_var"  # Outputs: I am global

# Attempting to access local variable outside the function will fail
echo "$local_var"  # Outputs nothing
```

How to Create and Run the Script:

Create the Script:

nano local_example.sh

Add the Script Content: Copy and paste the code above into the file.

Make the Script Executable:

chmod +x local_example.sh

Run the Script:

./local_example.sh

Output Example:

I am local
I am global

In this example, local_var is only accessible within the print_local function, and attempting to access it outside results in no output.

4. Scope and Lifetime of Variables

Understanding the scope and lifetime of variables is essential for effective scripting:

Scope: Refers to the context in which a variable can be accessed. Global variables have a script-wide scope, while local variables have function-specific scope.

Lifetime: Refers to how long a variable exists in memory. Global variables exist for the duration of the script, whereas local variables exist only while the function is executing. Once the function exits, the local variable is destroyed and cannot be accessed.

5. Modifying Global Variables Inside Functions

A function can modify a global variable directly, affecting its value throughout the script. However, to avoid confusion, it's often better to pass variables as arguments or return values.

Example: Modifying a global variable within a function.

```bash
#!/bin/bash

# Global variable
counter=0

function increment_counter() {
   counter=$(( counter + 1 ))  # Modify global variable
}

increment_counter
echo "Counter after increment: $counter"  # Outputs: Counter after increment: 1
```

How to Create and Run the Script:

Create the Script:

nano increment_example.sh

Add the Script Content: Copy and paste the code above into the file.

Make the Script Executable:

chmod +x increment_example.sh

Run the Script:

./increment_example.sh

Output Example:

Counter after increment: 1

In this example, the increment_counter function modifies the global counter variable, which is reflected outside the function.

6. Best Practices for Using Local and Global Variables

Limit Global Variables: Minimize the use of global variables to reduce potential conflicts and unintended side effects. Use them sparingly and only when necessary.

Use Local Variables in Functions: Always prefer local variables in functions to avoid polluting the global namespace and to make your functions more modular and easier to understand.

Document Variable Usage: Clearly comment on the purpose of global and local variables in your scripts, especially if a global variable is modified within a function.

Be Cautious with Variable Names: Choose variable names that are descriptive and unique to avoid naming collisions. Consider using prefixes or suffixes to distinguish between global and local variables.

Avoid Side Effects: When designing functions, avoid modifying global variables unless absolutely necessary. Instead, consider returning values or using arguments to pass data.

Understanding local and global variables in Bash is crucial for effective scripting. In this section, we covered:

- The definition and usage of global and local variables.
- The scope and lifetime of variables in Bash.
- How to modify global variables from within functions.
- Best practices for using variables to create maintainable and efficient scripts.

By mastering the use of local and global variables, you can write clearer and more predictable Bash scripts that avoid common pitfalls associated with variable scope and lifetime. This knowledge is foundational for creating robust scripts that perform complex tasks without unintended consequences.

5.5 Using Functions for Code Reuse and Organization

In Bash scripting, functions play a pivotal role in enhancing code reuse and organization, ultimately leading to cleaner, more maintainable scripts. Functions allow you to encapsulate blocks of code that perform specific tasks, enabling you to call these blocks whenever needed without rewriting the code. This section will explore the benefits of using functions for code reuse and organization, along with practical examples and best practices.

1. The Importance of Code Reuse

Code reuse is a fundamental programming principle that involves writing code once and using it multiple times throughout a script or program. The benefits of code reuse include:

Reduced Redundancy: Writing the same code multiple times can lead to errors and inconsistencies. Functions allow you to define a block of code once and reuse it as needed.

Simplified Maintenance: When you need to make changes, you only have to update the code in one place, reducing the risk of introducing bugs.

Enhanced Readability: Functions can make scripts easier to read and understand by breaking complex tasks into smaller, manageable pieces.

Improved Collaboration: In team environments, well-defined functions can help other developers understand and utilize your code more effectively.

2. Defining Functions in Bash

Defining a function in Bash is straightforward. You can use the following syntax:

```bash
function_name() {
    # Code block
}
```

Example: A simple function to greet a user.

```bash
#!/bin/bash

# Function to greet a user
greet_user() {
    local name="$1"
    echo "Hello, $name!"
}

# Call the function
greet_user "Shoichi"
```

How to Create and Run the Script:

Create the Script:

nano greet_example.sh

Add the Script Content: Copy and paste the code above into the file.

Make the Script Executable:

chmod +x greet_example.sh

Run the Script:

./greet_example.sh

Output Example:

Hello, Shoichi!

In this example, the greet_user function takes a name as an argument and prints a greeting.

3. Code Organization with Functions

Functions help organize your code by grouping related actions together. This modular approach makes it easier to manage and understand your scripts.

Example: A script that performs multiple calculations using functions.

```
#!/bin/bash

# Function to calculate the sum
calculate_sum() {
    local a=$1
    local b=$2
    echo $(( a + b ))
}

# Function to calculate the difference
calculate_difference() {
```

```bash
    local a=$1
    local b=$2
    echo $(( a - b ))
}

# Function to calculate the product
calculate_product() {
    local a=$1
    local b=$2
    echo $(( a * b ))
}

# Function to calculate the quotient
calculate_quotient() {
    local a=$1
    local b=$2
    if [[ $b -ne 0 ]]; then
        echo $(( a / b ))
    else
        echo "Division by zero is not allowed."
    fi
}

# Call the functions
num1=10
num2=5
echo "Sum: $(calculate_sum $num1 $num2)"
echo "Difference: $(calculate_difference $num1 $num2)"
echo "Product: $(calculate_product $num1 $num2)"
echo "Quotient: $(calculate_quotient $num1 $num2)"
```

How to Create and Run the Script:

Create the Script:

nano calculator_example.sh

Add the Script Content: Copy and paste the code above into the file.

Make the Script Executable:

```
chmod +x calculator_example.sh
```

Run the Script:

```
./calculator_example.sh
```

Output Example:

```
Sum: 15
Difference: 5
Product: 50
Quotient: 2
```

In this example, multiple functions encapsulate different mathematical operations, improving the organization and readability of the script.

4. Enhancing Code Reuse with Parameters

Functions can accept parameters, allowing you to customize their behavior based on the inputs provided. This feature enables the creation of flexible, reusable code.

Example: A function that formats and prints a user's information.

```bash
#!/bin/bash

# Function to print user info
print_user_info() {
    local name="$1"
    local age="$2"
    echo "Name: $name"
    echo "Age: $age"
}

# Call the function with different arguments
print_user_info "Shoichi" 30
print_user_info "Alice" 25
```

How to Create and Run the Script:

Create the Script:

nano user_info_example.sh

Add the Script Content: Copy and paste the code above into the file.

Make the Script Executable:

chmod +x user_info_example.sh

Run the Script:

./user_info_example.sh

Output Example:

Name: Shoichi
Age: 30
Name: Alice
Age: 25

In this example, the print_user_info function is reused to print information for different users, demonstrating code reuse.

5. Return Values for Enhanced Reusability

Functions can return values using echo, allowing you to capture results for further processing.

Example: A function that calculates the area of a rectangle and returns it.

```bash
#!/bin/bash

# Function to calculate the area of a rectangle
calculate_area() {
   local length=$1
   local width=$2
   echo $(( length * width ))
}
```

 # Call the function and capture the return value
area=$(calculate_area 10 5)
echo "The area of the rectangle is: $area"

How to Create and Run the Script:

Create the Script:

nano area_example.sh

Add the Script Content: Copy and paste the code above into the file.

Make the Script Executable:

chmod +x area_example.sh

Run the Script:

./area_example.sh

Output Example:

The area of the rectangle is: 50

In this example, the calculate_area function returns the area of the rectangle, demonstrating how functions can be reused to obtain results.

6. Best Practices for Using Functions

Keep Functions Focused: Each function should perform a single task or a closely related set of tasks. This approach enhances readability and maintainability.

Use Meaningful Names: Choose descriptive names for your functions that clearly indicate their purpose. This practice helps other developers (and your future self) understand the code better.

Document Function Behavior: Include comments to explain what each function does, its parameters, and its return values. This documentation is valuable for maintaining the code over time.

Limit Side Effects: Functions should ideally not modify global variables unless necessary. This approach helps keep functions independent and predictable.

Organize Functions Logically: Group related functions together in your scripts. Consider using separate files for large scripts to improve organization.

Using functions for code reuse and organization is a powerful practice in Bash scripting. In this section, we covered:

- The importance of code reuse and its benefits.
- How to define functions and encapsulate code.
- The significance of using parameters for flexible function behavior.
- Returning values from functions for enhanced reusability.
- Best practices for writing and organizing functions.

By incorporating these techniques into your Bash scripts, you can create cleaner, more efficient, and maintainable code that effectively handles complex tasks while promoting reusability and organization. This practice not only improves your scripting skills but also enhances collaboration with others in software development environments.

6. Command-line Arguments and User Input

In this chapter, you'll explore how to enhance your Bash scripts by handling command-line arguments and user input. You'll learn about positional parameters, which allow you to pass data directly to your scripts when you execute them. We'll also delve into the use of the getopts command for parsing options and flags, making your scripts more flexible and user-friendly. Additionally, you'll discover how to prompt users for input using the read command, enabling interactive scripts that respond to user actions. By the end of this chapter, you'll have the skills to create scripts that are not only powerful but also adaptable to user needs and command-line input.

6.1 Understanding Positional Parameters ($1, $2, etc.)

In Bash scripting, positional parameters provide a convenient way to pass arguments to scripts and functions. These parameters are referenced by special variables like $1, $2, $3, and so on, representing the first, second, third, and subsequent arguments, respectively. This section will delve into how to use positional parameters effectively, their advantages, and practical examples to illustrate their usage.

1. What are Positional Parameters?

Positional parameters are variables that store the arguments passed to a script or a function. When you invoke a script or function, you can provide values that these parameters can access, allowing for dynamic behavior based on user input.

Example: When running a script like ./script.sh arg1 arg2 arg3, the following positional parameters are defined:

$1 will be arg1
$2 will be arg2
$3 will be arg3

Note: The total number of positional parameters can be accessed using the special variable $#, which counts how many arguments were passed.

2. Accessing Positional Parameters

You can access positional parameters in your script using the $ symbol followed by the parameter number. Here's how you can use them:

```bash
#!/bin/bash

# Script to demonstrate positional parameters
echo "First Argument: $1"
echo "Second Argument: $2"
echo "Third Argument: $3"
echo "Total Number of Arguments: $#"
```

How to Create and Run the Script:

Create the Script:

nano positional_example.sh

Add the Script Content: Copy and paste the code above into the file.

Make the Script Executable:

chmod +x positional_example.sh

Run the Script with Arguments:

./positional_example.sh "Hello" "World" "!"

Output Example:

First Argument: Hello
Second Argument: World
Third Argument: !
Total Number of Arguments: 3

In this example, the script prints each argument passed to it, demonstrating how positional parameters work.

3. Using Positional Parameters in Functions

Positional parameters can also be used within functions, allowing you to pass arguments when calling the function.

Example: A function that calculates the area of a rectangle using positional parameters.

```bash
#!/bin/bash

# Function to calculate the area of a rectangle
calculate_area() {
    local length=$1  # First argument
    local width=$2   # Second argument
    echo $(( length * width ))  # Calculate area
}

# Call the function with arguments
area=$(calculate_area 10 5)
echo "The area of the rectangle is: $area"
```

How to Create and Run the Script:

Create the Script:

nano area_function_example.sh

Add the Script Content: Copy and paste the code above into the file.

Make the Script Executable:

chmod +x area_function_example.sh

Run the Script:

./area_function_example.sh

Output Example:

The area of the rectangle is: 50

In this example, the calculate_area function accepts two parameters, length and width, which are then used to compute the area.

4. Handling More Arguments

Bash allows you to handle more arguments than you explicitly define in your script. You can access them in a loop or by using the special variable $@ or $*.

- $@: Expands to all positional parameters as separate quoted strings.
- $*: Expands to all positional parameters as a single word.

Example: A script that prints all arguments.

```bash
#!/bin/bash

# Script to demonstrate $@ and $*
echo "Using \$@:"
for arg in "$@"; do
   echo "$arg"
done

echo "Using \$*:"
for arg in "$*"; do
   echo "$arg"
done
```

How to Create and Run the Script:

Create the Script:

nano all_arguments_example.sh

Add the Script Content: Copy and paste the code above into the file.

Make the Script Executable:

chmod +x all_arguments_example.sh

Run the Script with Multiple Arguments:

./all_arguments_example.sh "Hello" "World" "This" "Is" "Bash"

Output Example:

Using $@:
Hello
World
This
Is
Bash
Using $:*
Hello World This Is Bash

In this example, you can see how $@ and $* handle the arguments differently.

5. Validating Positional Parameters

Validating the number of positional parameters is essential to ensure that your script behaves correctly. You can use conditional statements to check the number of arguments passed.

Example: A script that checks if the correct number of arguments is provided.

```bash
#!/bin/bash

# Check if the correct number of arguments is passed
if [[ $# -ne 2 ]]; then
    echo "Usage: $0 <length> <width>"
    exit 1
fi

# Function to calculate area
calculate_area() {
    local length=$1
    local width=$2
    echo $(( length * width ))
}

# Call the function with arguments
area=$(calculate_area "$1" "$2")
echo "The area of the rectangle is: $area"
```

How to Create and Run the Script:

Create the Script:

nano validate_example.sh

Add the Script Content: Copy and paste the code above into the file.

Make the Script Executable:

chmod +x validate_example.sh

Run the Script with Incorrect Arguments:

./validate_example.sh 10

Output Example:

Usage: ./validate_example.sh <length> <width>

This script checks if exactly two arguments are provided. If not, it outputs a usage message and exits.

Understanding positional parameters is essential for effective Bash scripting. In this section, we explored:

- The definition and purpose of positional parameters.
- How to access and utilize them in scripts and functions.
- The use of special variables like $@ and $* to handle multiple arguments.
- Techniques for validating the number of arguments passed to ensure scripts run smoothly.

By mastering positional parameters, you can create more dynamic and user-friendly scripts that can adapt to various input scenarios, enhancing their functionality and usability. This foundational knowledge is a stepping stone toward building more complex Bash scripts that leverage user input effectively.

6.2 Using shift to Manage Command-line Arguments

In Bash scripting, managing command-line arguments effectively is crucial for creating flexible and robust scripts. The shift command is a powerful tool that allows you to manipulate the positional parameters by shifting them to the left. This section will cover how to use the shift command to manage command-line arguments effectively, including its syntax, practical examples, and common use cases.

1. Understanding the shift Command

The shift command is used to move the positional parameters to the left by a specified number of positions. When you use shift, the value of $1 is discarded, and the value of $2 becomes the new $1, the value of $3 becomes the new $2, and so on. The total number of positional parameters ($#) is decreased accordingly.

Syntax:

shift [n]

n: (optional) The number of positions to shift. If not specified, it defaults to 1.

2. Basic Usage of shift

Let's look at a simple example to demonstrate the use of shift.

Example: A script that processes command-line arguments one by one.

```bash
#!/bin/bash

# Script to demonstrate the use of shift
while [[ $# -gt 0 ]]; do
    echo "Processing argument: $1"
    shift  # Shift the positional parameters to the left
done

echo "All arguments processed."
```

How to Create and Run the Script:

Create the Script:

nano shift_example.sh

Add the Script Content: Copy and paste the code above into the file.

Make the Script Executable:

chmod +x shift_example.sh

Run the Script with Multiple Arguments:

./shift_example.sh "arg1" "arg2" "arg3" "arg4"

Output Example:

Processing argument: arg1
Processing argument: arg2
Processing argument: arg3
Processing argument: arg4
All arguments processed.

In this example, the script processes each argument individually by using shift to remove the processed argument from the list.

3. Managing Options with shift

Using shift is particularly useful when you have scripts that accept options or flags along with their arguments. This allows you to handle different types of input more flexibly.

Example: A script that processes flags and their values.

```bash
#!/bin/bash

# Script to demonstrate processing options
while [[ $# -gt 0 ]]; do
    case "$1" in
        -f|--file)
            FILE="$2"
            echo "File set to: $FILE"
            shift 2  # Shift past the flag and its argument
            ;;
        -v|--verbose)
```

```
            VERBOSE=true
            echo "Verbose mode activated."
            shift  # Shift past the flag
            ;;
        *)
            echo "Unknown option: $1"
            shift  # Shift past the unknown option
            ;;
    esac
done

echo "Finished processing options."
```

How to Create and Run the Script:

Create the Script:

nano options_example.sh

Add the Script Content: Copy and paste the code above into the file.

Make the Script Executable:

chmod +x options_example.sh

Run the Script with Options:

./options_example.sh -f myfile.txt -v

Output Example:

- File set to: myfile.txt
- Verbose mode activated.
- Finished processing options.

In this example, the script handles different options and their corresponding arguments using shift to move past processed flags.

4. Practical Use Case: Command-line Argument Validation

Using shift can also help in validating the arguments passed to your script. You can check for required parameters while iterating through the provided arguments.

Example: A script that requires a filename and an optional verbosity flag.

```bash
#!/bin/bash

# Check for required argument
if [[ $# -lt 1 ]]; then
    echo "Usage: $0 <filename> [-v | --verbose]"
    exit 1
fi

# Default values
VERBOSE=false

# Process arguments
while [[ $# -gt 0 ]]; do
    case "$1" in
        -v|--verbose)
            VERBOSE=true
            echo "Verbose mode activated."
            shift
            ;;
        *)
            FILENAME="$1"
            echo "Filename set to: $FILENAME"
            shift  # Move past the filename
            ;;
    esac
done

if $VERBOSE; then
    echo "Verbose mode is ON. Processing file: $FILENAME"
else
    echo "Processing file: $FILENAME"
fi
```

How to Create and Run the Script:

Create the Script:

nano validate_arguments_example.sh

Add the Script Content: Copy and paste the code above into the file.

Make the Script Executable:

chmod +x validate_arguments_example.sh

Run the Script with Required and Optional Arguments:

./validate_arguments_example.sh myfile.txt -v

Output Example:

- Verbose mode activated.
- Filename set to: myfile.txt
- Verbose mode is ON. Processing file: myfile.txt

In this example, the script requires a filename and allows for an optional verbosity flag. It uses shift to manage and validate the arguments efficiently.

5. Using shift in Loops for Batch Processing

Another common use case for shift is when you want to process a batch of arguments in a loop. This can be particularly useful for scripts that handle multiple files or other similar inputs.

Example: A script that copies multiple files to a target directory.

```bash
#!/bin/bash

# Check if at least two arguments (target directory and one file) are provided
if [[ $# -lt 2 ]]; then
    echo "Usage: $0 <target_directory> <file1> [file2 ...]"
    exit 1
fi

TARGET_DIR="$1"
```

```bash
shift  # Remove the target directory from the list of arguments

# Loop through the remaining arguments
while [[ $# -gt 0 ]]; do
   FILE="$1"
   if [[ -f "$FILE" ]]; then
      cp "$FILE" "$TARGET_DIR"
      echo "Copied $FILE to $TARGET_DIR"
   else
      echo "Warning: $FILE does not exist."
   fi
   shift  # Shift to the next file
done

echo "Finished copying files."
```

How to Create and Run the Script:

Create the Script:

nano copy_files_example.sh

Add the Script Content: Copy and paste the code above into the file.

Make the Script Executable:

chmod +x copy_files_example.sh

Run the Script with a Target Directory and Files:

./copy_files_example.sh /path/to/target_directory file1.txt file2.txt file3.txt

Output Example:

- Copied file1.txt to /path/to/target_directory
- Warning: file2.txt does not exist.
- Copied file3.txt to /path/to/target_directory
- Finished copying files.

In this example, the script takes a target directory as the first argument and then processes each subsequent argument as a filename to copy. It uses shift to move through the list of files.

The shift command is a valuable tool in Bash scripting for managing command-line arguments. In this section, we covered:

- The purpose and syntax of the shift command.
- Basic usage examples of shift in scripts.
- Processing options and flags using shift.
- Validating command-line arguments effectively.
- Batch processing of files or inputs with shift.

By mastering the shift command, you can enhance the flexibility and usability of your Bash scripts, allowing them to handle various input scenarios with ease. This skill is essential for creating dynamic and user-friendly scripts that respond intelligently to user input.

6.3 Parsing Options with getopts

In Bash scripting, handling command-line options and arguments efficiently is crucial for building flexible and user-friendly scripts. The getopts command is a built-in utility designed specifically for parsing command-line options, making it ideal for more complex argument handling. This section will introduce the getopts command, explain its usage, and provide practical examples for parsing options like flags and values in your Bash scripts.

1. What is getopts?

getopts is a tool for parsing command-line options in a standardized way, similar to how many Linux utilities handle options. It supports single-character options (such as -f or -v), optional arguments (like -o output.txt), and even error handling. It simplifies scripts that need to process options by automating the option parsing process.

Syntax:

- getopts optstring variable
- optstring: A string that defines the valid options.

- variable: The name of the variable that will hold the current option being processed.

2. The optstring: Defining Valid Options

The optstring is a critical component in getopts, as it defines what options your script will accept.

- Single-character options are listed without any additional characters.
- Options that require an argument are followed by a colon (:).

For example, if your script accepts the following options:

- -f (requires an argument)
- -v (no argument required)
- -o (requires an argument)

The optstring would be: "f:o:v"

3. Basic Example: Parsing Options with getopts

Here's a simple example to demonstrate how getopts works.

```bash
#!/bin/bash

# Simple example of getopts usage
while getopts "f:o:v" opt; do
   case "$opt" in
      f) # Option -f requires an argument
         filename="$OPTARG"
         echo "Filename: $filename"
         ;;
      o) # Option -o requires an argument
         output="$OPTARG"
         echo "Output: $output"
         ;;
      v) # Option -v does not require an argument
         verbose=true
         echo "Verbose mode activated"
         ;;
```

```
    \?)  # Invalid option
        echo "Invalid option: -$OPTARG" >&2
        ;;
  esac
done
```

How to Create and Run the Script:

Create the Script:

nano getopts_example.sh

Add the Script Content: Copy and paste the code above into the file.

Make the Script Executable:

chmod +x getopts_example.sh

Run the Script with Options:

./getopts_example.sh -f input.txt -o output.txt -v

Output Example:

- Filename: input.txt
- Output: output.txt
- Verbose mode activated

In this example:

- -f requires an argument, so it captures input.txt.
- -o requires an argument, so it captures output.txt.
- -v is a flag, so it simply activates the verbose mode.

4. Handling Invalid Options and Missing Arguments

When an invalid option or a missing argument is passed, getopts provides built-in error handling. Let's improve the previous example by adding better error messages for these scenarios.

Example: Handling missing arguments and invalid options.

```bash
#!/bin/bash

# Enhanced example with error handling
while getopts ":f:o:v" opt; do
    case "$opt" in
        f)
            if [[ -z "$OPTARG" ]]; then
                echo "Option -f requires an argument." >&2
                exit 1
            fi
            filename="$OPTARG"
            echo "Filename: $filename"
            ;;
        o)
            if [[ -z "$OPTARG" ]]; then
                echo "Option -o requires an argument." >&2
                exit 1
            fi
            output="$OPTARG"
            echo "Output: $output"
            ;;
        v)
            verbose=true
            echo "Verbose mode activated"
            ;;
        \?)
            echo "Invalid option: -$OPTARG" >&2
            exit 1
            ;;
        :)
            echo "Option -$OPTARG requires an argument." >&2
            exit 1
            ;;
    esac
done
```

Run the Script with Missing or Invalid Options:

./getopts_example.sh -f -o output.txt -v

Output Example:

Option -f requires an argument.

In this case:

The script checks if -f or -o are missing arguments and handles it appropriately.

It also detects invalid options and flags errors.

5. Using OPTARG for Argument Values

When an option requires an argument, getopts stores that argument in the special variable OPTARG. This allows you to access and process the argument inside your script.

Example: Using OPTARG to store and use option arguments.

```bash
#!/bin/bash

# Example of using OPTARG
while getopts "u:p:" opt; do
  case "$opt" in
    u)
      username="$OPTARG"
      ;;
    p)
      password="$OPTARG"
      ;;
    \?)
      echo "Invalid option: -$OPTARG" >&2
      exit 1
      ;;
    :)
      echo "Option -$OPTARG requires an argument." >&2
      exit 1
      ;;
  esac
```

done

echo "Username: $username"
echo "Password: $password"

Run the Script:

./getopts_example.sh -u admin -p secret

Output Example:

Username: admin
Password: secret

Here, -u and -p both require arguments, and getopts stores those arguments in OPTARG for use later in the script.

6. Handling Long Options in Bash

By default, getopts only supports short options (single-character options, like -f). If you want to handle long options (like --file or --verbose), you need to implement custom handling. A common approach is to process long options manually.

Example: Handling long options alongside getopts.

```bash
#!/bin/bash

# Custom long option handling combined with getopts
while [[ $# -gt 0 ]]; do
    case "$1" in
        --file)
            filename="$2"
            shift 2  # Shift past the option and its argument
            ;;
        --verbose)
            verbose=true
            shift  # Shift past the flag
            ;;
        -f)
            filename="$OPTARG"
```

```bash
            ;;
        -v)
            verbose=true
            ;;
        *)
            echo "Invalid option: $1" >&2
            exit 1
            ;;
    esac
done

echo "Filename: $filename"
if [[ $verbose == true ]]; then
    echo "Verbose mode is ON"
fi
```

Run the Script with Long and Short Options:

./getopts_long_example.sh --file myfile.txt --verbose

Output Example:

Filename: myfile.txt
Verbose mode is ON

In this example, long options like --file and --verbose are handled alongside traditional short options using a manual approach with case statements.

7. Combining Options and Arguments

Sometimes, you may want to combine options and their arguments, such as -f input.txt -v. getopts supports combining multiple options, allowing you to build more complex command-line interfaces.

Example: Combining options in a compact command line.

```bash
#!/bin/bash

while getopts "vf:o:" opt; do
    case "$opt" in
```

```
    v)
        verbose=true
        echo "Verbose mode activated."
        ;;
    f)
        filename="$OPTARG"
        echo "Filename: $filename"
        ;;
    o)
        output="$OPTARG"
        echo "Output: $output"
        ;;
    \?)
        echo "Invalid option: -$OPTARG" >&2
        exit 1
        ;;
    :)
        echo "Option -$OPTARG requires an argument." >&2
        exit 1
        ;;
  esac
done
```

Run the Script with Combined Options:

./getopts_combined_example.sh -vf input.txt -o output.txt

Output Example:

- Verbose mode activated.
- Filename: input.txt
- Output: output.txt

In this example, getopts processes multiple options (-v, -f, and -o) in a single command-line input, demonstrating its flexibility.

The getopts command is an essential tool for parsing command-line options in Bash scripts. It allows for handling both simple and complex options with ease, offering built-in error handling and argument validation. In this section, we covered:

- Basic usage of getopts for parsing options.
- Handling arguments with OPTARG.
- Error handling for missing arguments and invalid options.
- Combining options and arguments in a script.
- Handling long options with custom code.

Mastering getopts allows you to build more interactive and user-friendly scripts, making them easier to use and more powerful for real-world applications.

6.4 Validating and Handling User Input

When building robust Bash scripts, validating and handling user input is essential to ensure that your script behaves as expected and avoids errors caused by invalid or unexpected input. Proper input validation can prevent issues such as incorrect file paths, invalid command-line arguments, or unsafe user input that could cause script failure or even security vulnerabilities. This section will cover key techniques for validating user input in Bash, including checking for empty input, enforcing specific formats, and providing meaningful feedback to users.

1. Importance of Input Validation

Input validation ensures that the data provided by users or other programs conforms to the expected format, type, or range. Without validation, a script can break when it encounters unexpected data, leading to unpredictable behavior, crashes, or security risks. Validation is particularly crucial when accepting user input from sources such as:

- Command-line arguments.
- Interactive prompts.
- Configuration files or external data sources.

2. Basic Input Validation Techniques

There are several basic techniques you can use to validate user input in a Bash script, including checking for empty input, ensuring the input is of the correct data type (such as numeric or string), and verifying that the input meets specific criteria (like file existence or matching patterns).

2.1 Checking for Empty Input

One of the simplest forms of input validation is ensuring that the user provides a value and that the input is not empty. This is especially important for required arguments.

Example: Checking for non-empty input.

```bash
#!/bin/bash

# Ask the user for input
read -p "Enter your name: " name

# Validate the input: check if it's empty
if [[ -z "$name" ]]; then
    echo "Error: Name cannot be empty. Please enter a valid name."
    exit 1
else
    echo "Hello, $name!"
fi
```

In this example, the [[-z "$name"]] condition checks if the variable name is empty. If it is, the script exits with an error message.

2.2 Checking for Numeric Input

In some cases, you need to ensure that the user provides a numeric value, such as when accepting ages, quantities, or other numeric parameters.

Example: Checking for numeric input.

```bash
#!/bin/bash

read -p "Enter your age: " age

# Validate that the input is a number
if ! [[ "$age" =~ ^[0-9]+$ ]]; then
    echo "Error: Age must be a number."
    exit 1
else
    echo "You are $age years old."
fi
```

Here, the regular expression ^[0-9]+$ ensures that the input contains only digits (0-9). If the input is not a valid number, the script exits with an error message.

3. Validating Command-line Arguments

When accepting command-line arguments in a script, it's essential to validate them to avoid processing invalid data.

3.1 Validating Argument Count

A common validation task is ensuring that the correct number of arguments is passed to the script.

Example: Checking the number of command-line arguments.

```bash
#!/bin/bash

# Check if the script received exactly 2 arguments
if [[ $# -ne 2 ]]; then
    echo "Error: You must provide exactly 2 arguments."
    echo "Usage: $0 <arg1> <arg2>"
    exit 1
fi

echo "Argument 1: $1"
echo "Argument 2: $2"
```

In this script, [[$# -ne 2]] checks if the number of arguments passed ($#) is not equal to 2. If the wrong number of arguments is provided, the script outputs an error message and displays the correct usage.

3.2 Validating File Paths

When a script expects a file path as an argument, you should validate whether the file exists and is accessible.

Example: Validating file input.

```bash
#!/bin/bash
```

```bash
file="$1"

# Check if the file exists and is readable
if [[ ! -f "$file" ]]; then
    echo "Error: File '$file' does not exist."
    exit 1
fi

echo "Processing file: $file"
```

The condition [[! -f "$file"]] checks if the file exists and is a regular file. If the file does not exist, the script exits with an error message.

4. Validating User Input Formats

In some cases, you may need to validate that input matches a specific format, such as email addresses, IP addresses, or dates. Regular expressions are a powerful tool for performing such validations in Bash.

4.1 Validating an Email Address

Example: Validating an email format.

```bash
#!/bin/bash

read -p "Enter your email address: " email

# Validate the email address format using a regular expression
if ! [[ "$email" =~ ^[a-zA-Z0-9._%+-]+@[a-zA-Z0-9.-]+\.[a-zA-Z]{2,}$ ]]; then
    echo "Error: Invalid email address format."
    exit 1
fi

echo "Valid email: $email"
```

In this script, the regular expression checks that the input follows a common email address pattern: username@domain.extension. If the format is invalid, the script outputs an error.

4.2 Validating an IP Address

Example: Validating an IPv4 address.

```bash
#!/bin/bash

read -p "Enter an IP address: " ip

# Validate the IP address format
if ! [[ "$ip" =~ ^([0-9]{1,3}\.){3}[0-9]{1,3}$ ]]; then
    echo "Error: Invalid IP address format."
    exit 1
fi

echo "Valid IP address: $ip"
```

This regular expression checks if the input matches the typical format of an IPv4 address (x.x.x.x), where x is a number between 0 and 255.

5. Sanitizing User Input

In addition to validation, sanitizing input is crucial to prevent unwanted characters or potentially harmful input (like command injection) from causing security risks.

5.1 Removing Special Characters

If you need to ensure that the user input is free of special characters, you can sanitize it by stripping out or rejecting certain characters.

Example: Removing special characters from input.

```bash
#!/bin/bash

read -p "Enter your username: " username

# Sanitize input by removing special characters
sanitized_username=$(echo "$username" | tr -cd '[:alnum:]')

echo "Sanitized username: $sanitized_username"
```

In this example, the tr command removes all characters except alphanumeric ones, ensuring that the username contains only letters and numbers.

5.2 Preventing Command Injection

When dealing with user input that may be passed to system commands, it's essential to sanitize or escape the input to avoid command injection vulnerabilities.

Example: Preventing command injection.

```bash
#!/bin/bash

read -p "Enter a directory path: " dir

# Validate and sanitize input before using it in a system command
if [[ -d "$dir" ]]; then
    echo "Listing contents of directory: $dir"
    ls -- "$dir"
else
    echo "Error: Directory '$dir' does not exist."
    exit 1
fi
```

The ls -- "$dir" syntax ensures that even if the input contains special characters or malicious input, it is treated as a literal directory path and not executed as part of a command.

6. Providing User Feedback and Error Messages

Clear and informative error messages are essential for helping users understand why their input is invalid and how to correct it. When validating input, provide detailed feedback about what went wrong and offer guidance on valid input formats.

Example: Providing user feedback.

```bash
#!/bin/bash

read -p "Enter your age: " age

# Validate the input
```

```
if ! [[ "$age" =~ ^[0-9]+$ ]]; then
    echo "Error: Age must be a number between 0 and 120."
    exit 1
elif [[ "$age" -lt 0 || "$age" -gt 120 ]]; then
    echo "Error: Age must be between 0 and 120."
    exit 1
fi

echo "You are $age years old."
```

This script provides clear feedback when the age is not a number or when it falls outside a reasonable range, helping the user input valid data.

Validating and handling user input is an essential aspect of writing robust and secure Bash scripts. By implementing proper input validation techniques, you can ensure that your scripts handle data reliably and safely, improving both usability and security. In this section, we explored:

- The importance of input validation.
- Techniques for checking empty, numeric, and formatted input.
- Validating command-line arguments and file paths.
- Sanitizing input to prevent security risks.
- Providing clear feedback and error messages to guide users.

By mastering these validation techniques, you'll create more reliable and user-friendly Bash scripts that are resilient to errors and unexpected input.

6.5 Reading Input from the User with read

In Bash scripting, gathering input from users dynamically is a common and essential task, especially when writing interactive scripts. The read command provides a simple and effective way to prompt users for input, capture their responses, and store that input into variables for later use within the script. Whether you're asking for user preferences, passwords, filenames, or any other input, read offers various options to handle these scenarios efficiently.

1. Basic Usage of read

The read command is straightforward and typically follows this syntax:

read [options] variable_name

Here, variable_name is where the user input will be stored. After prompting the user, the input entered from the keyboard is assigned to this variable.

1.1 Example: Simple User Input

Let's begin with a basic example of using read to get user input.

```bash
#!/bin/bash

# Prompt the user for their name
read -p "Enter your name: " name

# Output the captured input
echo "Hello, $name!"
```

In this script:

-p "Enter your name: " allows us to display a prompt message to the user.

The input is stored in the variable name, which is then echoed back to greet the user. This example demonstrates how simple it is to get user input with the read command.

2. Using read with Multiple Variables

The read command can be used to gather multiple pieces of information at once by assigning user input to multiple variables.

2.1 Example: Reading Multiple Values

```bash
#!/bin/bash

# Prompt the user for first and last name
read -p "Enter your first and last name: " first_name last_name

# Display the input
echo "First Name: $first_name"
echo "Last Name: $last_name"
```

In this case, when the user enters two words separated by space (e.g., "John Doe"), first_name will store "John" and last_name will store "Doe". If the user enters more than two words, only the first two will be assigned, and the rest will be ignored.

3. Handling Silent Input with -s (Secret Input)

Sometimes, you need to collect sensitive information, such as passwords, where displaying the input on the terminal is undesirable. The -s option tells read to keep the input hidden while the user types.

3.1 Example: Reading a Password

```
#!/bin/bash

# Prompt the user for a password, hide the input
read -sp "Enter your password: " password

# Add a newline for formatting
echo

# Use the password in the script (for demo purposes, we'll just display its length)
echo "Password length: ${#password}"
```

In this example:

- The -s flag ensures the password is entered without being displayed.
- The echo command is used afterward to print a newline for formatting purposes.
- This is especially useful in scripts where security and confidentiality are important.

4. Setting a Timeout for Input with -t

Sometimes, scripts need to run interactively but can't afford to wait indefinitely for user input. The -t option allows you to specify a timeout in seconds. If the user does not provide input within the given time, the script will proceed.

4.1 Example: Input with Timeout

```
#!/bin/bash
```

```bash
# Prompt the user for input with a 10-second timeout
read -t 10 -p "Enter your name (10 seconds to respond): " name

# Check if the input was provided or the timeout expired
if [[ -z "$name" ]]; then
    echo "You didn't provide any input. Timeout expired."
else
    echo "Hello, $name!"
fi
```

In this script:

The -t 10 option sets a 10-second timer. If no input is received within that time, the variable name remains empty, and the script proceeds.

The script checks if name is empty ([[-z "$name"]]) and provides appropriate feedback.

5. Limiting Input Length with -n

If you want to restrict the number of characters a user can input, the -n option allows you to limit the input to a specific number of characters.

5.1 Example: Limiting Input Length

```bash
#!/bin/bash

# Prompt the user for input, but only allow 5 characters
read -n 5 -p "Enter a 5-character string: " input

# Output the captured input
echo
echo "You entered: $input"
```

In this example:

The -n 5 option restricts the user to inputting only 5 characters. After the user enters 5 characters, read automatically moves forward without the need to press Enter.

A newline (echo) is used after capturing input to format the output nicely.

6. Handling Default Values for Input

Sometimes, you may want to give the user the option to accept a default value if they press Enter without providing input. You can achieve this by checking if the input is empty and assigning a default value in that case.

6.1 Example: Providing a Default Value

```bash
#!/bin/bash

# Prompt the user for their favorite color, with a default value
read -p "Enter your favorite color (default is blue): " color

# If the user doesn't provide input, use "blue" as the default value
color=${color:-blue}

# Output the result
echo "Your favorite color is $color."
```

Here, ${color:-blue} sets the value of color to "blue" if the user leaves the input blank. This provides a simple way to offer default values in your scripts.

7. Reading Input from Files and Streams

In addition to reading input from users, read can also capture input from files or other streams. This is useful when processing data in files line by line.

7.1 Example: Reading Lines from a File

```bash
#!/bin/bash

# Read each line from a file and process it
while IFS= read -r line; do
    echo "Processing: $line"
done < input.txt
```

In this example:

- The while loop reads each line from input.txt using read -r, which prevents backslashes from being interpreted as escape characters.
- IFS=, the internal field separator, ensures that leading or trailing whitespace is preserved.
- This is particularly useful when writing scripts that handle configuration files, logs, or other structured data.

8. Reading User Input with Prompts in Loops

The read command can be used in loops to continuously ask for user input until a valid response is provided or a certain condition is met. This can enhance the interactivity of your script.

8.1 Example: Input Validation Loop

```
#!/bin/bash

while true; do
   read -p "Enter a number between 1 and 10: " number

   # Validate the input
   if [[ "$number" =~ ^[1-9]$|10 ]]; then
      echo "You entered a valid number: $number"
      break
   else
      echo "Invalid input. Please try again."
   fi
done
```

In this script:

- The loop repeatedly asks the user for a number between 1 and 10 until a valid input is provided.
- The condition [["$number" =~ ^[1-9]$|10]] uses a regular expression to check if the input is a number between 1 and 10.
- If the input is valid, the loop breaks, and the script proceeds. Otherwise, it continues prompting the user.

The read command is an incredibly versatile tool for capturing and handling user input in Bash scripts. Whether you're writing interactive scripts, processing sensitive data, or handling file input, read provides flexible options to meet a wide variety of needs. Key features include:

- Prompting users with customized messages (-p).
- Reading and hiding sensitive input like passwords (-s).
- Handling multiple inputs at once.
- Limiting input length or setting timeouts (-n and -t).
- Processing input from files or streams.

By mastering these features, you can create more dynamic and user-friendly Bash scripts that are capable of responding to real-time input efficiently and securely.

7. Working with Strings and Text Processing

In this chapter, you will delve into the essential skills of string manipulation and text processing in Bash. You'll learn how to perform basic string operations such as concatenation, substring extraction, and length calculation. We'll also explore pattern matching and regular expressions, which are invaluable for searching and validating text. Additionally, you will discover powerful tools like grep, sed, and awk for filtering, transforming, and reporting text data. By the end of this chapter, you'll be equipped with the techniques to effectively handle and process strings within your scripts, allowing you to manipulate data with precision and ease.

7.1 Basic String Operations: Concatenation, Length, and Substrings

Strings are one of the most common data types you will work with in shell scripting, and Bash provides several tools to manipulate strings efficiently. Whether you are combining (concatenating) strings, calculating their length, or extracting substrings, understanding how to perform these operations is essential for building robust and versatile shell scripts. In this section, we'll cover the basic string operations in Bash, including concatenation, length determination, and substring extraction.

1. String Concatenation in Bash

String concatenation refers to the process of joining two or more strings together to form a single string. Bash does not have a specific operator for concatenation, but strings can easily be concatenated by placing them next to each other.

1.1 Basic Concatenation

The simplest way to concatenate two or more strings is by using variables and the echo command.

```
#!/bin/bash

# Define two strings
str1="Hello"
str2="World"
```

```
# Concatenate the strings
result="$str1 $str2"

# Output the concatenated string
echo "$result"
```

In this example:

- Two variables, str1 and str2, hold the values "Hello" and "World" respectively.
- Concatenating the two strings involves placing them together inside the variable result and separating them with a space ("$str1 $str2").
- The final result is "Hello World".
- You can concatenate as many strings as you like by following the same pattern.

1.2 Concatenation with Additional Text

You can also concatenate strings with additional text, such as static text or special characters, in Bash.

```
#!/bin/bash

name="Alice"
greeting="Hello, $name! Welcome to Bash scripting."

echo "$greeting"
```

In this case, the variable name is combined with other static text to form a personalized greeting. The final output will be:

Hello, Alice! Welcome to Bash scripting.

This technique is useful for building dynamic strings that combine user input, command output, and static text.

2. Calculating String Length

In Bash, you can easily calculate the length of a string using a special syntax. Knowing the length of a string can be useful for validating input or performing operations based on string size.

2.1 Syntax for String Length

To find the length of a string, use the following syntax:

${#variable}

This returns the number of characters in the string stored in variable.

2.2 Example: String Length

```
#!/bin/bash

# Define a string
str="Bash scripting"

# Get the length of the string
length=${#str}

# Output the length
echo "The length of the string is: $length"
```

In this example:

- The variable str contains the string "Bash scripting".
- The expression ${#str} calculates the number of characters in the string, which in this case is 14.
- The result is printed as: The length of the string is: 14.

This technique is helpful when working with dynamic inputs or when the length of the string is important for decision-making in scripts.

3. Extracting Substrings in Bash

A substring is a portion of a string, extracted from a larger string. Bash provides a powerful syntax to extract specific parts of a string based on position and length.

3.1 Syntax for Substring Extraction

The general syntax for extracting a substring is:

${variable:offset:length}

Where:

- variable is the string from which you want to extract the substring.
- offset is the position in the string where the extraction should begin (0-based index).
- length is the number of characters to extract from the starting position.

If the length is omitted, Bash will extract all characters from the offset to the end of the string.

3.2 Example: Basic Substring Extraction

#!/bin/bash

 # Define a string
str="Bash scripting is powerful"

 # Extract a substring starting from position 5, for 9 characters
substring=${str:5:9}

 # Output the substring
echo "Extracted substring: $substring"

In this example:

- The variable str contains the string "Bash scripting is powerful".
- The substring ${str:5:9} extracts 9 characters starting from position 5, which results in the string "scripting".
- The output will be: Extracted substring: scripting.

3.3 Extracting from a Specific Offset to the End

You can extract a substring starting from a specific position and continuing to the end of the string by omitting the length parameter.

#!/bin/bash

 # Define a string

```
str="Learning Bash scripting"

# Extract from position 9 to the end
substring=${str:9}

# Output the substring
echo "Substring: $substring"
```

In this case, ${str:9} extracts the substring starting from the 9th position ("Bash scripting") and continues to the end of the string. The output will be:

Substring: Bash scripting

3.4 Extracting Substrings with Negative Indexing

Bash also allows negative indexing, where an offset can start counting from the end of the string. A negative offset starts at the last character and moves backward.

```
#!/bin/bash

# Define a string
str="Bash scripting is fun"

# Extract the last 3 characters
substring=${str: -3}

# Output the substring
echo "Last 3 characters: $substring"
```

In this example:

- The expression ${str: -3} extracts the last 3 characters of the string, resulting in "fun".
- Negative indexing is particularly useful when you need to extract elements from the end of a string without knowing the exact length of the string in advance.

Note the space between the colon and the minus sign (: -3). This prevents confusion between negative numbers and the substring syntax.

4. Combining String Operations

String concatenation, length calculation, and substring extraction can be combined to perform more complex string manipulations in your scripts.

4.1 Example: Complex String Manipulation

#!/bin/bash

 # Define a string
full_name="Alice Johnson"

 # Extract the first name and last name
first_name=${full_name:0:5}
last_name=${full_name:6}

 # Concatenate the extracted parts with additional text
greeting="Hello, $first_name! Your last name is $last_name."

 # Output the result
echo "$greeting"

In this example:

- The variable full_name contains "Alice Johnson".
- The first name is extracted using ${full_name:0:5}, and the last name is extracted using ${full_name:6}.

The final greeting is built by concatenating the extracted values with additional text, resulting in: Hello, Alice! Your last name is Johnson.

5. Summary

In this section, we explored the basic string operations in Bash, including:

- String concatenation: Joining strings together using simple syntax by placing them side by side.
- String length: Calculating the number of characters in a string using ${#variable}.
- Substring extraction: Extracting specific parts of a string using ${variable:offset:length}, with options for starting at specific positions or counting from the end.

These fundamental string operations are essential for processing user input, handling text data, and performing a wide variety of tasks in your Bash scripts. Mastering these techniques will help you write more dynamic and flexible scripts that can manipulate strings effectively.

7.2 Pattern Matching and Regular Expressions

In shell scripting, pattern matching and regular expressions are powerful tools that allow you to search for, identify, and manipulate text based on specific patterns. Whether you're working with file names, validating input, or processing text, understanding how to use pattern matching and regular expressions in Bash is essential for efficient scripting.

In this section, we will explore the basics of pattern matching in Bash, how regular expressions (regex) can be used, and the different ways they are applied in shell scripting.

1. Pattern Matching in Bash

Bash has its own built-in mechanisms for pattern matching, which are often used for filename expansion (globbing) and string matching in conditional expressions. Unlike regular expressions, Bash pattern matching is simpler and generally used to match filenames or sections of strings.

1.1 Wildcards for Pattern Matching

Wildcards are the most basic form of pattern matching in Bash. They allow you to match strings or filenames that fit a specific pattern.

The common wildcards used in Bash include:

- `*` – Matches any number of characters (including none).
- `?` – Matches exactly one character.
- `[ ]` – Matches any one of the enclosed characters.

1.1.1 Example: Using Wildcards

#!/bin/bash

```bash
# List all .txt files in the current directory
ls *.txt
```

In this example, *.txt uses the * wildcard to match any file that ends with .txt. The * means "any string of characters," so it will list all text files, regardless of their filenames.

1.2 Brace Expansion

Brace expansion allows you to generate multiple strings or filenames based on a pattern. It's useful when you need to perform operations on a set of similar files or strings.

1.2.1 Example: Brace Expansion

```bash
#!/bin/bash

# Create three files: file1.txt, file2.txt, file3.txt
touch file{1..3}.txt
```

In this case, file{1..3}.txt generates three filenames: file1.txt, file2.txt, and file3.txt. The brace expansion creates a sequence, which can be useful for working with groups of files or automating repetitive tasks.

1.3 Pattern Matching with case

Bash's case statement is a useful tool for pattern matching within scripts. It allows you to execute different code blocks depending on the pattern that matches the input.

1.3.1 Example: Pattern Matching with case

```bash
#!/bin/bash

read -p "Enter a file extension: " ext

case "$ext" in
  txt)
    echo "Text file"
    ;;
  jpg|jpeg)
```

```
        echo "Image file (JPEG)"
            ;;
    *)
        echo "Unknown file type"
            ;;
esac
```

In this example:

- The case statement checks the value of the ext variable.
- If the user enters txt, it identifies it as a "Text file".
- If the user enters jpg or jpeg, it matches either pattern and outputs "Image file (JPEG)".
- The * wildcard matches anything else and returns "Unknown file type."

2. Regular Expressions in Bash

Regular expressions (regex) offer much more sophisticated pattern matching capabilities than Bash's wildcards. They allow you to define complex search patterns and are widely used in text processing tasks like searching, validating, and manipulating strings. In Bash, regular expressions are commonly used with commands like grep, sed, awk, and even the [[ ]] conditional expression.

Regular expressions can be simple or very complex, depending on the task. They consist of literals (specific characters), meta-characters, and special syntax that form a pattern to search for or manipulate text.

2.1 Basic Regular Expression Syntax

Here are some common elements of regular expressions:

. – Matches any single character.
^ – Matches the beginning of a line.
$ – Matches the end of a line.
* – Matches zero or more occurrences of the preceding character.
+ – Matches one or more occurrences of the preceding character.
? – Matches zero or one occurrence of the preceding character.
[ ] – Matches any one of the characters enclosed in brackets.
( ) – Groups characters or expressions.
| – Acts as an OR operator.

2.2 Using grep with Regular Expressions

The grep command is one of the most common tools for searching through text using regular expressions.

2.2.1 Example: Searching with grep

#!/bin/bash

 # Search for lines containing "error" in a log file
grep "error" server.log

This example searches for the word "error" in the server.log file. By default, grep matches simple text, but you can use the -E flag to enable extended regular expressions.

2.2.2 Example: Extended Regular Expressions with grep -E

#!/bin/bash

 # Search for lines that start with a digit
grep -E "^[0-9]" server.log

In this example, the regular expression ^[0-9] matches lines that start with a digit (0-9). The caret ^ specifies the start of a line, and [0-9] matches any digit.

2.3 Regular Expressions with [[ ]] in Bash

In addition to external commands like grep, Bash itself can perform regex matching using the [[ ]] conditional expression and the =~ operator.

2.3.1 Example: Regex Matching in Bash

#!/bin/bash

read -p "Enter a string: " str

 # Check if the string contains only digits
if [["$str" =~ ^[0-9]+$]]; then

```
    echo "The string contains only digits."
else
    echo "The string contains non-digit characters."
fi
```

In this example:

- The expression ^[0-9]+$ checks if the entire string consists only of digits.
- ^ and $ ensure that the match applies to the whole string, and [0-9]+ matches one or more digits.
- The [["$str" =~ ^[0-9]+$]] syntax is used to test if the input string matches the pattern.

2.4 Using sed for Substitutions with Regular Expressions

The sed command (stream editor) is a versatile tool for manipulating text. It's often used for search-and-replace operations with regular expressions.

2.4.1 Example: Substituting Text with sed

```
#!/bin/bash

# Replace "foo" with "bar" in a text file
sed 's/foo/bar/g' input.txt
```

In this example:

- s/foo/bar/g is a substitution command where foo is replaced with bar in the input.txt file.
- The g flag indicates that all occurrences of "foo" should be replaced, not just the first one in each line.
- Regular expressions can be combined with sed for more complex text manipulation tasks, such as replacing patterns that match certain criteria.

2.5 Using awk for Pattern Matching and Text Processing

awk is another powerful text-processing tool that uses regular expressions to perform operations on text files or streams.

2.5.1 Example: Using awk for Pattern Matching

```bash
#!/bin/bash

# Print lines from a file that contain the word "error"
awk '/error/ { print }' log.txt
```

In this example:

- /error/ is the regular expression that matches any line containing "error".
- awk then prints the matching lines from log.txt.
- awk can be used to perform more advanced operations, such as extracting fields from CSV files, transforming data, and more.

3. Regular Expressions: Practical Use Cases

3.1 Validating Input

Regular expressions are often used to validate input in shell scripts. For example, you can use a regex to check if an email address is valid or if a string contains only specific characters.

3.1.1 Example: Email Validation

```bash
#!/bin/bash

read -p "Enter your email address: " email

# Validate email format using regex
if [[ "$email" =~ ^[a-zA-Z0-9._%+-]+@[a-zA-Z0-9.-]+\.[a-zA-Z]{2,}$ ]]; then
    echo "Valid email address."
else
    echo "Invalid email address."
fi
```

This script checks if the entered email matches a typical email format using regular expressions.

3.2 Text Parsing

Regular expressions are also useful for extracting specific information from text. For example, you can use regex to parse a log file and extract error messages or specific fields.

3.2.1 Example: Extracting Error Messages from a Log

#!/bin/bash

 # Extract error messages from a log file
grep -E "ERROR [0-9]{3}" server.log

In this example, the regular expression ERROR [0-9]{3} searches for lines containing the word "ERROR" followed by a three-digit error code.

Pattern matching and regular expressions are essential tools for any Bash programmer. While pattern matching with wildcards and case statements provides simple and effective ways to work with filenames and conditions, regular expressions offer a more powerful and flexible approach to searching, validating, and manipulating text. By mastering these techniques, you can create more efficient, dynamic, and robust shell scripts that handle a wide variety of tasks. Whether you are filtering log files, validating user input, or processing text data, the ability to harness pattern matching and regular expressions will significantly enhance your scripting capabilities.

7.3 grep: Searching for Patterns in Files

The grep command is one of the most powerful and widely used tools in the Unix/Linux command-line environment. Its primary purpose is to search for patterns (typically strings or regular expressions) within files or input streams. The name grep stands for Global Regular Expression Print, highlighting its ability to search text using regular expressions and print the matching lines.

In this section, we'll explore the functionality of grep, its syntax, options, and how it can be used to search for patterns effectively. Whether you're working with log files, filtering large datasets, or searching for specific data, grep is an indispensable tool for Bash programmers.

1. Basic Syntax of grep

The basic syntax of the grep command is as follows:

grep [options] pattern [file...]
pattern: The string or regular expression to search for.
[file...]: The file(s) in which to search. If no file is specified, grep searches from standard input.

1.1 Example: Simple Search

grep "hello" file.txt

In this example, grep searches for the string "hello" in the file file.txt. If any lines in file.txt contain "hello", grep prints them to the output.

2. Case Sensitivity in Searches

By default, grep performs case-sensitive searches, meaning "Hello" and "hello" are considered different strings. To perform a case-insensitive search, use the -i option.

2.1 Example: Case-Insensitive Search

grep -i "hello" file.txt

In this case, both "hello" and "Hello" (or any variation of capitalization) will match the search pattern.

3. Displaying Line Numbers with Matches

When working with large files, it can be helpful to know where in the file a match occurred. You can display the line numbers of matching lines using the -n option.

3.1 Example: Showing Line Numbers

grep -n "error" log.txt

This command searches for the word "error" in log.txt and outputs the matching lines along with their line numbers.

4. Matching Entire Words

Sometimes, you might want to search for a specific word rather than a substring. By default, grep matches substrings within larger words, but you can restrict the search to whole words using the -w option.

4.1 Example: Matching Whole Words

grep -w "error" log.txt

In this case, grep will match "error" only if it appears as a whole word (e.g., "error" but not "errors" or "supererror").

5. Recursive Search Through Directories

You can use grep to search through all files within a directory and its subdirectories by using the -r (or -R) option, which makes the search recursive.

5.1 Example: Recursive Search

grep -r "pattern" /path/to/directory

This command searches for "pattern" in all files within /path/to/directory and its subdirectories.

6. Counting Matches Instead of Printing Them

If you're only interested in how many times a pattern appears in a file, you can use the -c option. This option tells grep to count the number of matching lines instead of printing them.

6.1 Example: Counting Matches

grep -c "error" log.txt

This command outputs the number of lines in log.txt that contain the word "error".

7. Inverting the Match

There may be cases when you want to find lines that do not contain a certain pattern. The -v option inverts the match, meaning grep will display all lines that do not contain the pattern.

7.1 Example: Inverting the Match

grep -v "error" log.txt

This command prints all lines from log.txt that do not contain the word "error". It's useful when you want to filter out certain lines.

8. Using Regular Expressions with grep

One of grep's greatest strengths is its ability to use regular expressions (regex) for pattern matching, which makes it extremely versatile in searching for complex patterns.

8.1 Basic Regular Expressions in grep

grep "^error" log.txt

This regular expression matches any line that starts with the word "error" (^ represents the start of a line). You can use more complex regular expressions depending on the need.

8.2 Extended Regular Expressions with grep -E

To enable extended regular expressions, which support more complex regex features (like +, |, ()), use the -E option (equivalent to using egrep).

8.2.1 Example: Extended Regular Expression

grep -E "(error|warning)" log.txt

This example searches for lines that contain either "error" or "warning". The pipe symbol (|) acts as a logical OR in extended regex.

9. Highlighting Matches

Sometimes, it's helpful to visually distinguish the matching text. By default, grep doesn't highlight matches, but you can enable this feature with the --color option.

9.1 Example: Highlighting Matches

grep --color "error" log.txt

In this example, every occurrence of the word "error" in log.txt will be highlighted, making it easier to spot the matched text within the lines.

10. Searching for Multiple Patterns

grep allows you to search for multiple patterns simultaneously by using the -e option for each pattern. Alternatively, you can provide a list of patterns in a file.

10.1 Example: Multiple Patterns

grep -e "error" -e "warning" log.txt

This command searches for both "error" and "warning" in log.txt, printing any line that contains either word.

11. Fixed String Search

Sometimes, patterns can be interpreted as regular expressions, even though you only want to search for the exact string. In such cases, you can use the -F option (or use fgrep), which tells grep to treat the pattern as a fixed string, not a regex.

11.1 Example: Fixed String Search

grep -F "a+b" file.txt

Without -F, the pattern "a+b" would be interpreted as a regular expression where + has special meaning. With -F, grep will search for the literal string "a+b".

12. Suppressing Output with -q

There are times when you don't need to see the output but just want to know if a pattern exists. The -q option (quiet mode) suppresses all output and only returns the exit status of the search. This is useful in scripts where you only need a "yes" or "no" answer (success or failure).

12.1 Example: Silent Search in Scripts

if grep -q "error" log.txt; then

```
    echo "Errors found."
else
    echo "No errors found."
fi
```

In this script:

- The grep -q command checks for the existence of the word "error" in log.txt.
- If grep finds a match, it returns 0 (success), and the message "Errors found" is displayed.
- If no match is found, it returns 1 (failure), and "No errors found" is displayed.

13. Grep and Performance: The -f Option

When you need to search for a large number of patterns, it's more efficient to store the patterns in a file and use the -f option to specify the file.

13.1 Example: Using the -f Option

grep -f patterns.txt file.txt

This command searches for multiple patterns in file.txt, where the patterns are listed in patterns.txt. Each line in patterns.txt represents a pattern to search for.

14. Grep with Binary Files

By default, grep assumes it's working with text files. However, if you're searching in binary files, you can use the -a option, which treats binary files as text.

14.1 Example: Searching Binary Files

grep -a "pattern" binary_file.bin

This command searches for the string "pattern" in binary_file.bin, treating it as if it were a text file.

15. Summary

The grep command is an essential tool for searching and filtering text in files. From simple string searches to complex regular expression matching, grep provides numerous options to tailor its functionality to your needs. Whether you're troubleshooting log files, searching code repositories, or filtering large datasets, mastering grep will significantly improve your efficiency when working in Bash.

Key features of grep include:

- Case sensitivity: Default case-sensitive searches, with the option for case-insensitive (-i).
- Line numbers: Displaying line numbers of matches (-n).
- Recursive search: Searching through directories and subdirectories (-r).
- Pattern matching: Using regular expressions (grep, -E, -F).
- Highlighting and silent searches: Highlighting matches (--color) and suppressing output (-q).

Learning to use grep proficiently will enhance your text processing skills and help streamline many aspects of working with data in Bash.

7.4 sed: Stream Editing and Substitutions

The sed command (short for stream editor) is a powerful text processing tool in Unix/Linux environments. It's designed to make automated edits to text streams or files, making it extremely useful for tasks like text substitution, insertion, deletion, and more. While sed can perform basic operations like search-and-replace similar to a text editor's "find and replace" function, it operates directly on the input stream, allowing it to process large amounts of text efficiently.

In this section, we'll dive into the essential features of sed, focusing on its most common use case: substitutions. You'll learn how to modify text on the fly, transform data, and automate tedious tasks that involve text manipulation, all using the concise syntax of sed.

1. Basic Syntax of sed

The basic syntax of the sed command is as follows:

sed [options] 'command' file
[options]: Various options that modify the behavior of sed (e.g., to edit files in-place).
'command': The specific sed command to execute, often wrapped in single quotes.
file: The file or input stream on which to perform the operation.

1.1 Common Options:
-n: Suppresses automatic output. Used with p (print) to display only selected lines.
-i: Edits the file "in place" without creating a new copy.
-e: Allows multiple commands to be executed in a single invocation.

2. Performing Substitutions with sed

The most common operation with sed is substitution, where you replace occurrences of a string or pattern with a new value. The substitution syntax is as follows:

- sed 's/pattern/replacement/' file
- s: Stands for "substitute".
- pattern: The string or regular expression to be replaced.
- replacement: The string to replace the pattern with.
- The final / separates the components of the substitution command.

2.1 Example: Basic Substitution

sed 's/old/new/' file.txt

This command replaces the first occurrence of "old" with "new" in each line of file.txt. If multiple instances of "old" exist on a single line, only the first one will be substituted.

3. Global Substitution: Replacing All Occurrences

To replace all occurrences of a pattern in each line, you can use the g flag at the end of the command. Without this flag, sed only replaces the first match on each line.

3.1 Example: Global Substitution

sed 's/old/new/g' file.txt

This command replaces every instance of "old" with "new" on each line of file.txt.

4. Editing Files In-Place with sed

By default, sed outputs the result to standard output (the terminal), and the original file remains unchanged. To apply the changes directly to the file, you can use the -i option, which edits the file "in place."

4.1 Example: In-Place Editing

sed -i 's/old/new/g' file.txt

This command replaces all occurrences of "old" with "new" in file.txt and saves the changes directly to the file. No intermediate file is created.

5. Substitution with Delimiters Other than /

In sed, the / character is the default delimiter for substitution commands. However, if your pattern or replacement contains slashes (e.g., file paths), you can choose a different delimiter to avoid escaping characters.

5.1 Example: Using Alternative Delimiters

sed 's:/home/user:/home/newuser:g' file.txt

Here, the colon (:) is used as the delimiter instead of /. This makes the command cleaner and easier to read when dealing with paths that contain slashes.

6. Working with Regular Expressions in sed

sed supports regular expressions, allowing you to match complex patterns beyond simple text strings. You can leverage regular expressions to perform powerful text transformations.

6.1 Example: Using a Regular Expression

sed 's/[0-9]\{3\}-[0-9]\{2\}-[0-9]\{4\}/XXX-XX-XXXX/' file.txt

This example replaces Social Security numbers in the format XXX-XX-XXXX with the string XXX-XX-XXXX to anonymize sensitive data. The \{n\} syntax specifies the number of occurrences of the previous character or character set.

7. Limiting Substitutions to Specific Occurrences

If you want to replace only a specific occurrence of a pattern in each line (e.g., the second or third match), you can specify the occurrence number as an additional parameter.

7.1 Example: Replacing the Second Occurrence Only

sed 's/old/new/2' file.txt

This command replaces the second occurrence of "old" with "new" in each line of file.txt. Other occurrences are left unchanged.

8. Applying Substitutions to Specific Lines

Sometimes, you may only want to apply a substitution to certain lines of a file. sed allows you to target specific line numbers or ranges.

8.1 Example: Substituting on a Specific Line

sed '3s/old/new/' file.txt

This command replaces "old" with "new" only on the third line of file.txt.

8.2 Example: Substituting in a Range of Lines

sed '3,5s/old/new/' file.txt

Here, the substitution is applied only to lines 3 through 5.

9. Deleting Lines with sed

Besides substitution, sed can also delete lines that match a pattern. The command for deletion is d.

9.1 Example: Deleting Lines That Contain a Pattern

sed '/error/d' file.txt

This command deletes all lines in file.txt that contain the word "error".

9.2 Example: Deleting a Specific Line

sed '3d' file.txt

This command deletes the third line in file.txt.

10. Inserting and Appending Text

You can also use sed to insert or append text at specific points in a file. The i command inserts text before a matched line, while the a command appends text after the matched line.

10.1 Example: Inserting Text

sed '3i\This is a new line.' file.txt

This command inserts the text "This is a new line." before the third line of file.txt.

10.2 Example: Appending Text

sed '3a\This is an appended line.' file.txt

This command appends the text "This is an appended line." after the third line of file.txt.

11. Substituting Text Across Multiple Lines

sed normally operates on a line-by-line basis. However, with certain patterns, you may need to match text that spans multiple lines. To handle such cases, the N command in sed can be used to join multiple lines together before performing operations.

11.1 Example: Matching and Replacing Text Across Two Lines

sed '/pattern1/{N;s/pattern1.*pattern2/replacement/}' file.txt

This command looks for pattern1, then joins the next line (with the N command), and replaces the entire content between pattern1 and pattern2 with "replacement".

12. Combining Multiple Commands

You can chain multiple sed commands together in a single invocation by using the -e option, or you can use a semicolon (;) to separate commands within a single set of quotes.

12.1 Example: Multiple Substitutions

sed -e 's/old/new/g' -e 's/error/success/g' file.txt

This command performs two substitutions: first, it replaces "old" with "new", and then it replaces "error" with "success".

13. Summary

The sed command is an incredibly versatile tool for stream editing, allowing you to perform a wide range of text transformations efficiently. From simple substitutions to complex multi-line edits, sed is an essential utility for any Bash programmer dealing with text processing. Here's a quick summary of the key sed features:

- Substitutions (s): Replace text patterns with new values, with options for global or specific substitutions.
- Regular expressions: Use patterns to match and transform complex text.
- Line-specific operations: Target individual lines or ranges of lines for edits.
- Deletion and insertion: Remove or add text at specific points in the file.
- Multi-line processing: Join lines for more complex transformations.
- In-place editing: Modify files directly without creating new copies.

Mastering sed will significantly enhance your ability to automate and streamline text processing tasks, making it a vital skill for any shell scripting enthusiast.

7.5 awk: Powerful Text Processing and Reporting

awk is a versatile and powerful programming language designed for text processing and data extraction, especially useful when working with structured data such as tables or delimited files. Named after its creators—Alfred Aho, Peter Weinberger, and Brian Kernighan—awk excels in transforming data and generating reports through its concise syntax and robust features.

This section explores the fundamental capabilities of awk, including its syntax, common operations, and practical applications, making it an invaluable tool for anyone involved in shell scripting or data analysis.

1. Overview of awk

At its core, awk is a pattern scanning and processing language that operates on a line-by-line basis. It reads input files, processes each line, and applies user-defined actions to matching lines. The basic structure of an awk command can be summarized as follows:

awk 'pattern { action }' file

- **pattern**: A condition that determines when the specified action should be executed (e.g., line matches a regular expression).
- **action**: Commands to be executed for lines matching the pattern, which can include printing specific fields, performing calculations, etc.

If no pattern is specified, awk executes the action for every line.

2. Basic Syntax and Structure

The syntax for awk allows for both inline command execution and scripting through .awk files. A typical command looks like this:

awk '{ print $1 }' file.txt

This command prints the first field ($1) of each line in file.txt.

2.1 Fields in awk

In awk, fields are defined based on a field separator, which defaults to whitespace (spaces or tabs). You can access these fields using the $ symbol, followed by the field number (e.g., $1, $2, etc.).

To change the field separator, you can use the -F option:

awk -F, '{ print $1 }' file.csv

In this example, awk uses a comma as the field separator for processing a CSV file.

3. Printing Data with awk

One of the primary uses of awk is to extract and print specific columns or fields from input files. The print statement is commonly used for this purpose.

3.1 Example: Printing Specific Fields

awk '{ print $1, $3 }' file.txt

This command prints the first and third fields from each line in file.txt, separated by a space.

3.2 Example: Custom Formatting with printf

For more control over output formatting, you can use the printf function, similar to the C programming language.

awk '{ printf "Field 1: %-10s | Field 2: %s\n", $1, $2 }' file.txt

This command formats the output to align the fields neatly.

4. Using Patterns for Filtering

awk allows for powerful filtering capabilities based on patterns. You can specify conditions that determine whether an action should be taken on a given line.

4.1 Example: Filtering Lines with a Pattern

awk '/error/ { print $0 }' file.log

This command prints all lines in file.log that contain the word "error".

4.2 Example: Numeric Comparisons

You can also use numeric comparisons in your patterns:

awk '$3 > 100 { print $1, $3 }' file.txt

This command prints the first and third fields from lines where the third field is greater than 100.

5. Built-in Variables in awk

awk provides several built-in variables that enhance its functionality:

- **NR**: Represents the total number of records (lines) processed so far.
- **NF**: Indicates the number of fields in the current record.

- **$0**: Represents the entire line.

5.1 Example: Using Built-in Variables

awk '{ print NR, $0 }' file.txt

This command prepends the line number to each line of file.txt.

6. Control Structures in awk

Like many programming languages, awk supports control structures such as if, for, and while, allowing for more complex data processing.

6.1 Example: Conditional Statements

awk '{ if ($3 > 100) print $1 " exceeds 100." }' file.txt

This command checks if the third field is greater than 100 and prints a message if true.

6.2 Example: Loops

You can use loops to iterate over fields or records:

awk '{ for (i = 1; i <= NF; i++) print $i }' file.txt

This command prints each field on a new line for every line in file.txt.

7. Functions in awk

awk supports user-defined and built-in functions, enabling you to perform more complex calculations and manipulations.

7.1 Example: Using Built-in Functions

You can utilize various built-in functions like length, substr, and toupper:

awk '{ print toupper($1) }' file.txt

This command converts the first field of each line to uppercase.

7.2 Example: User-Defined Functions

You can also define your own functions to encapsulate reusable logic:

*function square(x) { return x * x }*

awk '{ print square($2) }' file.txt

This command defines a function to calculate the square of a number and uses it on the second field of file.txt.

8. Handling Multiple Input Files

awk can process multiple files simultaneously, applying the same operations across all specified files.

8.1 Example: Processing Multiple Files

awk '{ print FILENAME ": " $0 }' file1.txt file2.txt

This command prefixes each line with the name of the file it came from, allowing you to differentiate between input files.

9. Generating Reports with awk

awk is particularly effective for generating formatted reports from structured data. You can group data, perform calculations, and format the output accordingly.

9.1 Example: Summing Values

awk '{ sum += $3 } END { print "Total: ", sum }' file.txt

This command sums the values in the third field and prints the total at the end of processing.

9.2 Example: Grouping and Counting

awk '{ count[$1]++ } END { for (key in count) print key, count[key] }' file.txt

This command counts occurrences of each unique value in the first field and prints the results.

awk is a powerful tool for text processing and reporting, offering a rich set of features for manipulating structured data. Its strengths lie in its ability to easily filter, format, and report on data, making it an essential part of any data processing toolkit.

Key Features of awk:

- **Field-based processing**: Access and manipulate specific fields from structured input.
- **Pattern matching**: Apply actions based on patterns and conditions.
- **Control structures**: Utilize loops and conditionals for complex processing logic.
- **Functions**: Leverage built-in and user-defined functions for calculations and transformations.
- **Multi-file support**: Process multiple input files in a single command.

Mastering awk can significantly enhance your productivity and capabilities when working with data in shell scripts, making it an indispensable skill for any programmer or data analyst.

7.6 Combining Tools for Complex Text Manipulation

When working with text processing in the Bash environment, tools like awk, sed, grep, and others provide immense power individually, but their true strength lies in their ability to be combined for complex tasks. Bash scripting allows you to string together multiple utilities, creating efficient pipelines for extracting, transforming, and processing data in ways that would otherwise require significantly more effort in traditional programming languages.

This section will introduce the key strategies for combining tools like awk, sed, grep, and others to build more sophisticated text manipulation workflows. We'll also provide real-world examples to demonstrate how these tools can work together for maximum efficiency.

1. Piping and Redirection: The Foundation of Combining Tools

Before diving into specific combinations of tools, it's important to understand how piping (|) and redirection (>, >>, <) work in the Bash shell. Piping allows the output of one command to become the input of another, enabling seamless data processing across multiple utilities.

1.1 Example: Using Piping to Chain Commands

cat file.txt | grep "error" | awk '{ print $2, $5 }'

In this example:

- cat reads the content of file.txt.
- grep "error" filters lines that contain the word "error".
- awk '{ print $2, $5 }' extracts and prints the second and fifth fields from the matching lines.

This simple pipeline illustrates how combining multiple tools can create a more powerful processing chain than using each tool individually.

2. Combining grep and awk for Pattern Matching and Data Extraction

grep is often used to filter lines based on patterns, while awk is ideal for field-based data extraction. When used together, they allow you to first find relevant lines and then drill down into the specific data you need.

2.1 Example: Filtering and Extracting Data

grep "success" logs.txt | awk '{ print $3, $7 }'

This command:

Uses grep to filter lines containing the word "success".

Passes the matching lines to awk, which prints the third and seventh fields, perhaps representing timestamps and status codes.

3. Combining sed and awk for Stream Editing and Data Processing

sed excels at stream editing, such as performing substitutions, deletions, and text modifications. awk, on the other hand, is adept at processing structured text and performing field-based operations. Together, they provide a comprehensive solution for transforming and analyzing data.

3.1 Example: Text Substitution and Extraction

sed 's/failed/error/' report.txt | awk '{ print $1, $NF }'

This command:

- Uses sed to replace the word "failed" with "error" in report.txt.
- Passes the modified lines to awk, which prints the first and last fields of each line (e.g., the username and the status).
- This combination allows for both text replacement and structured extraction in one concise pipeline.

4. Combining grep, sed, and awk for Complex Data Transformation

Sometimes, you need to filter, transform, and extract data all in one go. By combining grep, sed, and awk, you can build highly specific data processing pipelines.

4.1 Example: Filtering, Replacing, and Extracting

grep "ERROR" system.log | sed 's/ERROR/FATAL/' | awk '{ print $1, $2, $NF }'

This command:

- Uses grep to find lines containing the word "ERROR".
- Uses sed to replace "ERROR" with "FATAL" in the matching lines.
- Passes the result to awk, which prints the first two fields (likely timestamps) and the last field (possibly an error message).
- In a single command, you've filtered specific log lines, updated their content, and extracted important information.

5. Using xargs to Pass Output as Arguments

While tools like grep, sed, and awk are useful for line-by-line operations, sometimes you need to pass the output of one command as arguments to another. This is where xargs comes into play—it takes input from standard output and converts it into arguments for other commands.

5.1 Example: Finding and Deleting Files

*grep -l "TODO" *.txt | xargs rm*

This command:

- Uses grep -l to list the names of all .txt files containing the word "TODO".
- Passes the resulting filenames to xargs, which feeds them to rm for deletion.
- By combining grep and xargs, you automate file cleanup based on content, rather than filenames.

6. Advanced Example: Combining awk, sort, and uniq for Data Summarization

You can combine awk, sort, and uniq to create a simple report by counting occurrences of values in a specific field.

6.1 Example: Summarizing Log File Entries

awk '{ print $5 }' access.log | sort | uniq -c | sort -nr

This pipeline:

- Uses awk to extract the fifth field (e.g., IP addresses) from access.log.
- Sorts the extracted IP addresses.
- Uses uniq -c to count occurrences of each IP.
- Sorts the result numerically in descending order (-nr), showing the most frequent IP addresses at the top.

In this example, you've created a concise log file report to summarize frequent visitors or potential attackers based on IP addresses.

7. Combining find with grep and sed for File Content Manipulation

The find command is essential for locating files based on various criteria, such as name, size, or modification date. When combined with grep and sed, you can locate files and manipulate their content in one pipeline.

7.1 Example: Finding and Replacing Text in Multiple Files

find . -name ".html" | xargs grep -l "old-link" | xargs sed -i 's/old-link/new-link/g'*

This pipeline:

- Uses find to locate all .html files in the current directory.
- Passes the filenames to grep -l to find files containing the string "old-link".
- Uses sed -i to perform an in-place substitution, replacing "old-link" with "new-link" in those files.

This combination allows you to automate the task of updating links across a large set of files.

8. Using paste and cut for Column-Based Operations

The cut command is used to extract specific columns from a file, while paste can combine columns from different files. These two commands are often combined when dealing with data in tabular formats.

8.1 Example: Merging Columns from Two Files

cut -f1 names.txt | paste - addresses.txt

This command:

Uses cut to extract the first field (e.g., names) from names.txt.

Uses paste to combine this list with the contents of addresses.txt, resulting in a file where each line contains a name and an address.

9. Combining tr, cut, and sort for Text Processing

The tr command is useful for translating or deleting characters. It's often used in conjunction with cut and sort to process columns of text.

9.1 Example: Processing CSV Data

cat data.csv | tr ',' '\t' | cut -f2 | sort | uniq

This pipeline:

- Uses tr to convert commas to tabs, making the CSV data easier to process.
- Uses cut to extract the second column.
- Sorts the data and uses uniq to remove duplicates.

10. Real-World Example: Processing and Reporting Log Files

Let's look at a more complex real-world example of log processing, where you combine several tools to extract meaningful information from a large log file.

10.1 Example: Extracting and Summarizing Errors

grep "ERROR" app.log | awk '{ print $1, $2, $3 }' | sort | uniq -c | sort -nr

This command:

- Uses grep to find lines containing the word "ERROR" in app.log.
- Passes the results to awk, which extracts the first three fields (perhaps the date and time).
- Sorts the extracted lines.
- Uses uniq -c to count occurrences of each unique error.

Finally, sorts the result in descending order, so the most frequent errors are listed at the top.

Combining text processing tools in Bash allows you to handle complex tasks efficiently by chaining together the strengths of each utility. Whether you are filtering data, performing bulk substitutions, or generating reports, tools like grep, awk, sed, and others, when used together, enable you to automate and streamline text processing workflows. This is essential for anyone dealing with large datasets, log files, or structured information.

By mastering the art of combining tools in Bash, you can unlock the full potential of shell scripting and achieve powerful, efficient solutions to a wide range of text manipulation tasks.

8. File Operations: Efficient File Handling

In this chapter, you'll learn how to efficiently manage files within your Bash scripts, a crucial skill for automating tasks and managing data. We'll begin with the basics of reading from and writing to files, including techniques for appending and overwriting content. You'll discover how to search for files using the find command, manage file permissions with chmod and chown, and work with compressed files using tools like tar and gzip. Additionally, we'll cover best practices for error checking and handling when performing file operations. By the end of this chapter, you'll have a comprehensive toolkit for working with files in Bash, empowering you to automate file management tasks seamlessly and efficiently.

8.1 Reading from and Writing to Files in Bash

Bash scripting provides a powerful way to interact with files, allowing you to read from and write to them seamlessly. Whether you're processing data, logging output, or generating reports, understanding how to manipulate files is crucial for effective shell scripting. This section will explore various methods for reading from and writing to files in Bash, showcasing practical examples and best practices.

1. Reading from Files

Reading data from files is a fundamental operation in Bash scripting. You can use several methods to read file contents, including cat, redirection, and the while loop with read.

1.1 Using cat

The simplest way to read a file's contents is by using the cat command. It concatenates and displays the content of one or more files.

Example:

cat myfile.txt

This command displays the entire content of myfile.txt to the standard output.

1.2 Using Input Redirection

Input redirection (<) allows you to read from a file within a command. For example, you can use it with a while loop to process each line of the file.

Example:

while read line; do
   echo "Line: $line"
done < myfile.txt

In this example:

- The while read line loop reads each line from myfile.txt.
- Each line is stored in the variable line, which can then be processed as needed.

1.3 Reading Specific Lines

You can also use sed or awk to read specific lines from a file.

Example: Using sed to Read Line 3

sed -n '3p' myfile.txt

This command prints only the third line of myfile.txt.

1.4 Reading All Lines into an Array

You can read all lines of a file into an array for further manipulation.

Example:

mapfile -t lines < myfile.txt
for line in "${lines[@]}"; do
   echo "Line: $line"
done

In this example, mapfile reads all lines into the lines array, which is then iterated through to display each line.

2. Writing to Files

Writing data to files in Bash can be achieved using redirection (> for overwriting and >> for appending), or by using commands like echo, printf, and file descriptors.

2.1 Overwriting a File

You can use the output redirection operator (>) to overwrite the contents of a file.

Example:

echo "This is a new line" > myfile.txt

This command writes "This is a new line" to myfile.txt, overwriting any existing content.

2.2 Appending to a File

To append data to an existing file, use the append operator (>>).

Example:

echo "This line will be appended." >> myfile.txt

This command adds "This line will be appended." to the end of myfile.txt without deleting the previous content.

2.3 Writing Multiple Lines

You can also write multiple lines to a file using cat with a heredoc.

Example:

cat <<EOL > myfile.txt
Line 1: This is the first line.
Line 2: This is the second line.
EOL

In this example:

- The <<EOL syntax allows you to write multiple lines until the EOL marker is encountered.

- All lines between the <<EOL and EOL markers are written to myfile.txt.

2.4 Using printf for Formatted Output

For more control over the formatting of the output, you can use printf.

Example:

printf "Name: %s\nAge: %d\n" "John Doe" 30 > myfile.txt

This command formats the output and writes it to myfile.txt. It will print:

Name: John Doe
Age: 30

3. File Descriptors

Bash supports multiple file descriptors, allowing you to handle standard input (stdin), standard output (stdout), and standard error (stderr). You can also create custom file descriptors.

3.1 Redirecting Standard Error

To redirect standard error messages to a file, use 2>.

Example:

ls non_existent_file 2> error.log

This command attempts to list a non-existent file and redirects the error message to error.log.

3.2 Redirecting Both Standard Output and Error

To redirect both stdout and stderr to the same file, use &> or 2>&1.

Example:

command &> output.log

or

command > output.log 2>&1

In both examples, any output and error messages from command are stored in output.log.

4. Best Practices for File Manipulation

When reading from and writing to files in Bash, consider the following best practices:

Check for File Existence: Before reading from or writing to a file, check if it exists to prevent errors.

if [[-f myfile.txt]]; then
   # Read from the file
else
   echo "File does not exist."
fi

Use Quotes: Always use quotes around variable expansions to prevent word splitting and globbing.

echo "$line" >> myfile.txt

Error Handling: Implement error handling to manage unexpected issues, such as failed writes or missing files.

if ! echo "Hello" > myfile.txt; then
   echo "Failed to write to the file."
fi

Close File Descriptors: If you open file descriptors, make sure to close them when done.

exec 3<> myfile.txt
 # Use the file descriptor
exec 3>&-

Understanding how to read from and write to files in Bash is a fundamental skill that enhances your scripting capabilities. Whether you are logging output, processing data, or generating reports, mastering these file manipulation techniques allows you to create powerful, efficient shell scripts. By leveraging redirection, file descriptors, and various command-line utilities, you can effectively manage and transform data in your Bash scripts.

8.2 Appending and Overwriting File Content

In Bash scripting, managing file content is crucial for tasks such as logging, data storage, and report generation. Understanding the difference between appending and overwriting file content allows you to control how data is added to or replaces existing information in files. This section will explore the various methods for appending to and overwriting files in Bash, along with practical examples.

1. Overwriting File Content

Overwriting a file in Bash means replacing the existing content with new data. This action is performed using the output redirection operator (>). When you redirect output to a file with >, any existing content in that file will be deleted, and the new content will take its place.

1.1 Basic Overwriting with echo

The simplest way to overwrite a file is by using the echo command with the output redirection operator.

Example:

echo "This is the new content." > myfile.txt

In this example, the command writes "This is the new content." to myfile.txt. If myfile.txt already contained data, that data will be lost, and only the new content will remain.

1.2 Overwriting with cat

You can also use cat with a heredoc to overwrite a file with multiple lines of content.

Example:

cat <<EOL > myfile.txt
This is the first line.
This is the second line.
EOL

This command creates (or overwrites) myfile.txt, placing the two specified lines into the file. If myfile.txt existed prior, its content will be replaced entirely by these two lines.

2. Appending to File Content

Appending to a file means adding new content to the end of the existing data without deleting what is already there. This can be accomplished using the append redirection operator (>>). Using >> will append the specified content rather than overwrite it.

2.1 Basic Appending with echo

To append a single line to a file, you can use echo with the append operator (>>).

Example:

echo "This line will be appended." >> myfile.txt

In this example, "This line will be appended." is added to the end of myfile.txt. If the file does not exist, it will be created automatically.

2.2 Appending Multiple Lines

To append multiple lines to a file, you can use cat in combination with a heredoc.

Example:

cat <<EOL >> myfile.txt

- This line is appended.
- This is another appended line.
- EOL

This command appends the two specified lines to myfile.txt. If myfile.txt did not exist before, it will be created.

3. Important Considerations

When managing file content, it's crucial to understand a few key points to avoid unintended data loss or corruption.

3.1 Use of Quotes

When using variables or file names that may contain spaces, it's good practice to enclose them in quotes to prevent issues with word splitting and globbing.

Example:

myfile="my file with spaces.txt"
echo "Some content" > "$myfile"

This ensures that the variable myfile is correctly interpreted as a single argument.

3.2 Checking File Existence

Before overwriting or appending to a file, you may want to check if it exists, especially if you're concerned about accidentally deleting important data.

Example:

if [-f myfile.txt]; then
*   echo "myfile.txt already exists. Proceeding to append."*
else
*   echo "myfile.txt does not exist. Creating a new file."*
fi
echo "Adding new content." >> myfile.txt

This script checks if myfile.txt exists and informs the user before appending new content.

3.3 Using tee for Overwriting and Appending

The tee command can be useful when you want to write output to a file and also display it on the screen. By default, tee overwrites files, but you can use the -a option to append instead.

Example:

echo "This will overwrite the file." | tee myfile.txt

This command will display the output on the screen and overwrite myfile.txt.

To append instead:

echo "This will be appended." | tee -a myfile.txt

In this case, the output is both displayed on the screen and added to the end of myfile.txt.

4. Real-World Scenarios

4.1 Logging Script Output

Appending is commonly used in scripts for logging purposes. By appending log entries to a log file, you can maintain a history of script runs without losing previous information.

Example:

echo "$(date): Script started" >> script.log
 # Some operations
echo "$(date): Script completed" >> script.log

This script logs the start and end times of a process, providing a clear history.

4.2 Configuration Files

When modifying configuration files, appending can be useful to add new settings without disrupting existing configurations.

Example:

echo "new_setting=true" >> config.txt

This command adds a new configuration setting to config.txt.

Understanding how to append and overwrite file content in Bash is essential for effective scripting. By mastering these techniques, you can efficiently manage file content for various tasks, such as logging, data storage, and configuration management. Always be cautious when overwriting files to prevent unintentional data loss, and utilize appending to maintain historical data and logs. With these practices, you can create robust and reliable Bash scripts that handle file operations effectively.

8.3 Using find to Search for Files by Name, Size, and Date

The find command is one of the most powerful and versatile tools in Bash for searching and locating files and directories within a file system. It provides various options to filter searches based on criteria such as file name, size, modification date, and more. This section will explore how to use find effectively to search for files based on these parameters.

1. Basic Syntax of the find Command

The general syntax of the find command is:

find [path] [expression]

- **path**: The directory path where the search should begin. Use . for the current directory or specify an absolute/relative path.
- **expression**: The conditions for filtering files (e.g., by name, size, or date).

2. Searching for Files by Name

One of the most common uses of find is to search for files by name using the -name option. This option allows you to specify the exact name of the file or use wildcards for partial matches.

2.1 Exact Name Search

To search for a file with an exact name, you can use the -name option followed by the file name.

Example:

find /path/to/search -name "filename.txt"

This command searches for filename.txt in the specified directory and all its subdirectories.

2.2 Case-Insensitive Search

If you want to perform a case-insensitive search, you can use the -iname option instead.

Example:

find /path/to/search -iname "filename.txt"

This command will match filename.txt, Filename.TXT, and any other case variations.

2.3 Wildcard Searches

You can also use wildcards to search for files with similar names. The asterisk (*) matches any number of characters, while the question mark (?) matches a single character.

Example:

find /path/to/search -name ".txt"*

This command finds all files ending with .txt.

find /path/to/search -name "file_??.txt"

This command searches for files with names like file_01.txt, file_02.txt, etc.

3. Searching for Files by Size

Another powerful feature of find is its ability to search for files based on their size. The -size option allows you to specify size criteria.

3.1 Specifying File Size

You can specify the file size using a combination of numeric values and suffixes. Common suffixes include:

- **c**: bytes
- **k**: kilobytes
- **M:** megabytes
- **G**: gigabytes

Example:

To find files larger than 1 megabyte:

find /path/to/search -size +1M

This command lists all files greater than 1 MB in the specified directory and its subdirectories.

3.2 Finding Smaller Files

To find files smaller than a specific size, use the - sign before the size value.

Example:

find /path/to/search -size -100k

This command finds all files smaller than 100 kilobytes.

3.3 Exact Size Matches

To find files of an exact size, use = before the size.

Example:

find /path/to/search -size 500M

This command lists files that are exactly 500 megabytes.

4. Searching for Files by Modification Date

The find command also allows you to filter files based on their last modification date using the -mtime, -atime, and -ctime options.

4.1 Modifying Time (-mtime)

The -mtime option is used to find files modified within a certain number of days. The numeric value can be:

- **Positive** (+n): More than n days ago.
- **Negative** (-n): Less than n days ago.
- **Exact** (n): Exactly n days ago.

Example:

To find files modified in the last 7 days:

find /path/to/search -mtime -7

To find files modified more than 30 days ago:

find /path/to/search -mtime +30

4.2 Access Time (-atime)

The -atime option allows you to search for files based on the last access time.

Example:

To find files accessed in the last 3 days:

find /path/to/search -atime -3

4.3 Change Time (-ctime)

The -ctime option is used to find files based on when their metadata (like permissions or ownership) was changed.

Example:

To find files whose metadata was changed in the last 10 days:

find /path/to/search -ctime -10

5. Combining Search Criteria

The find command allows you to combine multiple criteria using logical operators such as -and, -or, and -not. This feature lets you create more complex search queries.

5.1 Using -and

By default, multiple expressions are combined with -and, so you can simply list them.

Example:

find /path/to/search -name ".log" -mtime -5*

This command finds all .log files modified in the last 5 days.

5.2 Using -or

To search for files that match either of two criteria, use -or.

Example:

find /path/to/search -name ".jpg" -or -name "*.png"*

This command finds all .jpg or .png files.

5.3 Using -not

To exclude certain files from your search, use -not.

Example:

find /path/to/search -name ".tmp" -not -name "*.backup"*

This command finds all .tmp files that are not .backup files.

6. Executing Commands on Found Files

The -exec option allows you to execute a command on each file found. This feature is powerful for automating tasks on files that meet specific criteria.

Example:

find /path/to/search -name ".log" -exec rm {} \;*

This command finds all .log files and deletes them. The {} placeholder represents the found file, and \; indicates the end of the command.

7. Practical Applications of find

7.1 Finding Large Files

You can find large files to free up disk space.

Example:

find / -type f -size +100M

This command searches the entire file system for files larger than 100 MB.

7.2 Cleaning Up Old Files

You can automate the cleanup of old files.

Example:

find /path/to/temp -type f -mtime +30 -exec rm {} \;

This command finds and deletes files in the /path/to/temp directory that haven't been modified in over 30 days.

7.3 Searching for Recently Modified Files

You can search for files that have been modified recently, which is helpful for tracking changes.

Example:

find /path/to/project -type f -mtime -1

This command finds all files in the specified directory modified in the last day.

The find command is an essential tool for searching and managing files in Bash scripting. Its ability to search by name, size, and modification date makes it incredibly versatile for a variety of tasks, from simple file searches to complex file management operations. By mastering the find command and its options, you can enhance your productivity and effectively manage files in your system. Whether you're looking to delete old files, find large files, or locate files based on specific criteria, find offers a powerful solution to your file management needs.

8.4 Managing Compressed Files with tar, gzip, and zip

Managing compressed files is an essential skill for anyone working with the Linux command line. Compression is useful for reducing file size, saving disk space, and organizing files into a single archive for easier distribution. In this section, we'll cover three commonly used tools: tar, gzip, and zip. Each tool has its strengths and use cases, and understanding how to use them effectively will enhance your file management capabilities in Bash.

1. Introduction to File Compression

File compression reduces the size of files by eliminating redundant data. This process can significantly save storage space and speed up file transfer over networks. Different compression tools serve various purposes:

- **tar**: Primarily used for archiving files into a single file format, often combined with compression tools like gzip or bzip2.
- **gzip**: A compression tool that reduces the size of individual files but does not create an archive by itself.
- **zip**: Combines archiving and compression, allowing you to create a single compressed file containing multiple files and directories.

2. Working with tar

The tar (tape archive) command is used to create, manipulate, and extract archives. While it doesn't compress files on its own, it is often used in conjunction with compression tools to reduce the size of the resulting archive.

2.1 Creating a Tar Archive

To create a .tar archive, use the -c (create) option along with the -f (file) option to specify the output file name.

Example:

tar -cf archive.tar /path/to/directory

This command creates an archive named archive.tar that contains all files and subdirectories from /path/to/directory.

2.2 Creating a Compressed Tar Archive

To create a compressed archive, combine tar with gzip by using the -z option.

Example:

tar -czf archive.tar.gz /path/to/directory

This command creates a gzip-compressed archive named archive.tar.gz.

2.3 Extracting a Tar Archive

To extract the contents of a tar archive, use the -x (extract) option.

Example:

tar -xf archive.tar

To extract a gzip-compressed archive:

tar -xzf archive.tar.gz

2.4 Listing Contents of a Tar Archive

To view the contents of a tar archive without extracting, use the -t (list) option.

Example:

tar -tf archive.tar

For a compressed archive:

tar -tzf archive.tar.gz

3. Using gzip

The gzip (GNU zip) command is specifically designed for compressing individual files. It replaces the original file with a compressed version, appending the .gz extension.

3.1 Compressing a File

To compress a file using gzip, simply use the command followed by the file name.

Example:

gzip filename.txt

This command compresses filename.txt, creating filename.txt.gz and deleting the original file.

3.2 Decompressing a File

To decompress a gzip-compressed file, use the -d option or simply the gunzip command.

Example:

gzip -d filename.txt.gz

or

gunzip filename.txt.gz

Both commands will restore the original filename.txt.

3.3 Compressing Multiple Files

To compress multiple files at once, you can specify them all in the command.

Example:

gzip file1.txt file2.txt file3.txt

Each file will be compressed individually, resulting in file1.txt.gz, file2.txt.gz, and file3.txt.gz.

4. Working with zip

The zip command is a widely-used utility for compressing files and creating zip archives. Unlike tar, zip allows for the creation of a compressed archive while retaining the original files.

4.1 Creating a Zip Archive

To create a zip archive, use the zip command followed by the desired archive name and the files or directories to include.

Example:

zip archive.zip file1.txt file2.txt

This command creates a zip archive named archive.zip containing file1.txt and file2.txt.

4.2 Creating a Zip Archive with Directories

You can also include entire directories in a zip archive.

Example:

zip -r archive.zip /path/to/directory

The -r option indicates recursive compression, including all files and subdirectories.

4.3 Extracting a Zip Archive

To extract the contents of a zip archive, use the unzip command.

Example:

unzip archive.zip

This command extracts all files from archive.zip into the current directory.

4.4 Viewing Contents of a Zip Archive

To view the contents of a zip archive without extracting, use the -l (list) option.

Example:

zip -l archive.zip

6. Practical Use Cases

6.1 Backing Up Directories

You can use tar to create backups of important directories, compressing them to save space.

Example:

tar -czf backup.tar.gz /home/user/documents

6.2 Distributing Multiple Files

Using zip allows you to easily share multiple files and directories in a single compressed file.

Example:

zip -r project.zip /path/to/project

6.3 Reducing Disk Usage

By compressing large files or directories with gzip, you can free up disk space.

Example:

gzip largefile.iso

Managing compressed files is a vital skill for efficient file storage and organization. The tar, gzip, and zip tools each serve specific purposes and excel in different scenarios. By mastering these commands, you can effectively create, manipulate, and extract compressed files, enhancing your productivity on the Linux command line. Whether you're archiving data, sharing files, or managing disk space, these tools provide powerful solutions for your file management needs.

8.5 Handling File Permissions: chmod, chown, umask

File permissions are a crucial aspect of Unix-like operating systems, allowing users to control access to files and directories. Understanding how to manage permissions using commands like chmod, chown, and umask is essential for maintaining security and proper access levels on a system. In this section, we will explore these commands in detail and provide practical examples to illustrate their usage.

1. Introduction to File Permissions

Every file and directory in a Unix-like operating system has associated permissions that dictate who can read, write, or execute them. Permissions are divided into three categories:

- **User (Owner):** The creator of the file, typically has full control.
- **Group**: Users who belong to the same group as the file's owner, can have restricted access.
- **Others**: All other users on the system, typically have the least privileges.

Each of these categories can have three types of permissions:

- **Read (r):** Permission to read the contents of the file or list the contents of a directory.
- **Write (w):** Permission to modify the contents of the file or add/delete files in a directory.
- **Execute (x):** Permission to run a file as a program or script.

Permissions can be represented in two ways: symbolic notation (using letters) and numeric notation (using numbers).

2. Understanding chmod

The chmod (change mode) command is used to change the permissions of a file or directory. You can specify permissions using either symbolic or numeric notation.

2.1 Symbolic Notation

In symbolic notation, you specify which permission to change (read, write, or execute) and to which category (user, group, or others). The syntax is as follows:

chmod [who][operation][permission] file

- **who**: u (user), g (group), o (others), a (all).
- **operation**: + (add), - (remove), = (set exactly).
- **permission**: r (read), w (write), x (execute).

Example 1: Granting Execute Permission

To add execute permission for the user:

chmod u+x script.sh

Example 2: Removing Write Permission

To remove write permission for others:

chmod o-w document.txt

Example 3: Setting Exact Permissions

To set read and execute permissions for everyone, and remove write permissions:

chmod a=rx file.txt

2.2 Numeric Notation

In numeric notation, permissions are represented by three digits, with each digit ranging from 0 to 7. The digits correspond to the following permissions:

Read (r): 4
Write (w): 2
Execute (x): 1

The digits are combined to represent permissions for user, group, and others.

Example 4: Setting Permissions Using Numeric Notation

To set read and write permissions for the user, read permission for the group, and no permissions for others:

chmod 640 file.txt

Here, 6 (4 + 2) represents read and write for the user, 4 represents read for the group, and 0 represents no permissions for others.

3. Understanding chown

The chown (change owner) command changes the ownership of a file or directory. It can be used to change both the user owner and the group owner.

3.1 Changing the Owner

To change the owner of a file:

chown newuser file.txt

3.2 Changing the Group

To change the group of a file:

chown :newgroup file.txt

3.3 Changing Both User and Group

To change both the owner and group simultaneously, use the following syntax:

chown newuser:newgroup file.txt

Example 5: Changing Ownership Recursively

To change ownership for all files in a directory and its subdirectories, use the -R option:

chown -R newuser:newgroup /path/to/directory

4. Understanding umask

The umask (user file creation mask) command sets default permissions for newly created files and directories. It works by restricting the default permissions assigned to files.

4.1 Viewing the Current umask Value

To check the current umask value, run:

umask

This command returns a numeric value that represents the default permission mask.

4.2 Setting the umask Value

To set a new umask value, use the following command:

umask value

The value is typically a three-digit octal number that represents the permissions to be masked (i.e., removed) from the default.

Example 6: Setting umask to 027

To set the umask value to 027, which allows full permissions for the user, read and execute permissions for the group, and no permissions for others:

umask 027

4.3 Understanding umask Calculation

By default, files are created with the permissions 666 (read and write for user, group, and others) and directories with 777 (read, write, and execute for all). The umask value subtracts permissions from this base.

For example, a umask of 027 would mean:

For files: 666 - 027 = 640 (rw-r-----)
For directories: 777 - 027 = 750 (rwxr-x---)

5. Practical Examples

5.1 Securing a Script

Suppose you have a script that should only be executable by its owner. You could use:

chmod 700 script.sh

This command sets the permissions so that only the user can read, write, and execute the script.

5.2 Changing Ownership for a Shared Directory

If you have a shared directory, you may want to set the group ownership to allow others in the group to access it:

chown :developers /shared/directory

This command sets the group owner of /shared/directory to developers.

5.3 Applying umask to Ensure Security

To ensure that files created in your shell sessions are not world-readable, you can set the umask to 027:

umask 027

Now, any files created in the session will have restricted access for group and other users.

Handling file permissions is vital for maintaining security and ensuring that only authorized users can access, modify, or execute files on a system. By mastering commands like chmod, chown, and umask, you can effectively manage file permissions, control access levels, and ensure the integrity of your system. Understanding and implementing proper file permissions is essential for any user or administrator in a Unix-like environment.

8.6 Checking and Modifying File Metadata

File metadata provides essential information about files and directories, such as their size, permissions, ownership, modification time, and more. Understanding how to check and modify this metadata is crucial for effective file management in Unix-like operating systems. In this section, we will cover how to view file metadata using various commands and how to modify certain aspects of it when necessary.

1. Introduction to File Metadata

Metadata refers to data that describes other data. In the context of files, metadata includes information that describes the file's properties and characteristics. Some common types of metadata include:

- **File Size**: The size of the file in bytes.
- **Permissions**: The access rights associated with the file (who can read, write, or execute it).
- **Owner**: The user who owns the file.
- **Group**: The group associated with the file.
- **Timestamps**: Information regarding when the file was created, last modified, or last accessed.

This metadata is essential for understanding the status and properties of files and directories within the system.

2. Checking File Metadata

Several commands in Linux allow you to check various aspects of file metadata.

2.1 Using ls

The ls command is commonly used to list files and directories. It can also display metadata when used with specific options.

Example 1: Listing Files with Detailed Metadata

To list files along with their metadata, use the -l (long format) option:

ls -l

This command provides a detailed list of files, showing permissions, number of links, owner, group, size, and modification date.

Example 2: Including Hidden Files

To include hidden files (those starting with a dot), use the -a option:

ls -la

This will display all files, including hidden ones, along with their metadata.

2.2 Using stat

The stat command provides more detailed information about a file's metadata than ls. It shows all relevant metadata in a structured format.

Example 3: Viewing File Metadata

To view metadata for a specific file, run:

stat filename.txt

This command will display:

- File size
- Block size
- Number of blocks allocated
- File type
- Permissions
- User ID and group ID
- Timestamps for last access, modification, and status change

Example 4: Viewing Directory Metadata

You can also use stat to check the metadata of a directory:

stat /path/to/directory

2.3 Using file

The file command identifies the type of a file based on its content, rather than its extension. This can be useful for determining how to handle a file.

Example 5: Checking File Type

To check the type of a file:

file filename.txt

This command will return the file type, such as "ASCII text," "JPEG image data," or "directory."

3. Modifying File Metadata

While some metadata (like file size and type) cannot be directly modified, you can change aspects such as permissions, ownership, and timestamps using specific commands.

3.1 Modifying Permissions with chmod

As discussed in a previous section, the chmod command can change a file's permissions.

Example 6: Changing Permissions

To make a script executable by the owner, group, and others:

chmod 755 script.sh

3.2 Changing Ownership with chown

You can change the owner and group of a file using the chown command.

Example 7: Changing Owner and Group

To change the owner to newuser and the group to newgroup:

chown newuser:newgroup file.txt

Example 8: Changing Ownership Recursively

To change the ownership of all files in a directory:

chown -R newuser:newgroup /path/to/directory

3.3 Modifying Timestamps with touch

The touch command can be used to update the timestamps of a file or create a new empty file if it doesn't exist. You can also specify new timestamps.

Example 9: Updating the Access and Modification Time

To update the access and modification times to the current time:

touch filename.txt

Example 10: Setting Specific Timestamps

To set a specific timestamp, use the -t option:

touch -t 202401010000 filename.txt

This command sets the modification and access time of filename.txt to January 1, 2024, at midnight.

4. Other Metadata Modifications

In addition to the above commands, some other tools can help manage specific aspects of file metadata.

4.1 Using xattr

Extended attributes (xattr) allow you to associate additional metadata with a file, such as security labels or custom tags.

Example 11: Viewing Extended Attributes

To view extended attributes of a file:

getfattr -d filename.txt

Example 12: Setting Extended Attributes

To set an extended attribute:

setfattr -n user.comment -v "This is a text file" filename.txt

In this example, we add a user-defined comment to the file.

4.2 Using rename

The rename command is used to change file names, which indirectly modifies metadata by updating the file's name attribute.

Example 13: Renaming a File

To rename a file:

rename oldname.txt newname.txt

5. Practical Examples

5.1 Checking File Metadata Before Processing

Before processing files in a script, you might want to check their metadata:

for file in *.txt; do
  stat "$file"
done

This loop prints metadata for all .txt files in the current directory.

5.2 Changing Permissions for a Group of Files

To change permissions for all scripts in a directory, you could use:

chmod 755 *.sh

This command makes all shell scripts executable by the user and readable and executable by the group and others.

Understanding how to check and modify file metadata is essential for efficient file management in Unix-like operating systems. By using commands like ls, stat, chmod, chown, and touch, you can effectively manage the metadata associated with files and directories. Mastering these commands will help you maintain security, organization, and proper access controls within your file system, ultimately enhancing your productivity and system integrity.

9. Process Management in Bash

In this chapter, you'll explore the intricacies of process management within Bash, enabling you to control and monitor system processes directly from your scripts. We'll cover the difference between foreground and background processes, and you'll learn how to run commands in the background using the & operator. You'll discover tools like jobs, fg, and bg to manage these processes effectively. Additionally, we'll delve into process control commands such as kill and pkill for terminating unwanted processes. You'll also learn about process substitution for efficient data handling and how to use pipelines to connect multiple commands seamlessly. By the end of this chapter, you'll have a solid understanding of how to manage processes in Bash, allowing you to create scripts that can automate and streamline system tasks with confidence.

9.1 Understanding Processes: Foreground vs Background

In computing, a process is an instance of a program that is being executed. When you run a command in a Unix-like operating system, the shell creates a process for that command. Understanding the difference between foreground and background processes is crucial for effective shell scripting and command-line operations. This section will delve into these two types of processes, their characteristics, and how to manage them.

1. Definition of Processes

A process is a program in execution. It includes the program code, its current activity, and the resources it uses. Every process in a Unix-like system is assigned a unique Process ID (PID). Processes can be classified into two main categories based on their execution context: foreground and background.

2. Foreground Processes

A foreground process is one that runs in the foreground of the terminal. This means that the shell is actively waiting for the process to complete before you can enter any additional commands. The terminal is occupied by this process, and any output it generates is displayed directly in the terminal window.

2.1 Characteristics of Foreground Processes

- **Direct User Interaction**: Foreground processes can receive input from the user (e.g., prompts) and display output directly in the terminal.
- **Control**: The user has direct control over the process while it is running. You can stop it with Ctrl+C, which sends a termination signal.
- **Single Tasking**: While a foreground process is running, you cannot run other commands in the same terminal session until it completes.

Example of a Foreground Process:

When you run a command like ls, the shell waits for it to finish before you can enter the next command:

ls -l

Here, the ls command is a foreground process, and you can see the output in the terminal immediately.

3. Background Processes

A background process runs independently of the terminal session. When you execute a command in the background, the shell does not wait for it to finish; instead, it returns control to the user immediately, allowing you to run other commands simultaneously. Background processes are denoted by an & at the end of the command.

3.1 Characteristics of Background Processes

- **Independent Execution**: Background processes run without occupying the terminal. You can continue to use the terminal for other commands.
- **No Direct Interaction**: Unlike foreground processes, you cannot interact with background processes directly. They do not receive input from the terminal unless specifically programmed to do so.
- **Process Management**: You can check the status of background processes using the jobs command and bring them to the foreground with the fg command if needed.

Example of a Background Process:

To run a command like sleep in the background, you would use:

sleep 30 &

In this case, the sleep command runs for 30 seconds in the background. You can continue to use the terminal while this process runs.

4. Managing Processes

Understanding how to manage foreground and background processes is essential for effective shell usage.

4.1 Starting a Process in the Background

You can start any command in the background by appending an &:

command &

4.2 Stopping a Foreground Process

To stop a foreground process, you can use the keyboard shortcut Ctrl+C, which sends a termination signal to the process.

4.3 Suspending and Resuming Processes

Suspend a Foreground Process: You can suspend a foreground process by pressing Ctrl+Z. This stops the process and puts it in the background.

Example of Suspending a Process:

sleep 30

Pressing Ctrl+Z will stop the sleep process and display a message indicating that it has been suspended.

Resuming a Suspended Process: You can resume a suspended process in the background using the bg command:

bg %1

Here, %1 refers to the job number of the suspended process, which you can find by running the jobs command.

4.4 Bringing a Background Process to the Foreground

To bring a background process to the foreground, use the fg command:

fg %1

This will bring the first background job to the foreground, allowing you to interact with it directly.

5. Practical Examples

5.1 Running Multiple Commands

You can run multiple commands, both in the foreground and background, for effective multitasking:

```
# Run a long-running command in the background
long_running_command &

# Immediately run another command in the foreground
another_command
```

5.2 Managing Processes

After running some processes, you can check their status:

```
# List all jobs in the current terminal session
jobs
```

This will show the status of both foreground and background processes.

Understanding the distinction between foreground and background processes is crucial for efficient command-line operation and shell scripting. Foreground processes require user interaction and block the terminal until they finish, while background processes run independently, allowing you to multitask. Mastering process management commands will enhance your productivity and ability to work effectively in a Unix-like environment. Whether you are writing scripts or managing tasks, knowing how to handle processes can significantly improve your workflow.

9.2 Running and Controlling Background Jobs (&, jobs, fg, bg)

In Unix-like operating systems, background jobs are an essential aspect of process management, allowing users to run multiple tasks concurrently without blocking the terminal. This section explores how to run background jobs, check their status, and control them using the shell commands &, jobs, fg, and bg.

1. Understanding Background Jobs

When a process is run in the background, it executes independently of the terminal session, allowing you to continue using the terminal for other commands. Background jobs are particularly useful for long-running tasks that don't require immediate user interaction. This feature is a fundamental part of shell scripting and command-line operations.

2. Running Background Jobs

To run a command as a background job, append an & at the end of the command line. This tells the shell to execute the command in the background.

2.1 Basic Syntax

command &

Example:

To run a command like sleep for 30 seconds in the background:

sleep 30 &

After executing this command, the shell will immediately return control to you, allowing you to run additional commands while the sleep command is still executing.

2.2 Starting Multiple Background Jobs

You can start multiple background jobs in succession:

sleep 30 &
echo "Running sleep command in the background..."

sleep 20 &
echo "Running another sleep command in the background..."

In this example, both sleep commands run simultaneously, and you can execute other commands without waiting for them to complete.

3. Checking Background Jobs

Once you have started background jobs, you may want to check their status. The jobs command is used for this purpose.

3.1 Using the jobs Command

The jobs command lists all background jobs associated with the current terminal session.

Example:

jobs

This command will output something like:

[1]+ 12345 Running   sleep 30 &
[2]- 12346 Running   sleep 20 &

Here, the output indicates the job numbers (in brackets) and their corresponding process IDs (PIDs). The + and - symbols indicate the most recent foreground and background jobs, respectively.

4. Controlling Background Jobs

Once you have background jobs running, you may want to control them. You can do this using the bg and fg commands.

4.1 Suspending a Foreground Job

Before you can bring a job to the background or foreground, you might need to suspend it. You can suspend a foreground job by pressing Ctrl+Z. This will stop the job and place it in the background.

Example:

If you are running a foreground command like:

sleep 30

Pressing Ctrl+Z will suspend the command, and you will see output like:

[1]+ Stopped   sleep 30

4.2 Using the bg Command

After suspending a job, you can continue it in the background using the bg command:

bg %1

In this example, %1 refers to the job number of the suspended job, which you can find using the jobs command.

4.3 Using the fg Command

To bring a background job back to the foreground, use the fg command:

fg %1

This command brings the specified job (in this case, job number 1) back to the foreground, allowing you to interact with it directly.

5. Practical Examples

5.1 Starting and Managing Jobs

Here is a practical example demonstrating how to start, check, and control background jobs:

Start a Background Job:

sleep 60 &

After running this command, you'll get output similar to:

[1]+ 12345 &

Check Background Jobs:

jobs

The output will show the status of the job:

[1]+ Running   sleep 60 &

Suspend a Foreground Job:

While running a foreground job:

sleep 100

Press Ctrl+Z to suspend it:

[2]+ Stopped   sleep 100

Resume in the Background:

bg %2

You can check again with jobs to see that it is now running in the background.

Bringing Back to Foreground:

If you want to bring the suspended job back to the foreground:

fg %2

6. Additional Considerations

6.1 Job Numbers and Process IDs

- Each job started in a shell session is assigned a job number (e.g., %1, %2).

- Each job is also assigned a Process ID (PID), which is a unique number for identifying running processes. You can find the PID using the ps command or in the output of jobs.

6.2 Terminating Background Jobs

If you need to terminate a background job, you can do so using the kill command followed by the job's PID:

kill <PID>

For example:

kill 12345

If the job does not terminate, you can force it using:

kill -9 12345

Managing background jobs effectively is a vital skill in shell scripting and command-line usage. By understanding how to run jobs in the background using &, check their status with jobs, and control them with fg and bg, you can enhance your productivity and multitasking capabilities. These tools enable you to work efficiently, allowing you to keep multiple processes running without interrupting your workflow. Whether you are running scripts, performing data processing, or managing system tasks, mastering background job control is essential for a seamless command-line experience.

9.3 Terminating Processes with kill and pkill

In Unix-like operating systems, managing processes effectively is crucial for system performance and resource management. Sometimes, you may need to terminate processes that are not behaving as expected or are consuming excessive resources. The kill and pkill commands are powerful tools for this purpose. This section explores how to use these commands to terminate processes, along with examples and best practices.

1. Understanding Processes

Before delving into the commands for terminating processes, it's essential to understand the nature of processes in Unix-like systems. Each process is assigned a unique Process ID (PID), which is used to identify it within the system. Processes can run in the foreground or background, and there are various reasons why you might want to terminate them:

- The process is unresponsive or frozen.
- It is consuming too much CPU or memory.
- You no longer need the process to be running.

2. The kill Command

The kill command is used to send signals to processes, primarily for termination. Despite its name, kill can send various signals, not just termination signals.

2.1 Basic Syntax

The basic syntax for the kill command is:

kill [options] <PID>

Example:

To terminate a process with PID 1234, you would use:

kill 1234

This sends the default signal, SIGTERM, which gracefully requests the process to terminate. The process can catch this signal and perform cleanup before shutting down.

2.2 Common Signals

Here are some common signals you can send with the kill command:

- **SIGTERM (15):** The default signal that requests a process to terminate gracefully.
- **SIGKILL (9):** Forces a process to terminate immediately. This signal cannot be caught or ignored.
- **SIGHUP (1):** Often used to signal a process to reload its configuration.

To specify a different signal, use the -s option or the -SIGNAL syntax:

kill -s SIGKILL 1234

Or:

kill -9 1234

Note: Use SIGKILL with caution, as it does not allow the process to perform any cleanup, which can lead to data loss or corruption.

3. The pkill Command

The pkill command is more flexible than kill because it allows you to terminate processes based on criteria other than PID, such as the process name or user.

3.1 Basic Syntax

The basic syntax for the pkill command is:

pkill [options] <pattern>

Example:

To terminate all processes with the name firefox, you would use:

pkill firefox

This command sends the SIGTERM signal to all processes that match the pattern.

3.2 Pattern Matching

The pattern used in pkill can be a full or partial name of the process. You can also use regular expressions for more complex matching:

pkill -f "python script.py"

This command would terminate all Python scripts running script.py.

3.3 Sending Specific Signals with pkill

You can also specify which signal to send with pkill using the -signal option:

pkill -9 firefox

This sends the SIGKILL signal to all instances of Firefox, terminating them immediately.

4. Examples of Using kill and pkill

4.1 Finding a Process ID

Before using kill or pkill, you may need to find the PID of the process you want to terminate. You can use commands like ps or pgrep for this.

Using ps:

ps aux | grep firefox

This command lists all running processes and filters for those containing "firefox." The output will show you the PID of the Firefox process.

Using pgrep:

pgrep firefox

This command directly returns the PIDs of all processes matching "firefox."

4.2 Terminating a Process by PID

If you know the PID:

kill 1234

If the process does not respond, you can use:

kill -9 1234

4.3 Terminating Multiple Processes

Using pkill, you can terminate multiple processes at once:

pkill firefox

This command will terminate all instances of Firefox, making it a powerful option when dealing with multiple processes.

5. Best Practices

- **Use SIGTERM First**: Always start with SIGTERM (the default signal) to allow processes to terminate gracefully. Use SIGKILL only when necessary.
- **Double-Check PIDs**: Ensure you are terminating the correct process by checking the PID or name.
- **Avoid Wildcards**: Be cautious with patterns in pkill. Using broad patterns can unintentionally terminate critical processes.
- **Monitor System Performance**: Regularly check for unresponsive or resource-hogging processes to maintain system health.

Terminating processes using the kill and pkill commands is a vital skill for anyone working with Unix-like operating systems. Understanding how to send different signals and identify processes based on various criteria allows you to manage system resources effectively and resolve issues quickly. Whether you are a developer debugging an application or a system administrator maintaining a server, mastering these commands is essential for maintaining a healthy computing environment. Always approach process termination with caution, opting for graceful termination first and ensuring that you understand the impact of forcibly killing processes.

9.4 Process Substitution for Input/Output Redirection

Process substitution is a powerful feature in Unix-like operating systems that allows the output of a command to be treated as a file input for another command. This feature enhances the flexibility of shell scripting and command-line operations, enabling users to connect commands seamlessly. This section explores how process substitution works, its syntax, and practical use cases.

1. Understanding Process Substitution

In shell scripting, process substitution enables the output of one command to be used as an input to another command. This is particularly useful in scenarios where you want to process data generated by one command without creating temporary files.

1.1 Advantages of Process Substitution

- **Efficiency**: Reduces the need for temporary files, which can save disk space and I/O operations.
- **Convenience**: Simplifies command pipelines by allowing commands to interact directly.
- **Flexibility**: Facilitates complex operations that might require multiple steps in traditional command chaining.

2. Syntax of Process Substitution

The syntax for process substitution varies slightly depending on whether you're using it for input or output redirection.

2.1 Input Redirection

When using process substitution for input redirection, the syntax is as follows:

command <(command1)

In this case, command1 runs, and its output is provided as input to command.

Example:

Suppose you want to compare the output of two commands using diff:

diff <(ls /path/to/dir1) <(ls /path/to/dir2)

In this example, the ls command is executed for both directories, and diff compares their outputs without creating temporary files.

2.2 Output Redirection

For output redirection, the syntax is:

command >(command2)

Here, the output of command is sent as input to command2.

Example:

You can redirect the output of find to sort:

find . -name ".txt" > >(sort)*

In this command, find lists all .txt files, and the output is sorted in real time.

3. Practical Examples of Process Substitution

3.1 Comparing Files

One common use case for process substitution is comparing the contents of files. For instance, to compare two files without creating temporary files:

diff <(cat file1.txt) <(cat file2.txt)

This command runs cat on both files and compares their outputs directly.

3.2 Merging Data

Process substitution can also be helpful when merging data from different commands. For example, suppose you want to merge sorted lists from two different files:

sort <(cat file1.txt) <(cat file2.txt) > merged.txt

In this example, sort reads the output of cat commands and merges the sorted results into merged.txt.

3.3 Using with grep

Another useful scenario is searching for patterns across multiple commands. For example:

grep "error" <(tail -f log1.txt) <(tail -f log2.txt)

In this command, grep searches for "error" in the outputs of the two tail commands, allowing real-time monitoring of both log files.

4. Limitations of Process Substitution

While process substitution is powerful, it does come with some limitations:

- **Not Supported in All Shells**: Process substitution is supported in bash and some other shells, but not in all Unix shells. Always check compatibility.
- **Resource Limits**: Since process substitution uses a file descriptor to handle input/output, it may encounter issues with large data sets if system resource limits are exceeded.
- **Complexity**: While process substitution can simplify certain tasks, it can also make commands less readable. Overuse may lead to complex command lines that are difficult to understand.

Process substitution is a valuable feature that enhances the capabilities of shell scripting and command-line operations. By allowing users to redirect input and output between commands without creating temporary files, it simplifies many data processing tasks. Whether you're comparing files, merging data, or performing real-time searches, understanding and utilizing process substitution can significantly improve efficiency and streamline workflows. However, it's essential to be aware of its limitations and use it judiciously to maintain code clarity and maintainability.

9.5 Pipelining Processes for Efficient Data Flow (|)

Pipelining is one of the most powerful features of Unix-like operating systems that allows users to combine multiple commands into a single command line. This feature enables the output of one command to be fed directly as input to another command, creating a streamlined flow of data. The pipe operator (|) is the mechanism that facilitates this connection, enhancing the efficiency and flexibility of command-line operations and shell scripts.

1. Understanding Pipelining

At its core, pipelining allows for the output of one command to become the input of another, effectively chaining commands together. This means you can create complex data processing workflows by breaking down tasks into smaller, more manageable commands.

1.1 Advantages of Pipelining

- **Efficiency**: Reduces the need for temporary files, saving both disk space and I/O operations.
- **Speed**: Commands can run concurrently, which often results in faster overall execution compared to sequential processing.
- **Modularity**: Breaking tasks into smaller commands promotes code reuse and makes it easier to manage complex operations.

2. Basic Syntax of Pipelining

The basic syntax for creating a pipeline using the pipe operator (|) is straightforward:

command1 | command2 | command3

In this structure, command1 produces output, which becomes the input for command2, and so on. Each command in the pipeline runs simultaneously, processing data as it becomes available.

3. Practical Examples of Pipelining

Pipelining can be applied in numerous scenarios, allowing for efficient data processing. Here are some common use cases:

3.1 Searching and Counting

Suppose you want to find how many times the word "error" appears in a log file. You can use grep to search and wc to count:

grep "error" logfile.txt | wc -l

In this command, grep searches for "error," and its output is piped directly into wc, which counts the lines and provides the total.

3.2 Sorting and Displaying Unique Entries

You can combine sort and uniq to filter out duplicate entries from a list:

sort input.txt | uniq

This command sorts the contents of input.txt and pipes the sorted output to uniq, which displays only unique lines.

3.3 Monitoring System Resources

You can use top or htop alongside grep to monitor specific processes. For example:

ps aux | grep "httpd"

Here, ps aux lists all running processes, and grep filters the output to show only the processes related to httpd.

4. Combining Multiple Commands

You can create more complex pipelines by chaining multiple commands together. For example, to find the most frequently occurring IP addresses in a log file, you might use:

cat access.log | awk '{print $1}' | sort | uniq -c | sort -nr

In this example:

- cat outputs the contents of access.log.
- awk '{print $1}' extracts the first field (usually the IP address).
- sort arranges the IPs.
- uniq -c counts occurrences of each IP.

The final sort -nr sorts the results numerically in reverse order, showing the most frequent IPs at the top.

5. Handling Data Streams

Pipelining is particularly useful when working with large data streams, such as when processing files or logs. For instance, if you want to view the last 10 lines of a large file and search for a specific keyword:

tail -n 100 largefile.txt | grep "keyword"

In this command, tail outputs the last 100 lines of largefile.txt, and grep filters for the specified keyword, allowing you to efficiently analyze a subset of data without loading the entire file.

6. Limitations of Pipelining

While pipelining is a powerful feature, it does have some limitations:

- **Error Handling**: If one command in the pipeline fails, subsequent commands may still execute. It is essential to understand this behavior and handle errors appropriately.
- **Resource Management**: Pipelining can consume system resources, especially with large data sets. Be mindful of system limitations.
- **Command Compatibility**: Not all commands can be used in a pipeline. Commands that expect input from files rather than standard input may not work as intended.

Pipelining is a fundamental aspect of shell scripting and command-line operations that greatly enhances data processing capabilities. By using the pipe operator (|), users can create efficient workflows that allow for seamless data flow between commands, promoting modularity and efficiency. Whether you are performing simple tasks like counting occurrences or building complex data processing pipelines, mastering pipelining can significantly enhance your command-line proficiency and overall productivity. As you explore the power of pipelining, consider combining commands in creative ways to streamline your workflows and tackle even the most complex data manipulation tasks with ease.

9.6 Monitoring System Processes with top, htop, and ps

Monitoring system processes is crucial for maintaining performance and stability in Unix-like operating systems. Understanding how to utilize tools like top, htop, and ps allows users to effectively track system performance, diagnose issues, and manage running processes. This section explores these essential tools, their features, and practical usage examples.

1. Overview of Process Monitoring Tools

Each of these tools offers different capabilities and user interfaces, catering to various needs:

- **top**: A command-line utility that provides a real-time view of running processes and system resource usage.
- **htop**: An enhanced version of top with an improved user interface and additional features for easier interaction and management of processes.

- **ps**: A command that displays a snapshot of current processes, allowing users to view detailed information about each process.

2. The top Command

2.1 Features of top

- Displays real-time data about system processes, including CPU usage, memory consumption, and running time.
- Provides a dynamic, continuously updated view, allowing users to see changes in resource usage in real time.
- Allows sorting by various criteria, such as CPU or memory usage, and supports interactive commands for managing processes.

2.2 Basic Usage

To start top, simply enter the command in your terminal:

top

Upon execution, you'll see a continuously updating list of processes. The default columns typically include:

- **PID**: Process ID
- **USER**: User who owns the process
- **PR:** Priority of the process
- **NI**: Nice value
- **VIRT**: Virtual memory used
- **RES**: Resident memory used
- **SHR**: Shared memory used
- **S**: Process status (e.g., S for sleeping, R for running)
- **%CPU**: Percentage of CPU usage
- **%MEM**: Percentage of memory usage
- **TIME+:** Total CPU time used by the process
- **COMMAND**: Command name or path

2.3 Interactive Commands

While top is running, you can use various keyboard shortcuts to interact with the process list:

- **q**: Quit top.
- **h**: Display help.
- **k**: Kill a process by entering its PID.
- **r**: Renice (change the priority) a process.
- **M**: Sort processes by memory usage.
- **P**: Sort processes by CPU usage.

3. The htop Command

3.1 Features of htop

- Provides a more user-friendly interface compared to top, with color-coded output for better readability.
- Displays process trees, allowing users to see parent-child relationships between processes.
- Supports mouse interaction, making it easier to navigate and manage processes.
- Provides options to filter and search for specific processes.

3.2 Installation

On many systems, htop may not be installed by default. You can install it using package managers:

For Ubuntu/Debian:

sudo apt-get install htop

For CentOS/RHEL:

sudo yum install htop

3.3 Basic Usage

To launch htop, simply type:

htop

You will see a colorful display of system processes, similar to top, but with additional information, including:

- CPU and memory usage graphs.
- Swap usage.
- Process tree structure.

3.4 Interactive Commands

While htop is running, you can use the following commands:

- **F1**: Help.
- **F3**: Search for a process.
- **F4**: Filter processes.
- **F5**: Tree view.
- **F6**: Sort processes by different criteria.
- **F9**: Kill a process.
- **F10**: Quit htop.

4. The ps Command

4.1 Features of ps

- Provides a snapshot of current processes at the moment the command is executed.
- Offers various options to customize the output, including filtering by user, process status, and more.
- Useful for obtaining detailed information about specific processes or groups of processes.

4.2 Basic Usage

To display a list of currently running processes, simply use:

ps

This will show processes running in the current shell session. To see all processes running on the system, you can use:

ps aux

Here's what some of the columns represent in the output of ps aux:

- **USER**: The user who owns the process.
- **PID**: The unique identifier for each process.
- **%CPU**: Percentage of CPU usage.
- **%MEM**: Percentage of memory usage.
- **VSZ**: Virtual memory size.
- **RSS**: Resident Set Size (physical memory used).
- **STAT**: Process status.
- **START**: Start time of the process.
- **TIME**: Total CPU time used.
- **COMMAND**: The command that started the process.

4.3 Customizing Output

You can customize the output of the ps command with options:

To display processes in a hierarchical format, you can use:

ps -ef --forest

To filter processes by a specific user:

ps -u username

To search for a specific command:

ps aux | grep command_name

Monitoring system processes is essential for maintaining optimal performance and diagnosing issues in Unix-like systems. Tools like top, htop, and ps provide users with various capabilities for observing and managing processes effectively. Whether you prefer the real-time monitoring of top, the user-friendly interface of htop, or the snapshot capabilities of ps, understanding how to utilize these tools will enhance your ability to manage system resources efficiently. Regularly monitoring processes allows system administrators and users to ensure stability, troubleshoot problems, and optimize resource allocation, ultimately contributing to a more efficient computing environment.

10. Error Handling and Debugging

In this chapter, you'll learn the essential techniques for writing robust Bash scripts through effective error handling and debugging. We'll explore the significance of exit codes and how to use them to determine the success or failure of commands within your scripts. You'll discover methods for implementing error-checking mechanisms, including conditional statements to respond to failures gracefully. Additionally, we'll cover debugging tools such as set -x for tracing script execution and trap for catching errors and cleanup actions. You'll also learn how to write informative error messages to improve the user experience. By the end of this chapter, you'll be equipped with the skills to identify, troubleshoot, and handle errors in your scripts, ensuring they run smoothly and reliably in various scenarios.

10.1 Understanding Exit Codes and Return Values

Exit codes and return values are fundamental concepts in shell scripting and programming that provide essential information about the execution status of commands and scripts. Understanding how these codes work is crucial for effective error handling, debugging, and control flow in shell scripts.

1. What Are Exit Codes?

An exit code (also known as a return code or exit status) is a numerical value returned by a command or script upon its completion. This value indicates whether the command was executed successfully or if an error occurred. Exit codes are especially important for scripting, as they allow scripts to respond differently based on the success or failure of commands.

1.1 Convention of Exit Codes

- **Success**: By convention, an exit code of 0 signifies that a command has completed successfully without any errors.
- **Failure**: Any non-zero exit code indicates an error or an exceptional condition. The specific non-zero value can provide insight into the type of error that occurred.

For instance:

1: General errors (such as a command not found).

2: Misuse of shell builtins.

- **126**: Command invoked cannot execute.
- **127**: Command not found.
- **128+n**: Fatal error signal "n".
- **255**: Exit status out of range.

2. Understanding Return Values in Scripts

In addition to the exit codes from individual commands, shell scripts can also return exit codes to indicate their overall execution status. The return value of a script can be specified using the exit command.

2.1 Syntax for Exiting a Script

The syntax to return an exit code from a script is:

exit [N]

Where N is an optional integer. If N is omitted, the exit status of the last command executed in the script is used as the exit code.

Example:

```
#!/bin/bash

# A simple script to check if a directory exists
if [ -d "$1" ]; then
    echo "Directory exists."
    exit 0  # Success
else
    echo "Directory does not exist."
    exit 1  # Failure
fi
```

In this example:

- If the directory exists, the script exits with a code of 0.

- If it does not exist, it exits with a code of 1.

3. Checking Exit Codes

You can check the exit code of the last executed command in the shell by accessing the special variable $?. This variable holds the exit status of the most recently executed foreground command.

3.1 Example of Checking Exit Codes

```bash
#!/bin/bash

# Attempt to create a directory
mkdir /tmp/mydir

# Check if the command succeeded
if [ $? -eq 0 ]; then
    echo "Directory created successfully."
else
    echo "Failed to create directory."
fi
```

In this example, after attempting to create a directory, the script checks the exit code. If it is 0, it prints a success message; otherwise, it prints a failure message.

4. Using Exit Codes in Conditional Statements

Exit codes can be used in conditional statements to control the flow of a script based on the success or failure of commands.

4.1 Example with Conditional Execution

```bash
#!/bin/bash

# Update package manager
apt update

# Check if the update command was successful
if [ $? -eq 0 ]; then
    echo "Package manager updated successfully."
```

```
else
    echo "Failed to update package manager."
    exit 1  # Exit with failure status
fi
```

In this script, if the apt update command fails, the script outputs an error message and exits with a failure status.

5. Practical Use Cases for Exit Codes

Understanding and utilizing exit codes is crucial for writing robust and maintainable scripts. Here are some common use cases:

- **Error Handling**: Use exit codes to identify errors and take corrective actions in your scripts.
- **Conditional Logic**: Implement logic that depends on the success or failure of previous commands.
- **Debugging**: Exit codes can help diagnose problems in scripts, making it easier to understand where an issue occurred.

Exit codes and return values are critical components of shell scripting that provide essential feedback on command execution status. By understanding how to use and interpret these codes, you can enhance your scripts with robust error handling, control flow, and debugging capabilities. Effective use of exit codes leads to more reliable scripts that can adapt to varying conditions and handle errors gracefully, ensuring smoother and more efficient system operations. Whether you are writing simple scripts or complex automation tasks, mastering exit codes is a vital skill in the world of shell scripting.

10.2 Using set -e to Handle Errors Automatically

Error handling is a crucial aspect of writing robust shell scripts. One common approach to managing errors is the use of the set -e command. This built-in feature enables scripts to exit immediately when a command fails, simplifying error handling and reducing the need for verbose conditional checks. This section explores how to use set -e, its advantages, and best practices for incorporating it into your scripts.

1. Understanding set -e

The set -e command, when placed at the beginning of a shell script, instructs the shell to terminate the script immediately if any command within the script exits with a non-zero status (indicating an error). This behavior helps prevent subsequent commands from executing in an undesirable state, reducing the risk of cascading errors.

1.1 Basic Syntax

To enable this feature in a script, you simply include:

set -e

Typically, it's added at the top of your script to ensure that the behavior applies to all commands that follow.

2. How set -e Works

When set -e is enabled, the shell will check the exit status of each command. If a command returns a non-zero exit code, the shell will stop executing the script. This behavior helps to catch errors early, making debugging easier.

2.1 Example Without set -e

Consider a script that installs a package, creates a directory, and then writes to a file:

#!/bin/bash

apt-get install somepackage
mkdir /tmp/mydir
echo "Hello World" > /tmp/mydir/message.txt

If the package installation fails, the script will continue running, potentially leading to errors when trying to create a directory or write to a file.

2.2 Example With set -e

By adding set -e, you can prevent these potential issues:

#!/bin/bash

set -e

```
apt-get install somepackage
mkdir /tmp/mydir
echo "Hello World" > /tmp/mydir/message.txt
```

In this modified script, if apt-get install fails, the script will terminate immediately, preventing further commands from executing under a failed assumption.

3. Use Cases for set -e

Using set -e can be particularly beneficial in several scenarios:

- **Installation Scripts**: In scripts that install software or packages, failing at any point can leave the system in an inconsistent state. set -e ensures that the script halts on failure.
- **Automated Backups**: For backup scripts, if a command to copy files fails, continuing could result in partial backups or data loss.
- **CI/CD Pipelines**: In continuous integration and deployment, scripts should fail fast to allow for immediate feedback on the build process.

4. Limitations and Considerations

While set -e is useful, it's important to understand its limitations:

4.1 Commands That Do Not Cause Exit

Some commands are designed to fail gracefully or return a non-zero exit code intentionally, and set -e does not stop the script in these cases. For example:

Commands followed by a logical operator (like && or ||).

command1 || true

In this case, even if command1 fails, the script continues because the exit status is ignored due to || true.

4.2 Functions and Subshells

If a command in a function or subshell fails, it may not trigger set -e behavior. You may need to explicitly check exit codes in these cases.

4.3 Ignoring Specific Commands

If you want to allow a specific command to fail without terminating the script, you can disable set -e temporarily:

set +e # Disable set -e
command_that_may_fail
set -e # Re-enable set -e

5. Best Practices

Here are some best practices for using set -e effectively:

- **Use Early in Scripts**: Place set -e at the beginning of your script to ensure all subsequent commands are monitored for errors.
- **Combine with Exit Codes**: Although set -e automatically stops the script on error, consider also checking exit codes for commands that should not trigger a script termination.
- **Document Behavior**: Clearly document the behavior of your script, especially if using set -e, so users understand that the script will terminate on errors.
- **Test Thoroughly**: Ensure to test your scripts under various conditions to confirm that set -e behaves as expected, catching errors effectively.

The set -e command is a powerful tool for enhancing error handling in shell scripts. By instructing the shell to exit immediately on encountering an error, it promotes better script reliability and simplifies debugging efforts. However, it is essential to understand its limitations and use it in conjunction with proper exit code handling for the most effective results. Adopting set -e in your shell scripts will help ensure that your automation tasks run smoothly and consistently, providing a more robust scripting experience.

10.3 Trapping Signals with trap

In Unix-like operating systems, processes can receive signals that notify them of certain events. These signals can originate from the system or other processes, and they can affect the execution of your scripts. The trap command in Bash allows you to handle these signals gracefully, enabling you to execute specific actions when a signal is received. This section covers how to use trap effectively to manage signals, handle cleanup tasks, and improve the robustness of your shell scripts.

1. Understanding Signals

Signals are asynchronous notifications sent to processes to indicate that a specific event has occurred. Some common signals include:

- **SIGINT (Interrupt):** Sent when you press Ctrl+C, typically used to interrupt a running process.
- **SIGTERM (Terminate):** A request to terminate a process gracefully.
- **SIGQUIT (Quit):** Similar to SIGINT, but causes the process to produce a core dump.
- **SIGHUP (Hang Up):** Sent to a process when its controlling terminal is closed.
- **SIGKILL**: Cannot be caught or ignored; it forcibly kills a process.

Understanding how to respond to these signals can help prevent data loss, ensure cleanup tasks are executed, and improve user experience.

2. Using trap to Handle Signals

The trap command allows you to specify a command or set of commands that should be executed when the shell receives certain signals. This is particularly useful for cleanup tasks, like deleting temporary files or restoring the terminal state before exiting.

2.1 Basic Syntax

The basic syntax of the trap command is:

trap 'commands' SIGNALS

commands: The commands you want to execute when the specified signals are received.

SIGNALS: A list of one or more signals to trap, separated by spaces.

2.2 Example of Using trap

Here's a simple example that demonstrates how to use trap to catch the SIGINT signal:

```bash
#!/bin/bash

# Define a cleanup function
cleanup() {
    echo "Cleaning up before exit..."
    # Perform cleanup tasks, like removing temporary files
    rm -f /tmp/tempfile
    exit 1
}

# Trap the SIGINT signal (Ctrl+C) and call the cleanup function
trap cleanup SIGINT

echo "Running script. Press Ctrl+C to interrupt."

# Simulate a long-running process
while true; do
    sleep 1
    echo "Still running..."
done
```

In this script:

- The cleanup function is defined to perform necessary cleanup tasks when called.
- The trap command captures SIGINT and invokes the cleanup function when the user presses Ctrl+C.
- The script enters an infinite loop, continuously printing "Still running..." until interrupted.

3. Multiple Signals

You can trap multiple signals by specifying them in a space-separated list. For example:

trap cleanup SIGINT SIGTERM

This command will call the cleanup function when either SIGINT or SIGTERM is received.

4. Ignoring Signals

Sometimes you may want to ignore specific signals. You can do this by using an empty string as the command in the trap statement. For example:

trap " SIGINT

This command tells the shell to ignore SIGINT, meaning pressing Ctrl+C will have no effect.

5. Default Behavior

If you want to restore the default behavior for a signal after it has been trapped, you can do so by using the - option:

trap - SIGINT

This command removes the trap for SIGINT, reverting it to the default behavior.

6. Practical Use Cases for trap

Using trap is beneficial in various scenarios, including:

- **Cleanup Operations**: Ensure temporary files or resources are cleaned up when a script is interrupted.
- **User Experience**: Provide user-friendly messages before the script exits, explaining what is happening.
- **Graceful Shutdowns**: Allow for graceful handling of termination signals in long-running processes.

7. Example of Using trap in a Script

Here's a more complex example that demonstrates the use of trap for cleanup and signal handling in a script that downloads a file:

```
#!/bin/bash

# Temporary file for download
temp_file="/tmp/download.tmp"

# Cleanup function
cleanup() {
```

```
    echo "Cleaning up..."
    rm -f "$temp_file"
    echo "Exiting script."
    exit 1
}

# Trap SIGINT and SIGTERM to call cleanup
trap cleanup SIGINT SIGTERM

# Simulating a file download
echo "Starting download..."
echo "Downloading to $temp_file..."

# Fake download process
for i in {1..10}; do
    echo "Downloading... $((i * 10))%"
    sleep 1  # Simulate time taken for download
done

# Complete the download
echo "Download complete!"
rm -f "$temp_file"
```

In this script:

- The cleanup function ensures that the temporary file is removed if the script is interrupted.
- The script simulates a download process, and if the user interrupts it (e.g., by pressing Ctrl+C), the cleanup function is executed.

The trap command in Bash is a powerful tool for managing signals and ensuring that your scripts behave predictably under various conditions. By using trap, you can handle interruptions gracefully, perform cleanup operations, and provide a better user experience. Incorporating signal handling into your scripts can lead to more robust, user-friendly, and reliable shell scripts, especially for long-running processes or scripts that manipulate system resources. Understanding and effectively using trap will enhance your scripting capabilities and contribute to overall script reliability.

10.4 Debugging Scripts with set -x

Debugging is an essential part of developing shell scripts, as it helps identify and resolve issues that may arise during execution. One of the most powerful tools for debugging in Bash is the set -x command. This command enables a mode of debugging where the shell prints each command and its arguments to the standard error output before executing them. This visibility allows developers to trace the execution flow and pinpoint errors in their scripts. In this section, we will explore how to use set -x, its benefits, and best practices for effective debugging.

1. Understanding set -x

The set -x command is used to turn on a debugging feature in Bash scripts. When this mode is activated, each command that is executed is displayed in the terminal along with its arguments, prefixed by a + sign. This feature is particularly useful for understanding how a script is executing and for troubleshooting problems.

1.1 Basic Syntax

To enable debugging, simply include the following command at the beginning of your script:

set -x

To turn off debugging later in the script, you can use:

set +x

This allows you to control when you want the debugging output to appear.

2. Benefits of Using set -x

- **Visibility**: By displaying each command before it runs, set -x provides a clear view of what your script is doing at any given time.
- **Error Identification**: It helps identify where a script is failing, as you can see the exact command that was executed before the failure.
- **Understanding Flow**: It clarifies the execution flow of the script, which is especially beneficial in complex scripts with multiple branches and conditions.

3. Example of Using set -x

Here's a simple example to illustrate the use of set -x in a script:

```bash
#!/bin/bash

set -x  # Enable debugging

# Example variables
filename="example.txt"
backup_filename="example.bak"

# Create a file
echo "Creating file: $filename"
touch "$filename"

# Backup the file
echo "Backing up file to: $backup_filename"
cp "$filename" "$backup_filename"

# Remove the original file
echo "Removing the original file"
rm "$filename"

set +x  # Disable debugging
echo "Script execution completed."
```

3.1 Debugging Output

When you run this script, the output will look something like this:

```
+ filename=example.txt
+ backup_filename=example.bak
+ echo 'Creating file: example.txt'
```

Creating file: example.txt

```
+ touch example.txt
+ echo 'Backing up file to: example.bak'
```

Backing up file to: example.bak

```
+ cp example.txt example.bak
+ echo 'Removing the original file'
```

Removing the original file

```
+ rm example.txt
+ set +x
```

Script execution completed.

The + signs preceding each command indicate that debugging is enabled. This output shows exactly what commands are executed and in what order, making it easier to trace any potential issues.

4. When to Use set -x

Using set -x is particularly beneficial in the following scenarios:

- **Complex Scripts**: When dealing with scripts that have multiple functions, loops, or conditional statements.
- **Troubleshooting Errors**: When a script fails, and you need to determine which command caused the issue.
- **Learning and Development**: For beginners, using set -x can help understand how Bash processes scripts and how variable expansions occur.

5. Best Practices for Debugging with set -x

While set -x is a powerful tool for debugging, here are some best practices to consider:

5.1 Use Selectively

Instead of enabling debugging for the entire script, consider using it selectively for specific sections. This can be done by turning it on and off with set -x and set +x as needed.

set -x # Enable debugging for a specific block

 # Some commands to debug

set +x # Disable debugging

5.2 Combine with set -e

When debugging, you may still want to ensure that your script exits on errors. You can use set -e in conjunction with set -x:

set -e
set -x

This combination allows you to see commands and ensures that the script will stop on the first error encountered.

5.3 Clean Up Before Production

Before deploying scripts to production, it's a good practice to remove or comment out the set -x commands to prevent unnecessary output.

6. Example of a Complex Script with Debugging

Here's an example of a more complex script utilizing set -x for debugging:

```bash
#!/bin/bash

set -e
set -x  # Enable debugging

# Function to process files
process_file() {
    local file="$1"
    echo "Processing file: $file"
    # Simulate a command that might fail
    cp "$file" "/tmp/processed_$file" || { echo "Failed to process $file"; exit 1; }
}

# Main logic
for file in *.txt; do
    if [[ -f "$file" ]]; then
        process_file "$file"
    else
```

```
        echo "$file is not a valid file."
    fi
done

set +x  # Disable debugging
echo "All files processed."
```

In this script:

- The process_file function processes each .txt file.
- If the cp command fails, an error message is printed, and the script exits.
- Debugging output will show each command executed, helping to trace any issues.

Debugging shell scripts can be challenging, but the set -x command is a valuable tool that simplifies this process. By providing a clear view of the commands being executed, it allows developers to track down errors efficiently and understand the execution flow of their scripts. By using set -x judiciously, you can enhance your debugging capabilities and write more reliable, maintainable shell scripts. Whether you're a novice or an experienced developer, mastering debugging techniques with set -x will significantly improve your scripting proficiency.

10.5 Redirecting Errors to Logs

In shell scripting, managing error messages is crucial for developing robust and reliable scripts. Errors can occur for various reasons, such as missing files, permission issues, or syntax errors. By redirecting error messages to log files, you can keep your console output clean while retaining valuable debugging information. This section will cover how to redirect errors to logs, why it is important, and best practices for managing log files in your Bash scripts.

1. Understanding Standard Output and Standard Error

In Unix-like operating systems, every command produces two main types of output:

Standard Output (stdout): This is the default output stream where a command sends its normal output. It is represented by file descriptor 1.

Standard Error (stderr): This is the default output stream where a command sends its error messages. It is represented by file descriptor 2.

When running commands in a terminal, both stdout and stderr are displayed in the console. However, there are times when you may want to separate normal output from error messages, which is where redirection comes into play.

2. Basic Redirection Syntax

Bash provides several operators to redirect output streams. The most common operators are:

>: Redirects standard output to a file, overwriting the file if it exists.

>>: Redirects standard output to a file, appending to the file if it exists.

2>: Redirects standard error to a file, overwriting the file if it exists.

2>>: Redirects standard error to a file, appending to the file if it exists.

&>: Redirects both standard output and standard error to the same file (available in Bash).

3. Redirecting Standard Error to a Log File

To redirect error messages to a log file, you can use the 2> operator. Here's a basic example:

```
#!/bin/bash

# Redirecting stderr to a log file
command_that_may_fail 2> error.log
```

In this example, if command_that_may_fail produces any error messages, they will be captured in error.log instead of being displayed on the console.

3.1 Example of Error Redirection

Here's a practical example:

```bash
#!/bin/bash

# Redirect errors to a log file
log_file="script_errors.log"

# Attempt to create a directory that may fail
mkdir /root/protected_directory 2> "$log_file"

# Check if the directory was created
if [[ $? -ne 0 ]]; then
    echo "Error occurred. Check $log_file for details."
fi
```

In this script:

- The command attempts to create a directory in a protected location, which is likely to fail due to permission issues.
- Any error messages generated by the mkdir command are redirected to script_errors.log.
- After the command runs, the script checks the exit status ($?) and informs the user if an error occurred.

4. Redirecting Both stdout and stderr

Sometimes, you may want to capture both normal output and error messages in the same log file. You can achieve this using the &> operator or by combining redirection operators.

4.1 Using &>

Here's an example:

```bash
#!/bin/bash

# Redirect both stdout and stderr to a log file
log_file="script_output.log"

# Execute a command and redirect both outputs
command_that_may_fail &> "$log_file"
```

4.2 Using Separate Redirects

Alternatively, you can redirect stdout and stderr to the same file like this:

command_that_may_fail > output.log 2>&1

In this example:

- The command's normal output goes to output.log.
- The 2>&1 part tells the shell to redirect stderr (file descriptor 2) to the same location as stdout (file descriptor 1), effectively merging both streams into one file.

5. Rotating Log Files

When scripts are run frequently or generate a lot of output, the log files can quickly become large and unwieldy. Implementing a log rotation strategy can help manage file sizes and organize log files.

5.1 Using logrotate

On many systems, the logrotate utility is available to manage log file rotation automatically. You can configure logrotate to handle your script logs by creating a configuration file in /etc/logrotate.d/ that specifies when and how to rotate the logs.

Example configuration (/etc/logrotate.d/myscript):

/var/log/myscript.log {
　　daily
　　rotate 7
　　compress
　　missingok
　　notifempty
　　create 0640 root root
}

This configuration will:

- Rotate the log file daily.
- Keep the last 7 rotated logs.

- Compress old log files to save space.
- Skip rotation if the log file is missing or empty.

5.2 Manual Rotation

You can also implement manual log rotation within your script. Here's a simple approach:

log_file="script_output.log"

 # Rotate logs
if [[-f "$log_file"]]; then
   mv "$log_file" "$log_file.old"
fi

 # Redirect stdout and stderr to a new log file
exec > "$log_file" 2>&1

In this snippet:

- If the log file already exists, it is renamed to script_output.log.old.
- The exec command is then used to redirect both stdout and stderr to a new log file for the current execution of the script.

6. Best Practices for Logging in Scripts

Use Meaningful Log File Names: Include timestamps or other identifying information in your log file names to make it easier to manage and locate logs.

Log Verbosely, But Wisely: Ensure that logs contain relevant information for debugging but avoid excessive output that may clutter the logs.

Implement Log Rotation: Regularly rotate logs to prevent them from consuming too much disk space.

Separate Logs for Different Components: If your script has multiple functionalities, consider logging errors and output to separate files to enhance clarity.

Monitor Log File Size: Implement checks to monitor the size of log files and take action (e.g., rotating or compressing) if they exceed certain limits.

Redirecting errors to logs is an essential practice in shell scripting that enhances debugging and helps maintain clean output in the console. By understanding how to redirect standard error messages and using effective logging strategies, you can significantly improve the reliability and maintainability of your scripts. Whether you are developing simple scripts or complex automation tools, implementing robust error handling and logging practices will lead to better performance and easier troubleshooting.

10.6 Writing Defensive Code: Preventing Common Errors

When developing shell scripts, writing defensive code is crucial to ensure that scripts run smoothly and handle unexpected situations gracefully. Defensive programming involves anticipating potential issues and implementing strategies to prevent errors from occurring. This approach enhances the reliability, maintainability, and robustness of your scripts. In this section, we will explore common pitfalls in shell scripting and discuss techniques for writing defensive code to prevent these errors.

1. Common Errors in Shell Scripting

Understanding common errors is the first step to writing defensive code. Here are some frequent issues encountered in shell scripts:

1.1 Syntax Errors

Syntax errors occur when the script's syntax does not conform to the rules of the shell. These errors can prevent the script from running altogether.

1.2 Command Not Found

Attempting to execute a command that is not available in the system can lead to a "command not found" error. This may happen due to a typo, missing binaries, or improper path configurations.

1.3 File Not Found

Scripts that rely on external files (e.g., configuration files or input data) may fail if those files are missing or have incorrect paths.

1.4 Permission Issues

Scripts may attempt to read from or write to files for which they lack appropriate permissions, resulting in permission denied errors.

1.5 Variable Misuse

Using uninitialized or improperly scoped variables can lead to unexpected behavior or incorrect results.

2. Techniques for Writing Defensive Code

2.1 Use Set Commands for Safety

Using set commands at the beginning of your script can help catch errors early. Here are some useful options:

set -e: Exit immediately if a command exits with a non-zero status. This prevents the script from continuing execution when an error occurs.

set -u: Treat unset variables as an error when substituting. This helps catch issues where variables are not properly initialized.

set -o pipefail: Prevents the entire pipeline from succeeding if any command in the pipeline fails. This is particularly useful when chaining commands together.

Example:

#!/bin/bash

set -euo pipefail # Enable strict error handling

2.2 Validate Input

Always validate input before processing it. Check for expected formats, required fields, and whether the input meets your criteria.

if [[-z "$1"]]; then
   echo "Error: No input file provided."
   exit 1

fi

In this example, the script checks if a required input parameter is provided. If not, it displays an error message and exits.

2.3 Check for Required Commands

Before executing a command, check if it is available on the system using the command -v or type command.

```
if ! command -v git &> /dev/null; then
    echo "Error: git is not installed."
    exit 1
fi
```

This code checks for the presence of git and exits with an error message if it is not found.

3. Handling Files and Directories

3.1 Check for File Existence

Always check whether files and directories exist before attempting to read or write to them.

```
if [[ ! -f "config.txt" ]]; then
    echo "Error: config.txt file not found."
    exit 1
fi
```

This snippet verifies the existence of config.txt before attempting to access it.

3.2 Manage Permissions

Ensure that your script checks for the necessary permissions before performing operations that require them.

```
if [[ ! -w "output.log" ]]; then
    echo "Error: No write permission for output.log."
    exit 1
```

fi

This code checks if the script has permission to write to output.log.

4. Error Handling and Logging

4.1 Provide Meaningful Error Messages

When errors occur, it's essential to provide clear and actionable error messages. This helps users understand what went wrong and how to fix it.

command_that_may_fail || { echo "Error: Command failed with exit code $?"; exit 1; }

Using || allows you to handle errors immediately, providing a custom message while exiting gracefully.

4.2 Implement Logging

Consider logging errors to a file for later review. This can help with debugging and understanding script behavior over time.

log_file="script_errors.log"

command_that_may_fail 2>> "$log_file" || {
  echo "Error occurred. Check $log_file for details."
  exit 1
}

In this example, any errors generated by the command are appended to script_errors.log, while also notifying the user.

5. Example of Defensive Scripting

Here's a complete example that incorporates many of the defensive coding techniques discussed:

#!/bin/bash

set -euo pipefail # Enable strict error handling

```bash
# Function to check for command availability
check_command() {
    if ! command -v "$1" &> /dev/null; then
        echo "Error: $1 is not installed."
        exit 1
    fi
}

# Validate input
if [[ $# -ne 1 ]]; then
    echo "Usage: $0 <input_file>"
    exit 1
fi

input_file="$1"

# Check if input file exists
if [[ ! -f "$input_file" ]]; then
    echo "Error: Input file '$input_file' not found."
    exit 1
fi

# Check for required commands
check_command "awk"

# Process the file
output_file="output.txt"
if [[ ! -w "$output_file" ]]; then
    echo "Error: No write permission for '$output_file'."
    exit 1
fi

# Perform some processing
awk '{ print $1 }' "$input_file" > "$output_file" || {
    echo "Error: Processing failed."
    exit 1
}

echo "Processing completed successfully. Output written to '$output_file'."
```

Explanation of the Example

- **Strict Error Handling**: The script uses set -euo pipefail to handle errors effectively.
- **Input Validation**: It checks for the correct number of input parameters and whether the specified file exists.
- **Command Checks**: It verifies that the necessary commands are available before proceeding.
- **File Permissions**: The script checks if it can write to the output file before attempting to do so.
- **Error Logging**: Any errors encountered during processing are reported with clear messages.

Writing defensive code is a critical skill in shell scripting that helps prevent common errors and enhances the reliability of your scripts. By anticipating potential issues and implementing validation checks, error handling, and meaningful logging, you can create scripts that behave predictably, even in the face of unexpected situations. Adopting these practices not only improves your scripts' robustness but also makes them easier to maintain and troubleshoot in the long run. Whether you're a beginner or an experienced scripter, incorporating defensive programming techniques will greatly enhance the quality and reliability of your shell scripts.

11. Performance Optimization

In this chapter, you'll explore strategies for optimizing the performance of your Bash scripts, ensuring they run efficiently even under demanding conditions. We'll begin by discussing common performance bottlenecks and how to identify them using profiling techniques. You'll learn to minimize resource usage by optimizing loops, reducing unnecessary computations, and leveraging built-in Bash features for faster execution. We'll also cover the use of parallel processing with tools like xargs and GNU parallel to execute tasks simultaneously, significantly reducing overall runtime. Additionally, you'll discover techniques for minimizing I/O operations and managing memory usage effectively. By the end of this chapter, you'll have a comprehensive toolkit for enhancing the speed and efficiency of your scripts, enabling you to automate tasks more effectively and handle larger datasets with ease.

11.1 Profiling Scripts with time and bash -x

Profiling scripts is an essential practice for optimizing performance and ensuring that your Bash scripts run efficiently. By analyzing how long a script takes to execute and identifying which parts of the script consume the most time, you can make informed decisions on how to improve your scripts. This section will cover two primary methods for profiling Bash scripts: using the time command and the bash -x debugging option.

1. Understanding Profiling

Profiling refers to the process of measuring the space (memory) and time (CPU) complexity of a script or application. In the context of shell scripting, profiling allows you to:

- Identify bottlenecks and inefficient code paths.
- Understand resource consumption.
- Optimize performance for faster execution.

2. Using the time Command

The time command is a built-in utility in most Unix-like operating systems that allows you to measure the execution time of a command or script. It provides information on how long the command took to execute, including:

- **Real time**: The actual time taken from start to finish.
- **User CPU time**: The amount of CPU time spent in user mode (executing your code).
- **System CPU time**: The amount of CPU time spent in kernel mode (executing system calls on behalf of your code).

2.1 Basic Usage

To use the time command, simply prepend it to your script or command:

time ./your_script.sh

2.2 Example Output

When you run a script with time, you may see output similar to this:

real   0m0.025s
user   0m0.010s
sys   0m0.005s

real: Total elapsed time.
user: Time spent in user mode.
sys: Time spent in kernel mode.

This output provides a quick overview of how long your script took to execute and where the time was spent.

2.3 Advanced Usage

The time command can be customized to provide more detailed output. For instance, you can format the output using the -p option, which displays the time in a portable format:

/usr/bin/time -p ./your_script.sh

The output will look like this:

real 0.025
user 0.010
sys 0.005

Additionally, you can redirect the output of time to a file for further analysis:

`{ time ./your_script.sh; } 2> time_output.txt`

3. Using bash -x for Debugging

The bash -x option allows you to run your script in debug mode. This mode provides a detailed trace of the commands being executed, including their arguments, which can be invaluable for understanding script performance and flow.

3.1 Enabling Debug Mode

To enable debugging for your script, you can run it with the -x option:

`bash -x ./your_script.sh`

3.2 Example Output

When you run a script with bash -x, you will see output similar to the following:

```
+ echo 'Starting script...'
Starting script...
+ sleep 1
+ echo 'Script completed.'
Script completed.
```

The + sign before each command indicates the command being executed, along with its arguments. This output allows you to see how long each part of the script takes to run, which is useful for pinpointing bottlenecks.

3.3 Combining time with bash -x

For a more comprehensive analysis, you can combine both time and bash -x:

`{ time bash -x ./your_script.sh; } 2> time_output.txt`

In this case, you will get both the timing information and the debug output, enabling you to analyze performance alongside the execution trace.

4. Analyzing the Output

When profiling scripts, it's essential to analyze the output effectively:

Identify Slow Commands: Look for commands that take a long time to execute. Pay attention to their complexity and whether they can be optimized.

Inspect Loops and Conditions: If your script contains loops or conditional statements, ensure they aren't causing unnecessary delays. Consider whether they can be restructured for efficiency.

Evaluate External Calls: Commands that invoke external processes (like curl, wget, or database queries) may introduce latency. Assess whether these calls are necessary or if they can be consolidated.

5. Common Pitfalls to Avoid

When profiling your scripts, keep in mind the following common pitfalls:

Overhead of Debugging: Using bash -x adds some overhead to script execution. The additional time may be misleading if you're trying to measure performance.

Ignoring Real-World Conditions: Testing in a controlled environment may not accurately reflect real-world performance. Test your scripts under realistic load conditions.

Focusing Solely on Execution Time: While execution time is important, also consider other factors such as memory usage, CPU load, and the complexity of algorithms. An efficient algorithm may execute slower but use fewer resources overall.

Profiling your Bash scripts using time and bash -x is a fundamental practice for optimizing performance and ensuring that your scripts run efficiently. By measuring execution time and tracing command execution, you can identify bottlenecks and optimize your scripts accordingly. This practice not only enhances the performance of your scripts but also leads to better resource management and improved overall system performance. Adopting these profiling techniques will make you a more effective and efficient scripter.

11.2 Using Efficient Data Structures: Arrays and Strings

In Bash scripting, utilizing efficient data structures is crucial for optimizing performance and managing data effectively. Among the most commonly used data structures are arrays and strings. Understanding how to use and manipulate these structures can greatly enhance your scripts, making them more efficient and easier to maintain. This section will cover the basics of arrays and strings in Bash, including their creation, manipulation, and best practices for efficient usage.

1. Understanding Data Structures in Bash

Data structures are ways of organizing and storing data to facilitate efficient access and modification. In Bash scripting, arrays and strings are essential for handling collections of data and manipulating textual information.

1.1 Strings

Strings are sequences of characters used to represent text. In Bash, strings can be manipulated using various built-in commands and operators.

1.2 Arrays

Arrays are collections of variables accessed by an index. They allow you to group related data together, making it easier to manage and process.

2. Working with Strings in Bash

2.1 Creating and Initializing Strings

Strings in Bash can be created and initialized in various ways. The simplest method is by assigning a value to a variable:

my_string="Hello, World!"

You can also use single quotes to prevent variable expansion:

my_string='Hello, $USER!'

2.2 String Operations

Bash provides several operations to manipulate strings:

Length of a String: You can get the length of a string using the ${#variable} syntax.

length=${#my_string}
echo "Length: $length"

Substring Extraction: Extract a substring using the syntax ${variable:start:length}.

substring=${my_string:7:5} # Extracts 'World'

echo "Substring: $substring"

String Replacement: Replace occurrences of a substring using the syntax ${variable//search/replace}.

new_string=${my_string//World/Bash}
echo "$new_string" # Outputs: Hello, Bash!

2.3 String Comparison

String comparison can be performed using conditional expressions:

if [["$my_string" == "Hello, World!"]]; then
*   echo "The strings are equal."*
fi

For checking if a string is empty, you can use:

if [[-z "$my_string"]]; then
*   echo "String is empty."*
fi

3. Working with Arrays in Bash

3.1 Creating and Initializing Arrays

Arrays in Bash can be declared using parentheses. You can assign values to them at the time of creation or later.

```
my_array=(apple banana cherry)  # Declare and initialize an array
```

```
# Assigning values to specific indices
my_array[3]="date"  # Adds 'date' at index 3
```

3.2 Accessing Array Elements

You can access array elements using their index, which starts at 0:

```
echo "${my_array[0]}"  # Outputs: apple
```

To get all elements in the array, you can use the * or @ notation:

```
echo "${my_array[*]}"  # Outputs: apple banana cherry date
```

3.3 Array Length

To find the length of an array (the number of elements), use the syntax ${#array[@]}:

```
length=${#my_array[@]}
echo "Array length: $length"  # Outputs: Array length: 4
```

3.4 Iterating Over Arrays

You can iterate over array elements using loops. The for loop is commonly used:

```
for item in "${my_array[@]}"; do
   echo "$item"
done
```

3.5 Associative Arrays

Bash also supports associative arrays (hash maps), where keys can be strings instead of just integers. You can declare associative arrays using declare -A:

```
declare -A fruit_colors
fruit_colors=( ["apple"]="red" ["banana"]="yellow" ["cherry"]="red" )
```

```
# Accessing elements
echo "Apple is ${fruit_colors[apple]}."
```

4. Best Practices for Using Data Structures

4.1 Use Arrays for Grouping Related Data

When dealing with collections of related data, use arrays instead of individual variables. This makes your code cleaner and easier to maintain.

 # Instead of
apple="red"
banana="yellow"
cherry="red"

 # Use
declare -A fruit_colors
fruit_colors=(["apple"]="red" ["banana"]="yellow" ["cherry"]="red")

4.2 Minimize String Manipulations

String operations can be expensive, especially in large loops. Try to minimize unnecessary string manipulations. For example, instead of modifying a string multiple times in a loop, consider building it once:

result=""
for item in "${my_array[@]}"; do
   result+="$item, "
done
result=${result%, } # Remove trailing comma

4.3 Use Associative Arrays for Key-Value Pairs

When you need to map keys to values, associative arrays are more efficient and clearer than using two parallel arrays:

declare -A user_info
user_info=(["name"]="John Doe" ["age"]="30" ["city"]="New York")

4.4 Consider Memory Usage

Be mindful of memory usage when working with large arrays or strings. While Bash is efficient for small to medium-sized data sets, other languages may be better suited for handling large datasets or complex data structures.

Utilizing efficient data structures such as arrays and strings is essential for writing optimized Bash scripts. Understanding how to create, manipulate, and access these structures enables you to manage data effectively and improve your script's performance. By following best practices, you can ensure that your scripts are not only efficient but also clean and maintainable. With a solid grasp of these concepts, you will be well-equipped to tackle more complex scripting tasks and enhance the overall functionality of your shell scripts.

11.3 Optimizing Loops and Conditionals

Loops and conditionals are fundamental constructs in Bash scripting that allow you to control the flow of your scripts. However, inefficient use of these constructs can lead to performance bottlenecks, especially in large scripts or those that process substantial data sets. This section will discuss techniques for optimizing loops and conditionals, helping you write more efficient Bash scripts.

1. Understanding Loops and Conditionals

1.1 Loops

Loops enable you to execute a block of code multiple times. The primary types of loops in Bash include:

- **for Loops**: Iterate over a list of items or a sequence of numbers.
- **while Loops**: Continue executing as long as a condition is true.
- **until Loops**: Execute until a specified condition becomes true.

1.2 Conditionals

Conditionals allow your script to make decisions based on specific criteria. Common conditional statements include:

- **if Statements**: Execute a block of code if a condition is true.
- **case Statements**: Select from multiple possible blocks of code based on a variable's value.

2. Optimizing Loops

2.1 Use for Loops for Simple Iteration

When iterating over a fixed list or a range of numbers, use a for loop. This is generally more efficient than using while or until loops, especially when the number of iterations is known in advance.

 # Efficient for loop
for i in {1..10}; do
   echo "Iteration $i"
done

2.2 Avoid Unnecessary Subshells

Bash creates a subshell when using commands like $(...) or backticks (` `), which can slow down your script if used within a loop. Instead, capture the output of a command outside of the loop.

Inefficient:

for file in $(ls); do
   echo "Processing $(basename "$file")"
done

Efficient:

files=($(ls)) # Capture output outside the loop
for file in "${files[@]}"; do
   echo "Processing $(basename "$file")"
done

2.3 Minimize Loop Iterations

If possible, reduce the number of iterations by filtering data before entering the loop. For example, if you only need to process certain files, filter them first.

 # Filter files first
for file in *.txt; do

 # Process only text files
done

2.4 Use break and continue Wisely

In cases where you can terminate a loop early or skip an iteration, use break or continue. This can save time and resources.

for i in {1..100}; do
   if ((i == 50)); then
      break # Exit the loop early
   fi
   echo "$i"
done

2.5 Use Built-in Commands When Possible

Bash provides several built-in commands that are generally faster than external commands. Whenever possible, prefer using built-in commands to improve performance.

 # Using built-in commands
count=0
for file in *.txt; do
   ((count++))
done
echo "Total text files: $count"

3. Optimizing Conditionals

3.1 Combine Conditions

When checking multiple conditions, combine them to reduce the number of tests. Use logical operators like && (AND) and || (OR) to streamline your conditionals.

Inefficient:

if [[$var -eq 1]]; then
   echo "Var is 1"
fi

```
if [[ $var -eq 2 ]]; then
   echo "Var is 2"
fi
```

Efficient:

```
if [[ $var -eq 1 || $var -eq 2 ]]; then
   echo "Var is either 1 or 2"
fi
```

3.2 Use case Statements for Multiple Conditions

When you have multiple values to check against a single variable, use a case statement instead of several if statements. This can make your code cleaner and potentially faster.

```
case $var in
   1)
      echo "Var is 1"
      ;;
   2)
      echo "Var is 2"
      ;;
   *)
      echo "Var is something else"
      ;;
esac
```

3.3 Avoid Nested Conditionals

Nested conditionals can make your code complex and harder to read. Try to flatten your conditional logic where possible to improve readability and efficiency.

Inefficient:

```
if [[ $var -eq 1 ]]; then
   if [[ $other_var -eq 2 ]]; then
      echo "Both conditions are met."
   fi
fi
```

Efficient:

```
if [[ $var -eq 1 && $other_var -eq 2 ]]; then
    echo "Both conditions are met."
fi
```

3.4 Short-Circuit Evaluation

Bash supports short-circuit evaluation for && and || operators. This means that in an expression like condition1 && condition2, if condition1 is false, condition2 will not be evaluated, potentially saving time and resources.

```
# Short-circuit example
[[ -f "$file" && -r "$file" ]] && echo "$file is readable."
```

4. Profiling and Measuring Performance

To assess the performance of your optimized loops and conditionals, utilize the time command. Measure execution time before and after optimization to quantify improvements.

```
# Measure execution time
time {
    # Original loop or conditional code here
}
```

Optimizing loops and conditionals in your Bash scripts is crucial for enhancing performance and resource efficiency. By employing best practices such as using appropriate loop types, minimizing iterations, and leveraging built-in commands, you can significantly improve the performance of your scripts. Additionally, optimizing conditionals through careful structuring and combining checks can make your code cleaner and faster. Adopting these techniques will lead to more efficient, maintainable, and faster Bash scripts, ultimately improving the overall effectiveness of your scripting endeavors.

11.4 Parallel Processing with xargs and Background Jobs

Parallel processing is a powerful technique in Bash scripting that allows you to execute multiple commands simultaneously, making your scripts more efficient and responsive. This is especially useful when dealing with tasks that are independent of each other, such as processing files or making network requests. In this section, we will explore two primary methods for achieving parallel processing in Bash: using the xargs command and managing background jobs.

1. Understanding Parallel Processing

Parallel processing enables your scripts to perform multiple operations concurrently rather than sequentially. This can significantly reduce execution time, particularly for I/O-bound tasks or operations that can run independently. By leveraging Bash's built-in capabilities and external tools like xargs, you can harness the full power of your system's CPU and resources.

2. Using xargs for Parallel Execution

2.1 What is xargs?

xargs is a command-line utility that builds and executes command lines from standard input. It is particularly useful for processing large amounts of data in parallel, as it can efficiently handle input from pipes and arguments from other commands.

2.2 Basic Usage of xargs

To use xargs, you can pipe output from a command into it, which then processes the input in batches. For example, if you have a list of files and want to apply a command to each:

```
ls *.txt | xargs -n 1 echo "Processing file:"
```

This command will take each .txt file from the ls output and run the echo command on it.

2.3 Parallel Execution with xargs

The -P option allows you to run multiple commands in parallel with xargs. You can specify the number of processes to run simultaneously. For example, to compress multiple files in parallel:

```
ls *.txt | xargs -P 4 -n 1 gzip
```

In this command, gzip will be executed on up to 4 files at a time, significantly speeding up the compression process compared to processing files one by one.

2.4 Error Handling with xargs

When using xargs, it's important to handle errors that may occur during execution. You can achieve this by checking the exit status of the commands. For example:

ls *.txt | xargs -P 4 -n 1 gzip || echo "Error occurred during compression"

This way, if any compression fails, you will be informed without interrupting the entire batch process.

3. Managing Background Jobs

3.1 What are Background Jobs?

In Bash, you can run processes in the background by appending an ampersand (&) to the command. This allows the shell to execute the command without waiting for it to complete, freeing up the terminal for other tasks.

3.2 Starting Background Jobs

To start a command in the background:

gzip file1.txt &
gzip file2.txt &

Both gzip commands will run simultaneously in the background.

3.3 Monitoring Background Jobs

You can monitor your background jobs using the jobs command, which lists the currently running jobs:

jobs

This will show you a list of jobs along with their statuses.

3.4 Bringing Background Jobs to the Foreground

If you want to bring a background job to the foreground, you can use the fg command followed by the job number:

fg %1 # Bring job number 1 to the foreground

3.5 Terminating Background Jobs

To terminate a background job, use the kill command followed by the job's PID (process ID). You can find the PID by using the jobs command or the ps command:

kill %1 # Terminate job number 1

You can also use the pkill command to terminate jobs by name:

pkill gzip # Terminate all gzip processes

4. Combining xargs and Background Jobs

You can combine the functionality of xargs and background jobs to create highly efficient scripts. For example, if you want to process a large number of files using a script and run each instance in the background:

find . -name '.txt' | xargs -P 4 -n 1 bash process_file.sh &*

In this case, process_file.sh will be run in parallel for up to 4 files at a time.

5. Use Cases for Parallel Processing

5.1 Data Processing

When processing large datasets, such as logs or images, parallel processing can help speed up tasks significantly. For example, resizing images or parsing large log files can be performed concurrently.

find images/ -name '.jpg' | xargs -P 8 -n 1 convert -resize 50% {} resized/{}*

This command resizes images in parallel, improving the overall execution time.

5.2 Network Operations

When making multiple network requests (e.g., downloading files), using background jobs can maximize network utilization:

curl -O url1 & curl -O url2 & curl -O url3 &

Each curl command runs in the background, allowing multiple downloads to happen concurrently.

Parallel processing is a powerful technique that can greatly enhance the performance of your Bash scripts. By utilizing xargs for efficient command execution and managing background jobs, you can execute multiple operations simultaneously, significantly reducing processing time. Understanding how to effectively implement parallel processing in your scripts can lead to more responsive and efficient automation, especially when handling large volumes of data or performing repetitive tasks. By mastering these techniques, you will improve your Bash scripting skills and take full advantage of your system's capabilities.

11.5 Reducing Disk I/O and Memory Usage

In Bash scripting, efficient resource management is crucial for maximizing performance and ensuring that your scripts run smoothly, particularly when handling large datasets or executing complex tasks. Two critical aspects of performance optimization in scripting are minimizing disk input/output (I/O) operations and managing memory usage effectively. This section will explore strategies for reducing disk I/O and memory consumption in your Bash scripts.

1. Understanding Disk I/O and Memory Usage

1.1 Disk I/O

Disk I/O refers to the read and write operations performed on a disk. High disk I/O can slow down your scripts and overall system performance. Minimizing unnecessary reads and writes is essential for improving script efficiency.

1.2 Memory Usage

Memory usage pertains to how much RAM your script consumes while executing. High memory usage can lead to slow performance and, in extreme cases, cause scripts to fail if the system runs out of available memory. Effective memory management ensures that your scripts run efficiently and do not exceed system resources.

2. Strategies for Reducing Disk I/O

2.1 Minimize File Reads and Writes

One of the primary ways to reduce disk I/O is to minimize the number of times your script reads from or writes to the disk. You can achieve this through various techniques:

Batch Processing: Instead of processing files individually, batch process them to reduce the number of read/write operations.

```
# Inefficient file processing
for file in *.txt; do
    process_file "$file" > "${file%.txt}_processed.txt"
done

# Efficient batch processing
process_files *.txt > processed_files.txt
```

In-Memory Operations: If your script requires reading data multiple times, consider loading it into memory once and then operating on the in-memory data.

```
data=$(cat large_file.txt)  # Load data into memory
echo "$data" | process_data
```

2.2 Use Temporary Files Wisely

When your script requires intermediate data storage, use temporary files efficiently. Ensure that temporary files are created in a fast storage location (like /tmp) and removed after their usage to avoid unnecessary disk clutter.

```
temp_file=$(mktemp)  # Create a temporary file
# Perform operations and write to the temporary file
cat large_file.txt > "$temp_file"
# Process the temporary file
process_temp_file "$temp_file"
```

rm "$temp_file" # Remove temporary file when done

2.3 Reduce Log File Writes

Frequent logging can lead to high disk I/O, especially if your script runs for a long time. Instead of writing logs for every operation, consider:

Aggregating Logs: Write log entries in batches or at specific intervals.

echo "$(date): Processed $file" >> log.txt

Conditional Logging: Log only when necessary (e.g., on errors or key events).

if [[$status -ne 0]]; then
    echo "$(date): Error processing $file" >> error_log.txt
fi

3. Strategies for Reducing Memory Usage

3.1 Optimize Data Structures

Using efficient data structures is essential for reducing memory consumption. Avoid loading large datasets into memory unless necessary.

Use Streams: Instead of loading entire files into memory, process data in a streaming fashion.

 # Using a while loop to read a file line by line
while IFS= read -r line; do
    process_line "$line"
done < large_file.txt

3.2 Free Up Memory

When handling large arrays or variables, ensure you free up memory when they are no longer needed. You can do this by unsetting variables.

unset large_array # Free memory used by the array

3.3 Use Built-in Commands

Bash provides built-in commands that are generally more memory-efficient than external commands. Whenever possible, use these built-in commands to minimize memory usage.

```
# Using built-in read instead of external command
while read -r line; do
    process_line "$line"
done < large_file.txt
```

3.4 Avoid Unnecessary Forking

Each time you call an external command, Bash forks a new process, which can increase memory usage. Minimize forking by using built-in commands or optimizing command usage.

Inefficient:

```
for file in *.txt; do
    cat "$file" | grep "search_term"
done
```

Efficient:

```
for file in *.txt; do
    grep "search_term" "$file"
done
```

4. Profiling and Measuring Resource Usage

To assess the effectiveness of your optimizations, profile your scripts to measure disk I/O and memory usage. Use tools such as time, vmstat, or iotop to gather statistics.

```
# Measure execution time and memory usage
/usr/bin/time -v ./your_script.sh
```

5. Use Cases for Reducing Disk I/O and Memory Usage

5.1 Processing Large Log Files

When processing large log files, it is crucial to read and write data efficiently. Instead of loading an entire log file into memory, read it line by line, process it, and write results to a summary file.

 # Efficient log processing
while IFS= read -r line; do
   process_log "$line" >> summary.log
done < access.log

5.2 Image Processing

For image processing scripts, minimize disk I/O by processing images in batches and utilizing memory efficiently. For example, use temporary files for intermediate results and remove them when no longer needed.

*for img in *.png; do*
   convert "$img" -resize 50% "/tmp/resized_$img" &
done
wait # Wait for all background processes to finish

Reducing disk I/O and memory usage is vital for optimizing Bash scripts and enhancing performance. By implementing strategies such as minimizing file operations, using temporary files wisely, optimizing data structures, and avoiding unnecessary forking, you can significantly improve the efficiency of your scripts. These optimizations will lead to faster execution times, reduced resource consumption, and improved overall system performance. By mastering these techniques, you will become more proficient in writing effective and efficient Bash scripts that can handle demanding tasks without straining system resources.

11.6 Avoiding Subshells and Unnecessary Processes

In Bash scripting, performance is often impacted by how efficiently your scripts execute commands and manage processes. One common pitfall that can lead to degraded performance is the excessive creation of subshells and unnecessary processes. This section will explore the importance of minimizing these elements, their implications on resource usage, and strategies for writing more efficient scripts.

1. Understanding Subshells

1.1 What is a Subshell?

A subshell is a child process created by a shell (parent process) to execute commands in a separate environment. When a subshell is invoked, it inherits variables and the current environment from the parent shell but operates independently. While subshells are useful for certain tasks, they can introduce overhead, consume additional resources, and complicate variable scoping.

1.2 When Are Subshells Created?

Subshells are automatically created in several scenarios, including:

Command Substitution: Using backticks (`` `command` ``) or $(command) to capture command output.

output=$(ls -l) # Creates a subshell

Pipes: Using the pipe (|) operator to connect the output of one command to the input of another.

ls -l | grep "file" # Creates a subshell for grep

Grouping Commands: Enclosing commands in parentheses ().

(result=$(echo "Hello") && echo "$result") # Creates a subshell

2. Implications of Subshells

2.1 Performance Overhead

Creating subshells incurs performance overhead because each subshell is a separate process that requires system resources. Excessive use of subshells can slow down script execution, especially in loops or when processing large datasets.

2.2 Variable Scope Issues

Variables defined in a subshell are not accessible in the parent shell. This can lead to unexpected behavior or bugs in your scripts if you rely on variables defined within subshells.

```
result=$(echo "Hello")  # result is only accessible in the subshell
echo "$result"          # This will be empty
```

3. Strategies for Avoiding Subshells

3.1 Use Process Substitution

Instead of using pipes that create subshells, consider using process substitution. Process substitution allows you to redirect input/output of a command without creating a separate subshell.

```
# Instead of this:
ls -l | grep "file"

# Use process substitution:
grep "file" <(ls -l)  # No subshell created
```

3.2 Avoid Command Substitution for Simple Commands

If you only need the exit status of a command, avoid command substitution and use conditional constructs instead.

```
# Instead of this:
result=$(some_command)

# Use this:
if some_command; then
    echo "Command succeeded"
else
    echo "Command failed"
fi
```

3.3 Use Loops Efficiently

When iterating over files or items, avoid using command substitution or pipes that create subshells. Instead, read directly from the file or use a for loop.

```
# Inefficient: creates a subshell
for file in $(ls *.txt); do
    echo "$file"
```

```
done
```

```
# Efficient: directly reads from the file list
for file in *.txt; do
    echo "$file"
done
```

3.4 Use Here Documents

For multi-line input to commands, consider using here documents (<<) instead of subshells or pipes.

```
# Instead of this:
echo "line 1" | command
echo "line 2" | command
```

```
# Use here document:
command <<EOF
line 1
line 2
EOF
```

4. Managing Unnecessary Processes

4.1 Identify Unnecessary Processes

Unnecessary processes can include background jobs that are not needed, repeated calls to external commands, or redundant computations. Identifying and removing these can lead to more efficient scripts.

4.2 Optimize Command Usage

Instead of repeatedly calling an external command, cache its output or perform the operation in a single call. This reduces the overhead of creating new processes.

```
# Instead of calling external command multiple times:
for i in {1..5}; do
    external_command arg1 arg2
done
```

```
# Cache the output:
output=$(external_command arg1 arg2)
for i in {1..5}; do
    process "$output"
done
```

4.3 Use Built-in Commands

Whenever possible, prefer Bash built-in commands over external commands, as built-ins do not require the overhead of process creation.

```
# Instead of using external command for file size:
size=$(wc -c < file.txt)  # External command

# Use built-in parameter expansion:
size=${#var}  # Built-in variable length
```

5. Performance Profiling

To evaluate the efficiency of your scripts, profile them to identify where subshells and unnecessary processes are being created. Use tools like time, ps, or top to monitor resource usage.

```
# Measure execution time and memory usage
/usr/bin/time -v ./your_script.sh
```

6. Use Cases for Avoiding Subshells and Unnecessary Processes

6.1 File Processing Scripts

In file processing scripts, avoiding subshells can significantly improve performance. Instead of using ls with command substitution or pipes, directly iterate over files.

```
# Inefficient:
for file in $(ls *.txt); do
    process_file "$file"
done

# Efficient:
for file in *.txt; do
```

```
    process_file "$file"
done
```

6.2 Data Aggregation

When aggregating data from multiple sources, avoid spawning multiple processes. Instead, use built-in capabilities to handle data efficiently.

```
# Inefficient: creates multiple subshells
for line in $(cat data.txt | grep "pattern"); do
    echo "$line"
done

# Efficient: avoids subshells
while IFS= read -r line; do
    echo "$line"
done < data.txt | grep "pattern"
```

Avoiding subshells and unnecessary processes is essential for writing efficient Bash scripts. By understanding when subshells are created, their implications on performance, and implementing strategies to minimize their usage, you can enhance the efficiency of your scripts. Techniques such as process substitution, efficient looping, and utilizing built-in commands will help you manage system resources effectively and ensure that your scripts run smoothly. By mastering these practices, you will not only improve script performance but also reduce the complexity and potential pitfalls associated with resource management in Bash.

12. Working with External Tools

In this chapter, you'll learn how to extend the capabilities of your Bash scripts by integrating external tools and utilities. We'll explore essential command-line utilities like curl and wget for downloading files from the web, as well as how to interact with APIs to retrieve and send data. You'll also discover how to automate workflows using tools like cron for scheduling tasks and ssh for remote command execution. We'll discuss how to pipe data between commands, enabling you to create powerful one-liners and complex workflows. Additionally, you'll learn about using version control systems, such as Git, to manage your scripts efficiently. By the end of this chapter, you'll be equipped to enhance your Bash scripts with external tools, allowing for more complex automation and data processing tasks that leverage the full power of the command line.

12.1 Using curl and wget for Network Requests

In the realm of shell scripting and command-line operations, network requests play a crucial role in fetching data, interacting with web APIs, and managing remote resources. Two of the most commonly used tools for making network requests in a Bash environment are curl and wget. Both tools offer powerful functionalities, but they cater to slightly different use cases. In this section, we will explore their features, use cases, and practical examples for making network requests efficiently.

1. Introduction to curl and wget

1.1 What is curl?

curl (Client URL) is a command-line tool and library for transferring data with URLs. It supports a wide range of protocols, including HTTP, HTTPS, FTP, and many others. curl is widely used for making requests to web services, downloading files, and sending data over various protocols. Its versatility and flexibility make it a preferred choice for developers and system administrators.

Key Features of curl:

- Support for multiple protocols (HTTP, HTTPS, FTP, etc.)
- Ability to send and receive data (GET, POST, PUT, DELETE, etc.)
- Extensive options for customizing requests, including headers, cookies, and data formats

- Supports SSL/TLS for secure communication
- Output control options for displaying or saving results

1.2 What is wget?

wget is another command-line utility for retrieving files from the web using HTTP, HTTPS, and FTP protocols. Unlike curl, which is designed for data transfer and interaction with APIs, wget focuses primarily on downloading files and can resume interrupted downloads. It's particularly useful for batch downloading or mirroring websites.

Key Features of wget:

- Recursive downloading for fetching entire directories or websites
- Resuming downloads that were interrupted
- Downloading in the background
- Simple command structure and fewer options than curl, making it user-friendly for basic tasks
- Capability to save files with their original names

2. Basic Usage of curl

2.1 Making Simple GET Requests

To perform a simple HTTP GET request, you can use curl followed by the target URL:

curl http://example.com

This command retrieves the content of the specified URL and displays it in the terminal.

2.2 Saving Output to a File

To save the output of a request to a file, use the -o option:

curl -o output.txt http://example.com

This command will save the content of http://example.com to a file named output.txt.

2.3 Sending Data with POST Requests

You can send data using the POST method by using the -d option:

curl -X POST -d "name=John&age=30" http://example.com/api/users

This command sends the specified data to the provided URL, typically for creating or updating resources on a server.

2.4 Adding Headers

To include custom headers in your request, use the -H option:

curl -H "Authorization: Bearer YOUR_TOKEN" http://example.com/api/resource

This command includes an Authorization header, commonly required for accessing protected resources.

3. Basic Usage of wget

3.1 Downloading a Single File

To download a file using wget, simply specify the URL:

wget http://example.com/file.zip

This command downloads the specified file and saves it with its original name in the current directory.

3.2 Resuming Downloads

If a download is interrupted, you can resume it using the -c option:

wget -c http://example.com/file.zip

This command resumes the download from where it left off, preventing the need to start over.

3.3 Recursive Downloading

You can download an entire website or directory using the -r option:

wget -r http://example.com/some-directory/

This command will download all files from the specified directory, preserving the structure of the website.

3.4 Downloading in the Background

To run wget in the background, use the -b option:

wget -b http://example.com/largefile.zip

This command starts the download in the background, allowing you to continue using the terminal for other tasks.

4.2 Choosing Between curl and wget

- Use curl when you need to interact with web APIs, send data in various formats, or require extensive customization of requests.
- Use wget when your primary goal is to download files, especially when you need to download entire directories or resume interrupted downloads.

5. Practical Examples

5.1 Example 1: Fetching JSON Data with curl

You can fetch JSON data from a REST API using curl:

curl -H "Accept: application/json" http://example.com/api/data

This command requests data in JSON format from the specified API endpoint.

5.2 Example 2: Downloading a File with wget

To download a PDF file from the web:

wget https://example.com/document.pdf

This command downloads the PDF file to the current directory.

curl and wget are powerful tools for making network requests and downloading files in the Bash environment. Understanding their capabilities and differences allows you to choose the right tool for your tasks effectively. Whether you're interacting with APIs using curl or downloading files and mirroring websites with wget, mastering these tools enhances your scripting abilities and enables you to automate various network-related tasks seamlessly. By incorporating these tools into your Bash scripts, you can create efficient and powerful scripts to interact with online resources.

12.2 Integrating Bash with APIs: JSON Parsing with jq

In today's development landscape, Application Programming Interfaces (APIs) play a crucial role in enabling communication between different systems. When working with APIs, especially those that return data in JSON format, the ability to parse and manipulate this data effectively is essential. Bash scripting can be seamlessly integrated with APIs, and the powerful tool jq makes JSON parsing straightforward and efficient. This section will cover the fundamentals of using Bash with APIs, the capabilities of jq, and practical examples of how to integrate these tools.

1. Understanding JSON and APIs

1.1 What is JSON?

JSON (JavaScript Object Notation) is a lightweight data interchange format that is easy for humans to read and write and easy for machines to parse and generate. It is commonly used for APIs to exchange data between a server and a client. JSON structures data in key-value pairs, making it highly readable and flexible.

Example of a JSON object:

```
{
  "name": "John Doe",
  "age": 30,
  "is_student": false,
  "courses": ["Math", "Science"]
}
```

1.2 What is an API?

An API is a set of rules that allows different software applications to communicate with each other. APIs can provide access to various functionalities, such as retrieving data, updating records, or triggering events in another application. Many APIs return data in JSON format, which can be easily processed and utilized in scripts.

2. Using curl to Make API Requests

Before parsing JSON, you need to make a request to an API using curl. The typical workflow involves sending a request, receiving the response, and then parsing the JSON data.

2.1 Making a GET Request

Here's how to make a simple GET request to an API using curl:

curl -s http://api.example.com/users

The -s option tells curl to operate silently, omitting progress and error messages, which is useful when you're interested only in the output.

2.2 Making a POST Request

To send data to an API, you might use a POST request:

curl -s -X POST -H "Content-Type: application/json" -d '{"name":"John Doe","age":30}' http://api.example.com/users

This command sends a JSON object containing user information to the specified endpoint.

3. Introducing jq

3.1 What is jq?

jq is a powerful command-line tool for processing JSON data. It allows you to filter, transform, and extract data from JSON structures with a simple syntax. Whether you're retrieving specific fields, modifying data, or performing calculations, jq provides the functionality to manipulate JSON efficiently.

Key Features of jq:

- Powerful filtering and querying capabilities
- Supports complex operations on JSON data
- Allows for formatting and transforming output
- Lightweight and easy to integrate with Bash scripts

4. Basic jq Operations

4.1 Installing jq

Before using jq, you need to install it. On most Linux distributions, you can use the package manager:

 # For Debian/Ubuntu-based systems

sudo apt-get install jq

 # For macOS using Homebrew

brew install jq

4.2 Filtering JSON Data

Once you have jq installed, you can start filtering JSON data. Here's how to retrieve specific fields:

Given a JSON response from an API:

```
{
  "users": [
    {
      "name": "John Doe",
      "age": 30
    },
    {
      "name": "Jane Smith",
      "age": 25
    }
  ]
}
```

You can retrieve the names of users with the following command:

```
curl -s http://api.example.com/users | jq '.users[].name'
```

This command extracts the names of all users from the JSON response.

4.3 Using Filters

You can use various filters to manipulate JSON data:

To get all user ages:

```
curl -s http://api.example.com/users | jq '.users[].age'
```

To filter users based on a condition (e.g., age greater than 28):

```
curl -s http://api.example.com/users | jq '.users[] | select(.age > 28)'
```

4.4 Formatting Output

jq can also format the output for better readability. Use the -r option to output raw strings:

```
curl -s http://api.example.com/users | jq -r '.users[].name'
```

This will print each name on a new line without quotes.

5. Practical Examples of Integrating Bash with APIs

5.1 Example 1: Fetching User Data

Let's say you want to fetch user data from an API and display the names and ages of all users:

```bash
#!/bin/bash

response=$(curl -s http://api.example.com/users)
echo "$response" | jq -r '.users[] | "\(.name): \(.age) years old"'
```

This script fetches user data and formats the output neatly.

5.2 Example 2: Posting Data to an API

Here's how you can post data to an API and retrieve the response:

```bash
#!/bin/bash

response=$(curl -s -X POST -H "Content-Type: application/json" -d '{"name":"John Doe","age":30}' http://api.example.com/users)
echo "$response" | jq -r '.message'
```

This script sends a new user to the API and prints the response message.

6. Advanced jq Techniques

6.1 Nested JSON Structures

When dealing with nested JSON, you can traverse the structure using dot notation:

Given a more complex JSON response:

```
{
  "status": "success",
  "data": {
    "users": [
      {
        "id": 1,
        "name": "John Doe",
        "details": {
          "age": 30,
          "email": "john@example.com"
        }
      },
      {
        "id": 2,
        "name": "Jane Smith",
        "details": {
          "age": 25,
          "email": "jane@example.com"
```

```
      }
    }
  ]
 }
}
```

To extract names and email addresses:

curl -s http://api.example.com/users | jq -r '.data.users[] | "\(.name): \(.details.email)"'

6.2 Combining jq with Other Tools

You can combine jq with other command-line tools for enhanced functionality. For example, to count the number of users:

curl -s http://api.example.com/users | jq '.data.users | length'

Integrating Bash with APIs using curl and jq allows for powerful and flexible data manipulation capabilities. By mastering these tools, you can automate interactions with web services, efficiently retrieve and process JSON data, and streamline your scripting tasks. Whether you're building a simple data-fetching script or developing complex automation tasks, understanding how to leverage APIs and JSON parsing with jq is an invaluable skill for any developer or system administrator. This integration opens up endless possibilities for automating workflows and enhancing productivity in your Bash scripting endeavors.

12.3 Automating System Tasks with Cron Jobs

Automation is a key aspect of system administration, enabling you to streamline routine tasks and improve efficiency. One of the most powerful tools for automating system tasks in a Linux environment is Cron, a time-based job scheduler. With Cron, you can schedule scripts, commands, and other tasks to run at specified intervals, making it easier to manage repetitive tasks such as backups, updates, and monitoring. This section will explore the fundamentals of Cron jobs, how to create and manage them, and practical examples of automation in action.

1. Understanding Cron and Cron Jobs

1.1 What is Cron?

Cron is a daemon (background process) that runs on Unix-like operating systems. It allows users to schedule jobs (commands or scripts) to run automatically at specified times or intervals. This scheduling is done through a configuration file known as the crontab (cron table), which defines when and how often jobs are to be executed.

1.2 What are Cron Jobs?

A Cron job is a scheduled task defined in a crontab file. Each job specifies a command or script to run and a timing schedule. Cron jobs are ideal for automating various tasks, such as:

- Backing up files
- Running system updates
- Cleaning up temporary files
- Monitoring system performance
- Sending reports via email

2. Cron Syntax

Cron jobs are defined using a specific syntax that determines when the job should run. Each line in a crontab file follows this format:

* * * * * *command_to_execute*

Where the five asterisks represent:

- Minute (0-59)
- Hour (0-23)
- Day of Month (1-31)
- Month (1-12 or Jan-Dec)
- Day of Week (0-7 where both 0 and 7 represent Sunday)

2.1 Example

For example, to run a script every day at 3:30 AM, you would use:

*30 3 * * * /path/to/your/script.sh*

This line means that at 30 minutes past the third hour of every day, the specified script will execute.

3. Managing Cron Jobs

3.1 Viewing and Editing Crontab

To view the current user's crontab, use the following command:

crontab -l

To edit the crontab, use:

crontab -e

This opens the crontab in the default text editor, allowing you to add, modify, or remove jobs.

3.2 Removing Cron Jobs

To remove a specific job, simply edit the crontab using crontab -e and delete the corresponding line. You can also remove all jobs for the current user with:

crontab -r

4. Examples of Common Cron Jobs

4.1 Backing Up Files

You can schedule a backup of a directory every night at 2 AM:

*0 2 * * * tar -czf /backup/my_backup_$(date +\%F).tar.gz /path/to/my_directory*

This command creates a compressed tarball of the specified directory, using the current date as part of the filename.

4.2 Running System Updates

To update your system packages every Sunday at 4 AM, use:

*0 4 * * 0 sudo apt-get update && sudo apt-get upgrade -y*

This command checks for updates and installs them automatically.

4.3 Cleaning Temporary Files

You can set up a job to clean up temporary files every day at 1 AM:

*0 1 * * * find /tmp -type f -mtime +7 -exec rm {} \;*

This command removes files older than seven days from the /tmp directory.

5. Redirecting Output

When running cron jobs, it's essential to manage output, especially if the commands generate logs or errors. By default, any output from a cron job is sent via email to the user who owns the crontab. You can redirect output to a log file or suppress it entirely.

5.1 Redirecting to a Log File

To redirect both standard output and error messages to a log file:

*0 3 * * * /path/to/script.sh >> /var/log/my_script.log 2>&1*

This appends all output and errors to my_script.log.

5.2 Suppressing Output

To suppress all output, you can redirect it to /dev/null:

*0 3 * * * /path/to/script.sh > /dev/null 2>&1*

This prevents any output from being sent via email or written to a log.

6. Using Environment Variables in Cron Jobs

When running cron jobs, the environment may differ from your user shell. To ensure your scripts have access to the necessary environment variables, you can set them directly in the crontab.

6.1 Example

PATH=/usr/local/sbin:/usr/local/bin:/usr/sbin:/usr/bin:/sbin:/bin

*0 3 * * * /path/to/script.sh*

This sets the PATH variable for the cron job, ensuring it can find executables.

7. Advanced Cron Scheduling

7.1 Using Special Strings

Cron supports special strings that can simplify scheduling:

@reboot: Run once at startup
@yearly or *@annually*: Run once a year
@monthly: Run once a month
@weekly: Run once a week
@daily or *@midnight*: Run once a day
@hourly: Run once an hour

Example: Run a script at system startup

@reboot /path/to/startup_script.sh

Cron jobs are an essential tool for automating system tasks in a Linux environment. By scheduling commands and scripts to run automatically, you can reduce the manual effort involved in routine maintenance, backups, and updates. Understanding the syntax and management of Cron jobs, along with practical examples, enables you to leverage this powerful scheduling tool effectively.

Integrating Cron jobs into your workflows can lead to significant improvements in efficiency and reliability, allowing you to focus on more critical tasks while ensuring that your system runs smoothly and tasks are executed as intended. Whether you're a system administrator, developer, or casual user, mastering Cron will enhance your scripting capabilities and automate your daily operations.

12.4 Interacting with Cloud Platforms (AWS CLI, GCP SDK)

In today's technology landscape, cloud platforms like Amazon Web Services (AWS) and Google Cloud Platform (GCP) have become integral to deploying, managing, and scaling applications. Command-Line Interfaces (CLIs) provide powerful tools for interacting with these cloud services programmatically, enabling developers and system administrators to automate workflows, manage resources, and streamline operations. In this section, we'll explore how to interact with AWS using the AWS CLI and with GCP using the Google Cloud SDK (gcloud), along with practical examples to illustrate their capabilities.

1. Understanding Cloud Command-Line Interfaces

1.1 What is AWS CLI?

The AWS Command Line Interface (CLI) is a unified tool that allows you to interact with all AWS services using a command-line interface. It simplifies the management of AWS resources and services, allowing you to automate tasks via scripts. The AWS CLI is available on various operating systems and can be easily installed and configured.

1.2 What is Google Cloud SDK (gcloud)?

The Google Cloud SDK (gcloud) is a set of command-line tools for Google Cloud Platform. It includes the gcloud CLI for managing GCP resources, the gsutil tool for working with Google Cloud Storage, and the bq tool for BigQuery. The gcloud command-line interface enables users to automate and manage GCP resources effectively.

2. Setting Up AWS CLI

2.1 Installation

To install the AWS CLI, follow these steps:

For Linux/macOS: You can use pip to install the AWS CLI:

pip install awscli --upgrade --user

For Windows: You can download the AWS CLI MSI installer from the official AWS website.

2.2 Configuration

After installing the AWS CLI, you need to configure it with your AWS credentials:

aws configure

This command prompts you to enter:

- AWS Access Key ID
- AWS Secret Access Key
- Default region name (e.g., us-west-2)
- Default output format (e.g., json, text, table)

This configuration file is stored in ~/.aws/config and ~/.aws/credentials.

3. Using AWS CLI

3.1 Listing AWS S3 Buckets

To list all S3 buckets in your account:

aws s3 ls

This command will display the names and creation dates of all S3 buckets associated with your account.

3.2 Uploading Files to S3

To upload a file to an S3 bucket:

aws s3 cp /path/to/local/file.txt s3://your-bucket-name/

This command copies a local file to the specified S3 bucket.

3.3 Launching an EC2 Instance

To launch a new EC2 instance, you can use the following command:

aws ec2 run-instances --image-id ami-0123456789abcdef0 --count 1 --instance-type t2.micro --key-name MyKeyPair

Replace the --image-id with the appropriate Amazon Machine Image (AMI) ID, and specify your instance type and key pair name.

4. Setting Up Google Cloud SDK (gcloud)

4.1 Installation

To install the Google Cloud SDK, you can follow these steps:

For Linux: Use the following command to install:

curl https://sdk.cloud.google.com | bash

exec -l $SHELL

For Windows: Download the Google Cloud SDK installer from the official website.

4.2 Configuration

Once installed, you can initialize the SDK with:

gcloud init

This command will prompt you to log in with your Google account and set your project.

5. Using gcloud

5.1 Listing Google Cloud Storage Buckets

To list all Google Cloud Storage buckets in your project:

gsutil ls

This command will display the names of all buckets in the active project.

5.2 Uploading Files to Google Cloud Storage

To upload a file to a Cloud Storage bucket:

gsutil cp /path/to/local/file.txt gs://your-bucket-name/

This command copies a local file to the specified Google Cloud Storage bucket.

5.3 Deploying an App Engine Application

To deploy an application to Google App Engine, navigate to your application's directory and run:

gcloud app deploy

This command deploys the application to Google Cloud's App Engine.

6. Automating Cloud Tasks with Scripts

Both AWS CLI and gcloud CLI can be incorporated into Bash scripts for automation. Here's how you can create a simple script to automate cloud tasks.

6.1 Example: Automating S3 Backup

Here's an example script that creates a backup of a local directory to an S3 bucket:

```bash
#!/bin/bash

# Variables
BUCKET_NAME="your-bucket-name"
LOCAL_DIR="/path/to/local/directory"
DATE=$(date +%F)

# Create a backup directory
BACKUP_DIR="${LOCAL_DIR}/backup_${DATE}"
mkdir -p "$BACKUP_DIR"

# Copy files to backup directory
cp -r "$LOCAL_DIR/"* "$BACKUP_DIR"

# Upload backup to S3
aws s3 cp "$BACKUP_DIR" "s3://$BUCKET_NAME/backup_${DATE}/" --recursive

echo "Backup completed and uploaded to S3 bucket $BUCKET_NAME."
```

6.2 Example: Deploying to GCP

Here's a simple script that deploys an application to Google App Engine:

```bash
#!/bin/bash

# Variables
APP_DIR="/path/to/your/app"

# Navigate to the application directory
cd "$APP_DIR" || exit

# Deploy the application
gcloud app deploy

echo "Application deployed to Google App Engine."
```

7. Best Practices for Using Cloud CLIs

7.1 Use IAM Roles

When interacting with AWS, it's a best practice to use IAM roles with the least privilege necessary for your tasks. This enhances security by limiting access to only the required resources.

7.2 Monitor Usage

Regularly monitor the usage of your cloud resources to avoid unexpected costs. Both AWS and GCP provide tools for tracking resource utilization.

7.3 Use Environment Variables

When automating tasks, use environment variables to store sensitive information (like credentials) instead of hardcoding them into your scripts.

Interacting with cloud platforms like AWS and GCP through their command-line interfaces is a powerful way to automate tasks, manage resources, and streamline workflows. By leveraging the AWS CLI and Google Cloud SDK, you can execute commands programmatically, integrate them into your scripts, and manage cloud resources efficiently.

Understanding how to use these tools effectively not only enhances your productivity but also equips you with the skills necessary to thrive in cloud-based environments. Whether you're deploying applications, managing storage, or automating routine tasks, mastering these command-line interfaces will be invaluable in your cloud computing journey.

12.5 Using External Tools for System Monitoring (df, du, iostat)

Effective system monitoring is essential for maintaining the health and performance of a Linux system. Understanding how to analyze system resources, such as disk space, memory usage, and input/output operations, enables administrators to optimize system performance and prevent potential issues before they escalate. In this section, we will explore three powerful external tools—df, du, and iostat—that provide insights into disk usage and performance monitoring.

1. Overview of System Monitoring Tools

System monitoring tools allow you to gather real-time statistics about various system resources. Each tool has its specific focus:

- **df**: Reports the amount of disk space used and available on file systems.
- **du**: Estimates file and directory space usage.
- **iostat**: Monitors system input/output device loading by observing the time devices are active relative to their average transfer rates.

Understanding how to use these tools can help you maintain optimal system performance and ensure that resources are allocated effectively.

2. Using df - Disk Free

2.1 What is df?

The df (disk free) command provides a summary of available and used disk space on all mounted file systems. It is particularly useful for quickly checking how much disk space is left on your system.

2.2 Basic Usage

To display disk usage in a human-readable format (using MB or GB), you can run:

df -h

This command shows the filesystem, size, used space, available space, and the mount point of each filesystem.

2.3 Understanding the Output

The output of the df -h command typically includes the following columns:

- **Filesystem**: The name of the mounted filesystem.
- **Size**: The total size of the filesystem.
- **Used**: The amount of disk space currently used.
- **Available**: The amount of disk space that is still available.
- **Use%:** The percentage of disk space that is used.
- **Mounted on**: The directory where the filesystem is mounted.

2.4 Example Output

Here's an example of what you might see:

```
Filesystem     Size  Used Avail Use% Mounted on
/dev/sda1      50G   20G  30G   40%  /
tmpfs          1.0G  0    1.0G  0%   /dev/shm
/dev/sdb1      100G  75G  25G   75%  /mnt/data
```

In this example, the root filesystem /dev/sda1 has used 20GB out of 50GB, with 30GB available.

3. Using du - Disk Usage

3.1 What is du?

The du (disk usage) command estimates and displays the amount of disk space used by files and directories. It helps identify large files and directories that may be consuming significant disk space.

3.2 Basic Usage

To view the disk usage of a directory and its contents in a human-readable format, use:

du -h /path/to/directory

This command will provide a summary of the disk usage for the specified directory and its subdirectories.

3.3 Summary of Disk Usage

To display only the total size of a directory without listing every file:

du -sh /path/to/directory

The -s flag gives a summary (only the total), and the -h flag makes the output human-readable.

3.4 Example Output

Here's an example of how the du -h command might output:

```
4.0K    /path/to/directory/subdir1
2.5G    /path/to/directory/subdir2
2.5G    /path/to/directory
```

In this example, the total disk usage of /path/to/directory is 2.5GB, with subdir1 using 4KB and subdir2 using 2.5GB.

4. Using iostat - Input/Output Statistics

4.1 What is iostat?

The iostat (input/output statistics) command is part of the sysstat package and provides information about CPU and input/output statistics for devices and partitions. It helps in monitoring the system's performance by analyzing the input/output load on disks.

4.2 Installation

If iostat is not already installed, you can typically install it using the package manager. For example, on Debian/Ubuntu systems:

sudo apt-get install sysstat

On Red Hat/CentOS systems:

sudo yum install sysstat

4.3 Basic Usage

To display I/O statistics for all devices, use:

iostat

This command will provide a summary of CPU usage and disk I/O statistics.

4.4 Understanding the Output

The output includes the following columns:

- **Device**: The name of the device (e.g., sda, sdb).
- **tps**: Transactions per second (I/O requests).
- **kB_read/s:** Kilobytes read per second.
- **kB_wrtn/s:** Kilobytes written per second.
- **kB_read**: Total kilobytes read.
- **kB_wrtn**: Total kilobytes written.

4.5 Example Output

Here's an example output of the iostat command:

Linux 5.4.0-42-generic (hostname)   10/17/2024   _x86_64_   (4 CPU)

avg-cpu: %user   %nice %system %iowait %steal   %idle
*   12.34   0.00   5.67   2.34   0.00   79.65*

Device:	tps	kB_read/s	kB_wrtn/s	kB_read	kB_wrtn
sda	15.23	150.34	200.45	15003450	20004500
sdb	5.67	50.56	25.34	5056000	2534000

In this example, you can see the average CPU usage and the disk activity for devices sda and sdb.

5. Combining Tools for Comprehensive Monitoring

While each of these tools provides valuable information on their own, combining them can give you a comprehensive view of system health and performance. For instance, you can use df to check overall disk space availability, du to locate space hogs, and iostat to monitor the performance impact of I/O operations on your system.

5.1 Example Script

Here's a sample Bash script that combines these tools to report on disk usage and I/O performance:

```bash
#!/bin/bash

echo "Disk Space Usage:"
df -h

echo -e "\nDirectory Usage:"
du -sh /path/to/directory/*

echo -e "\nI/O Statistics:"
iostat -x 1 3
```

This script provides a clear overview of disk space, usage by directory, and I/O statistics every second for three iterations.

System monitoring is vital for maintaining optimal performance and reliability in a Linux environment. Tools like df, du, and iostat equip you with the ability to monitor disk space, file usage, and input/output operations effectively.

By mastering these tools, you can proactively manage your system resources, identify potential issues before they become critical, and ensure that your system runs smoothly. Whether you're a system administrator, developer, or power user, understanding these monitoring tools will enhance your ability to maintain and optimize system performance in the cloud or on-premises.

12.6 Packaging and Distributing Shell Scripts

Shell scripts are an invaluable part of the Unix/Linux ecosystem, providing automation and streamlining of various tasks. However, sharing and distributing these scripts effectively requires consideration of various factors, including dependencies, environment compatibility, and ease of use. In this section, we'll explore best practices for packaging and distributing shell scripts, enabling you to ensure that your scripts can be easily shared, installed, and executed by others.

1. Why Package Shell Scripts?

Packaging shell scripts serves several purposes:

- **Ease of Distribution**: A well-packaged script can be easily shared and installed across different systems.
- **Dependency Management**: Packaging allows you to specify dependencies, ensuring that required tools and libraries are available.
- **Version Control**: Proper packaging enables you to manage versions of your scripts, making it easier to track changes and updates.
- **User Convenience**: Simplifying the installation and execution process enhances user experience, especially for those who may not be familiar with shell scripting.

2. Choosing a Packaging Format

When it comes to packaging shell scripts, there are several formats to consider:

- **Tarball (.tar.gz):** A common method for distributing scripts along with any related files (like README or configuration files). You can compress the tarball to save space.
- **Debian Package (.deb):** Useful for Debian-based systems (like Ubuntu). It allows you to create a package that can be easily installed with dpkg or apt.
- **RPM Package (.rpm):** Suitable for Red Hat-based systems (like Fedora). Similar to Debian packages, it provides a way to manage installations.
- **Python Package (.whl):** If your shell script relies on Python scripts or libraries, consider packaging it as a Python package, allowing for easy distribution through PyPI.
- **Docker Container**: For more complex applications, packaging your shell script within a Docker container can encapsulate all dependencies and ensure consistency across environments.

3. Structuring Your Package

Regardless of the format you choose, it's important to have a well-defined structure for your package. Here's a common structure for a shell script tarball:

```
my_script/
├── bin/
│   └── my_script.sh
├── etc/
│   └── my_script.conf
├── README.md
├── LICENSE
└── CHANGELOG.md
```

- **bin/**: Contains the main shell script and any executable files.
- **etc/**: Contains configuration files and templates.
- **README.md**: Provides an overview of the script, installation instructions, usage examples, and any dependencies.
- **LICENSE**: Outlines the licensing terms for your script.
- **CHANGELOG.md**: Documents changes and updates to the script over time.

4. Writing Installation Scripts

If your shell script requires specific setup procedures, consider writing an installation script. This script can automate the installation of dependencies, configuration, and other tasks. Here's a simple example:

```bash
#!/bin/bash

echo "Installing My Script..."

# Check for required commands
for cmd in curl jq; do
    if ! command -v $cmd &> /dev/null; then
        echo "Error: $cmd is not installed. Please install it."
        exit 1
    fi
done

# Copy script to /usr/local/bin
```

sudo cp bin/my_script.sh /usr/local/bin/my_script
sudo chmod +x /usr/local/bin/my_script

echo "My Script has been installed successfully!"

5. Version Control and Distribution Platforms

Using version control systems like Git can help you manage changes and distribute your script efficiently. Here are a few platforms to consider:

- **GitHub**: A popular platform for hosting repositories, enabling easy sharing and collaboration. Users can clone your repository and contribute to the script's development.
- **GitLab**: Similar to GitHub, GitLab offers additional features like CI/CD integration, allowing you to automate testing and deployment.
- **Bitbucket**: Another Git-based repository platform, supporting private repositories for collaborative projects.

6. Creating a README File

A well-crafted README file is essential for effective distribution. Here's what to include:

- **Title and Description**: Clearly state the name and purpose of the script.
- **Installation Instructions**: Provide step-by-step instructions on how to install and set up the script, including any dependencies.
- **Usage Examples**: Include examples demonstrating how to use the script, showcasing its functionality.
- **Configuration Options**: Document any configuration files or options available to the user.
- **Contribution Guidelines**: If you welcome contributions, provide instructions on how others can contribute to the project.
- **License Information**: State the licensing terms and any relevant attributions.

7. Testing on Different Environments

Before distributing your shell script, it's crucial to test it across various environments to ensure compatibility. Here are some key considerations:

- **Operating Systems**: Test your script on different Linux distributions (e.g., Ubuntu, CentOS) and macOS. Be mindful of variations in command behavior or installed utilities.
- **Shell Compatibility**: Ensure your script works with the target shell environments, particularly if users might run it in shells other than Bash (e.g., Zsh, Fish).
- **Dependency Availability**: Verify that required dependencies are available on the target systems, or provide clear installation instructions.

8. Publishing Your Package

After thoroughly testing your package, it's time to publish it. Depending on your chosen format, here are a few publishing options:

- **For tarballs**, upload them to your website or a file-sharing service and provide download links in your README.
- **For Debian or RPM packages**, consider submitting them to the respective repositories or hosting them on your GitHub releases page.
- **For Docker containers**, publish your image to Docker Hub or any other container registry.
- **For Python packages**, upload your package to PyPI using tools like twine.

9. Supporting Users

Once your shell script is out in the wild, consider how you'll support users:

- **Issue Tracking**: Utilize GitHub or GitLab's issue tracking to allow users to report bugs or request features.
- **Documentation**: Maintain comprehensive documentation, including FAQs and troubleshooting sections, to assist users.
- **Community Engagement**: Foster a community around your script where users can share tips, tricks, and modifications.

Packaging and distributing shell scripts is a crucial skill for developers and system administrators. By following best practices for structuring, documenting, and sharing your scripts, you can ensure that they are easy to install, understand, and use.

Whether you are creating a simple utility script or a complex application, proper packaging not only enhances the usability of your script but also encourages collaboration and community contributions, ultimately leading to a more robust and reliable tool.

13. Advanced Scripting Techniques

In this chapter, you'll delve into advanced scripting techniques that will elevate your Bash skills to the next level. We'll explore the use of arrays to store and manipulate collections of data, allowing for more sophisticated data handling within your scripts. You'll learn about subshells and how to use them for command grouping and creating temporary environments without affecting the main shell. We'll also cover advanced features like parameter expansion, string manipulation, and command substitution to enhance your scripting capabilities. Additionally, you'll discover best practices for writing secure scripts, including input validation and avoiding command injection vulnerabilities. By the end of this chapter, you'll have a deeper understanding of advanced Bash constructs and techniques, empowering you to write more complex and efficient scripts that can handle a variety of tasks with ease.

13.1 Working with Arrays and Associative Arrays

Bash scripting allows for the use of arrays, providing a powerful way to handle collections of data. Arrays can store multiple values under a single variable name, making it easier to manage and manipulate data in scripts. In this section, we will explore how to work with both indexed (regular) arrays and associative arrays in Bash, discussing their syntax, operations, and practical examples.

1. What are Arrays in Bash?

An array is a variable that can hold multiple values, allowing you to store a list of items. In Bash, arrays are zero-indexed, meaning that the first element is accessed with index 0, the second with index 1, and so forth. Bash supports two types of arrays:

- **Indexed Arrays**: These use numerical indices.
- **Associative Arrays**: These use string keys for indexing.

2. Declaring and Initializing Indexed Arrays

You can declare an indexed array in Bash using the following syntax:

```
# Declaring an indexed array
my_array=(value1 value2 value3)
```

To initialize an indexed array with specific values:

```
# Initializing an indexed array
fruits=("apple" "banana" "cherry")
```

You can also declare an empty array and add elements later:

```
# Declaring an empty array
my_array=()
my_array[0]="first"
my_array[1]="second"
```

3. Accessing Array Elements

You can access individual elements of an indexed array using the syntax ${array_name[index]}. For example:

```
echo ${fruits[1]} # Output: banana
```

To access all elements of the array, you can use:

```
echo ${fruits[@]} # Output: apple banana cherry
```

You can also get the number of elements in an array using:

```
echo ${#fruits[@]} # Output: 3
```

4. Modifying Array Elements

You can modify the value of a specific element in the array by assigning a new value:

```
fruits[1]="blueberry"
echo ${fruits[@]} # Output: apple blueberry cherry
```

You can add new elements to the end of the array using the syntax:

```
fruits+=("orange")
```

5. Looping Through Indexed Arrays

Looping through the elements of an indexed array can be done using a for loop:

```
for fruit in "${fruits[@]}"; do
    echo $fruit
done
```

6. Associative Arrays

Associative arrays are indexed by strings rather than numbers. To declare an associative array, use the declare -A command:

```
declare -A colors
```

You can then add key-value pairs:

```
colors=(["red"]="#FF0000" ["green"]="#00FF00" ["blue"]="#0000FF")
```

To access an element in an associative array, use:

```
echo ${colors["green"]} # Output: #00FF00
```

7. Looping Through Associative Arrays

You can loop through the keys and values of an associative array using a for loop:

```
for key in "${!colors[@]}"; do
    echo "$key: ${colors[$key]}"
done
```

8. Common Operations with Arrays

8.1. Length of an Array

You can get the length of an array using ${#array_name[@]}:

```
echo "Number of fruits: ${#fruits[@]}"
```

8.2. Removing Elements

To remove an element from an array, use the unset command:

unset fruits[1] # Removes "blueberry"

To clear all elements in an array, you can do:

fruits=() # Resets the array

9. Practical Examples

Example 1: Shopping List

Here's a simple example of using an indexed array to manage a shopping list:

```
# Shopping list
shopping_list=("milk" "bread" "eggs")

# Adding an item
shopping_list+=("butter")

# Display the list
for item in "${shopping_list[@]}"; do
    echo "Buy: $item"
done
```

Example 2: User Information with Associative Arrays

In this example, we'll use an associative array to store user information:

```
declare -A user_info
user_info=(["name"]="Alice" ["age"]=30 ["city"]="New York")

# Accessing values
echo "User: ${user_info["name"]}, Age: ${user_info["age"]}, City: ${user_info["city"]}"

# Adding another user
user_info["job"]="Engineer"
echo "Job: ${user_info["job"]}"
```

Working with arrays and associative arrays in Bash is a powerful feature that can help streamline data management in your scripts. Whether you are dealing with a list of items or key-value pairs, understanding how to declare, initialize, modify, and loop through these data structures will greatly enhance your scripting capabilities. Mastering these concepts will enable you to create more dynamic and efficient shell scripts, making your tasks easier to automate and manage. As you progress in your Bash scripting journey, experimenting with arrays will open new avenues for data handling and manipulation.

13.2 Using Subshells and Command Grouping (() and {})

In Bash scripting, subshells and command grouping are essential techniques that enhance the power and flexibility of your scripts. They allow you to control the execution of commands, manage variables, and organize code more effectively. In this section, we will explore the concepts of subshells and command grouping, illustrating their syntax, use cases, and best practices.

1. What is a Subshell?

A subshell is a separate instance of the shell that executes a group of commands. Any variables or changes made in a subshell do not affect the parent shell. This isolation can be useful for temporary modifications that you want to discard after execution.

2. Creating a Subshell

You can create a subshell in Bash by enclosing commands in parentheses ():

(result=$(command1) && command2)

Here's a simple example of a subshell that lists files in a directory:

#!/bin/bash

 # Create a subshell to list files and count them
(file_list=$(ls) && echo "Files: $file_list")

 # Attempting to access file_list here will fail because it's defined in the subshell
echo "File list in subshell: $file_list" # Output will be empty

In this example, the variable file_list is defined in the subshell and is not available outside it.

3. Benefits of Subshells

- **Isolation**: Changes made to variables or the environment in a subshell do not affect the parent shell. This is useful for testing commands or temporary changes.
- **Parallel Execution**: Subshells can run commands in parallel, which can be beneficial for performance in scripts that involve multiple independent tasks.

4. Command Grouping

Command grouping allows you to group commands together for execution within the current shell context. This can be done using curly braces {}. Unlike subshells, variables defined within a command group remain accessible after execution.

5. Creating a Command Group

To create a command group, use curly braces {}:

{ command1; command2; command3; }

Here's an example of a command group:

```bash
#!/bin/bash

# Using command grouping to set multiple variables
{
   var1="Hello"
   var2="World"
   echo "$var1 $var2"
}

# Accessing variables outside the command group
echo "$var1 $var2" # Output: Hello World
```

In this case, var1 and var2 are accessible after the command group executes, demonstrating that command grouping operates within the current shell.

7. Practical Use Cases

Use Case 1: Using Subshells for Temporary Changes

Suppose you want to modify a variable temporarily within a subshell:

```bash
#!/bin/bash

my_var="Original Value"
echo "Before subshell: $my_var"

# Modify variable in subshell
(
   my_var="Modified Value"
   echo "Inside subshell: $my_var"
)

echo "After subshell: $my_var" # Output: Original Value
```

Here, changes to my_var inside the subshell do not affect its value outside.

Use Case 2: Command Grouping for Better Organization

Using command grouping can help you organize code that should be executed together:

```bash
#!/bin/bash

# Grouping commands for clarity
{
   echo "Starting process..."
   sleep 2
   echo "Process completed."
}

echo "The script continues..."
```

This example clearly groups the process-related commands, making the script more readable.

8. Combining Subshells and Command Grouping

You can also combine subshells and command grouping in more complex scripts. For instance:

```
#!/bin/bash

# Grouping commands in a subshell
(
  {
    echo "Running in subshell..."
    date
  }
)

# The subshell has completed execution
echo "Back to the main shell."
```

In this example, the commands inside the subshell are grouped, and their execution context is isolated.

9. Performance Considerations

While subshells and command grouping are powerful, it's essential to use them judiciously. Creating a subshell involves more overhead than command grouping because a new instance of the shell must be created. Therefore, use subshells when you need isolation, but prefer command grouping for simple group executions where variable persistence is needed.

Understanding subshells and command grouping is crucial for writing efficient and effective Bash scripts. Subshells provide isolation for temporary changes and can run commands in parallel, while command grouping allows for better organization of code and retains variable scope. By mastering these concepts, you can create scripts that are not only functional but also clean and maintainable, enabling you to tackle complex tasks with ease. As you continue your journey in Bash scripting, experiment with these techniques to enhance the robustness and clarity of your scripts.

13.3 Dynamic Code Execution with eval

The eval command in Bash is a powerful and often misunderstood tool that allows for the dynamic execution of commands and code. It takes a string as an argument, evaluates it as a command, and executes it in the current shell context. This can be particularly useful for situations where command names or parameters are generated at runtime, but it also comes with certain risks and best practices that you should be aware of.

1. What is eval?

The eval command evaluates its arguments as a Bash command and executes the resulting command line. Essentially, it allows you to build a command dynamically and then run it as if you had typed it directly into the shell.

2. Basic Syntax

The basic syntax of the eval command is:

eval command_string

Where command_string can be any valid Bash command.

3. How eval Works

When you pass a command string to eval, it does the following:

- It expands all the variables in the command string.
- It then executes the expanded command in the current shell context.

4. Example: Basic Usage of eval

Let's look at a simple example to demonstrate how eval works:

#!/bin/bash

command="echo Hello, World!"
eval $command

In this example, eval takes the string stored in the variable command, evaluates it, and executes it. The output will be:

Hello, World!

5. Building Dynamic Commands

One of the main advantages of eval is its ability to construct and execute commands dynamically. This can be useful in situations where the command is not known until runtime.

Example: Dynamic Variable Assignment

```bash
#!/bin/bash

var_name="greeting"
var_value="Hello, World!"

# Create a command to assign a value to a variable
command="declare $var_name='$var_value'"
eval $command

# Now we can use the dynamically created variable
echo $greeting # Output: Hello, World!
```

In this example, eval allows us to dynamically create a variable named greeting and assign it a value. This can be useful when dealing with variable names that are generated during the execution of the script.

6. Using eval with Arrays

You can also use eval with arrays to manipulate them dynamically:

```bash
#!/bin/bash

# Create an array of names
names=("Alice" "Bob" "Charlie")

# Build a command to print each name
for i in "${!names[@]}"; do
    eval "echo \${names[$i]}"
done
```

This example uses eval to access array elements dynamically. However, note that using eval in this way can lead to complex and hard-to-read code, so it should be used judiciously.

7. Safety Concerns with eval

While eval is powerful, it poses several risks:

Security Risks: If user input is directly passed to eval, it can lead to command injection vulnerabilities. Always validate or sanitize inputs that are passed to eval.

Readability and Maintainability: Overusing eval can make your code difficult to read and understand. It's usually better to use other constructs like functions or arrays unless dynamic execution is truly necessary.

8. Best Practices for Using eval

Limit Use: Only use eval when absolutely necessary. Explore other alternatives like functions, arrays, or indirect expansion.

Validate Inputs: If you need to use user input, ensure it is validated or sanitized to prevent code injection vulnerabilities.

Comment Your Code: If you use eval, provide comments explaining why it is necessary and what the dynamic code is intended to do.

9. Advanced Example: Using eval for Command-line Options

Suppose you want to dynamically construct a command that takes multiple command-line options. You can use eval for this purpose:

```bash
#!/bin/bash

options="--verbose --output=results.txt"
command="ls $options"

# Execute the command dynamically
eval $command
```

In this case, eval allows you to construct a command string with options that can change based on runtime conditions.

The eval command in Bash provides a powerful mechanism for dynamic code execution, allowing you to build and execute commands on the fly. However, with great power comes great responsibility. Understanding the risks and best practices associated with eval is essential for writing secure, maintainable, and efficient Bash scripts. As you continue your journey in Bash scripting, use eval judiciously, and always consider whether there are alternative approaches that might be safer or clearer.

13.4 Using exec to Replace the Current Shell Process

The exec command in Bash is a powerful utility that allows you to replace the current shell process with a specified command or program. This can be particularly useful in scripting and system administration, as it can streamline execution and conserve system resources by eliminating the need for a subshell. In this section, we will explore the exec command in detail, discussing its syntax, use cases, and practical examples.

1. What is exec?

The exec command in Bash is used to execute a command in place of the current shell process. When exec is invoked, the current shell is replaced by the specified command, meaning that after the command completes, the shell does not return to the original command line. This behavior is different from executing a command normally, where a new process is created, and control returns to the shell after the command finishes.

2. Basic Syntax

The syntax for using exec is as follows:

exec command [arguments...]

3. How exec Works

When you use exec, the shell performs the following:

- The command specified is executed.
- The current shell process is replaced by the new command, meaning that it takes over the current shell's PID (Process ID).

- There is no return to the original shell after the command completes; it effectively terminates the original shell.

4. Example: Basic Usage of exec

To demonstrate the basic usage of exec, let's consider a simple example:

#!/bin/bash

echo "This will execute 'ls' and replace the current shell."
exec ls -l
echo "This message will not be printed."

In this example, the exec ls -l command replaces the current shell process with the ls -l command. Because of this, the message after exec will not be printed, as the shell no longer exists in its original form after executing ls.

5. Use Cases for exec

Use Case 1: Running a New Command in Place of the Shell

One of the most common use cases for exec is to run a new command that should take the place of the shell itself. For instance, if you are creating a script that is intended to run a single command:

#!/bin/bash

 # This script runs a Python script
exec python3 my_script.py

After the Python script completes, there is no shell to return to since it has been replaced. This is useful for scripts that do not require further interaction with the shell after executing the command.

Use Case 2: Redirecting Input/Output Streams

exec can also be used to redirect file descriptors. For example, if you want to redirect all output from the script to a file:

#!/bin/bash

```
# Redirect all output to output.log
exec > output.log

# All subsequent commands' output will go to output.log
echo "This will be written to output.log."
echo "So will this."
```

In this case, the exec command redirects standard output (stdout) to output.log, so any subsequent output from the script will be captured in that file.

6. Replacing the Shell with an Interactive Command

If you want to replace the shell with an interactive program, such as a text editor, you can use exec as follows:

```
#!/bin/bash

# Replace the shell with nano text editor
exec nano myfile.txt
```

Once the user exits nano, there will be no return to the original shell session.

7. Using exec with Environment Variables

You can also set environment variables for a command executed with exec:

```
#!/bin/bash

# Set an environment variable and replace the shell with a command
exec MY_VAR="Hello" bash -c 'echo $MY_VAR'
```

In this example, the variable MY_VAR is set for the command executed by exec, which prints its value.

8. Performance Benefits of Using exec

Using exec can improve performance in certain scenarios:

Resource Efficiency: Since exec replaces the shell process, it eliminates the overhead associated with creating a new shell process. This can be advantageous in scripts that run commands where no return to the original shell is needed.

Simpler Control Flow: When a script is designed to run a single command, using exec can simplify the script's control flow by avoiding unnecessary complexity.

9. Limitations of exec

While exec has many benefits, it also comes with limitations:

No Return: After executing a command with exec, the original shell is terminated, and there is no way to return to it. This can be problematic if you want to run multiple commands sequentially.

Not Suitable for All Scripts: Scripts that require further interaction with the shell after executing a command may not be suitable for exec.

The exec command in Bash is a powerful tool for replacing the current shell process with a specified command. It allows for efficient execution, redirection of input/output, and can simplify control flow in scripts designed for single commands. However, it should be used with caution, as it terminates the original shell process and prevents any subsequent commands from executing in that shell context. By understanding the uses and implications of exec, you can make informed decisions when designing your Bash scripts, enhancing their efficiency and functionality.

13.5 Writing Secure Scripts: Input Validation and Permissions

When writing Bash scripts, security is a critical consideration that can't be overlooked. Poorly written scripts can expose systems to various vulnerabilities, including command injection, data corruption, and unauthorized access. This section will delve into two essential aspects of writing secure Bash scripts: input validation and permissions. By implementing robust input validation and managing permissions effectively, you can significantly reduce the risk of security breaches.

1. The Importance of Security in Bash Scripting

As systems become increasingly interconnected, scripts can be vulnerable entry points for attackers. A malicious user can exploit flaws in your scripts to execute arbitrary commands, access sensitive data, or cause other types of harm. Ensuring your scripts are secure is essential for protecting your system and its data.

2. Input Validation

Input validation is the process of ensuring that the data received by your script is appropriate, safe, and expected. This step is crucial for preventing attacks like command injection, where an attacker might supply malicious input that the script inadvertently executes.

2.1 Types of Input Validation

Type Checking: Ensure that input data is of the expected type (e.g., integer, string).

Length Checking: Limit the length of input to prevent buffer overflows or excessive resource consumption.

Format Checking: Use regular expressions to enforce specific formats (e.g., email addresses, IP addresses).

Whitelist Validation: Accept only known, safe values. For example, if a script accepts command options, only allow those predefined options.

2.2 Example: Basic Input Validation

Here's an example that demonstrates how to perform input validation in a Bash script:

```bash
#!/bin/bash

# Function to validate input
validate_input() {
   if [[ ! "$1" =~ ^[0-9]+$ ]]; then
      echo "Error: Input must be a positive integer."
      exit 1
   fi
}

# Get user input
```

```
read -p "Enter a positive integer: " user_input
```

```
# Validate the input
validate_input "$user_input"
echo "You entered: $user_input"
```

In this script, the validate_input function checks if the input is a positive integer using a regular expression. If the input does not match, it displays an error message and exits the script.

2.3 Command Injection Prevention

To prevent command injection attacks, always quote your variables when passing them to commands. For example:

```
#!/bin/bash

# Accept a filename from user input
read -p "Enter the filename to delete: " filename

# Validate and use the filename in a command
if [[ -e "$filename" ]]; then
    rm "$filename"  # Safely using the variable
else
    echo "Error: File does not exist."
fi
```

By quoting $filename, you prevent unexpected characters in the input from being interpreted as commands.

3. Managing Permissions

Proper management of file permissions is another crucial aspect of script security. The way you set permissions on your scripts can protect them from unauthorized access or modifications.

3.1 Understanding File Permissions

In Unix-like systems, file permissions determine who can read, write, or execute a file. Permissions are represented by three categories:

- **User**: The owner of the file.
- **Group**: A set of users assigned to the file.
- **Others**: All other users.

Permissions are typically represented in a format like rwxr-xr--, where:

r stands for read, w for write, and x for execute.

The first set of three characters represents the owner's permissions, the second set for the group, and the last set for others.

3.2 Setting Permissions

To set permissions on a script, use the chmod command. For example, to make a script executable only by the owner:

chmod 700 my_script.sh

This command sets the permissions to read, write, and execute for the owner only, denying access to group and others.

3.3 Owner and Group Management

Use the chown command to change the ownership of a script:

chown username:groupname my_script.sh

By assigning ownership appropriately, you can control who can modify or execute the script.

3.4 Restricting Environment Variables

When executing scripts, be mindful of which environment variables are available to them. Avoid exposing sensitive data, such as passwords or API keys, through environment variables. You can use the env -i command to execute a script in a clean environment, thus minimizing the risk of accidental exposure.

4. Additional Security Practices

Use ShellCheck: This is a tool that helps identify potential security issues and other problems in your Bash scripts. Running your scripts through ShellCheck can help catch common mistakes.

Avoid Using eval: The eval command can introduce significant security vulnerabilities if not used carefully. If possible, avoid it altogether or ensure that any variables passed to it are sanitized.

Limit Script Capabilities: Run scripts with the least privileges necessary. For instance, if a script only needs read access to certain files, don't give it write access.

Regular Audits: Periodically review your scripts for vulnerabilities, especially when updating them or when the environment changes.

Writing secure Bash scripts is essential in safeguarding systems from unauthorized access and potential attacks. By implementing robust input validation techniques and managing file permissions effectively, you can minimize vulnerabilities and enhance the overall security posture of your scripts. Always be vigilant and proactive in assessing security risks, applying best practices, and adapting to evolving security landscapes. By doing so, you not only protect your systems but also foster a culture of security awareness within your development practices.

13.6 Static Analysis of Bash Scripts with shellcheck

Static analysis is a crucial step in the development lifecycle of any software, including Bash scripts. It involves examining the code without executing it to identify potential issues, vulnerabilities, and adherence to coding standards. One of the most popular tools for static analysis of Bash scripts is ShellCheck. This section will explore the purpose of ShellCheck, its features, how to use it effectively, and best practices for integrating it into your workflow.

1. What is ShellCheck?

ShellCheck is a static analysis tool designed specifically for shell scripts. It analyzes scripts for a wide range of potential issues, including syntax errors, stylistic problems, and common pitfalls. By providing warnings and suggestions for improvement, ShellCheck helps developers write cleaner, more robust, and more maintainable Bash scripts.

2. Key Features of ShellCheck

- **Error Detection**: ShellCheck identifies syntax errors, misplaced commands, and unsupported syntax that could lead to runtime failures.
- **Common Pitfall Warnings**: The tool highlights common mistakes, such as unquoted variables that could lead to command injection vulnerabilities.
- **Suggestions for Best Practices**: ShellCheck offers best practices for writing Bash scripts, improving readability, and ensuring maintainability.
- **Line-by-Line Feedback**: It provides detailed feedback on specific lines of code, making it easier to pinpoint issues.
- **Compatibility**: ShellCheck works with various shell scripts, including those written for bash, sh, ksh, and dash.

3. Installing ShellCheck

ShellCheck can be installed on various platforms, including Linux, macOS, and Windows. Here's how to install it on each platform:

On Ubuntu/Debian

sudo apt-get install shellcheck

On macOS (using Homebrew)

brew install shellcheck

On Windows (via Chocolatey)

choco install shellcheck

Alternatively, you can download precompiled binaries from the ShellCheck GitHub Releases page.

4. Using ShellCheck

Once installed, using ShellCheck is straightforward. You can analyze a Bash script by running the following command in your terminal:

shellcheck my_script.sh

This command will output warnings, errors, and suggestions based on the content of my_script.sh. Here's an example of what the output may look like:

In my_script.sh line 5:
if [$var = "test"]; then
    ^-- SC2039: In POSIX sh, '=' is not a valid operator. Use '==' instead.

5. Interpreting ShellCheck Output

The output from ShellCheck includes several components:

- **Line Number**: The specific line in the script where the issue is located.
- **Warning/Error Code**: A code that represents the type of issue (e.g., SC2039).
- **Description**: A brief explanation of the issue.
- **Suggestion**: Recommendations for how to fix the problem.

Understanding these components allows you to quickly identify and address issues in your scripts.

6. Common Issues Identified by ShellCheck

ShellCheck can identify various types of issues, including:

Unquoted Variables: ShellCheck warns when variables are not quoted, which can lead to unexpected behavior:

echo $var # Warning: Unquoted variable

Command Substitution: It can detect issues with command substitution syntax, such as using backticks instead of $(...):

output=`command` # Warning: Use $(...) instead

Use of eval: ShellCheck will flag the use of eval due to its potential for security vulnerabilities:

eval "some command" # Warning: Avoid using eval

Incorrect Conditionals: It checks for proper syntax in conditional statements, ensuring best practices are followed:

if ["$var" == "value"]; then # Warning: Use single = for POSIX compliance

7. Integrating ShellCheck into Your Workflow

Integrating ShellCheck into your development workflow can significantly enhance script quality. Here are some ways to do this:

Pre-commit Hook: Set up a pre-commit hook in your version control system (e.g., Git) to run ShellCheck on your scripts before allowing commits. This ensures that only validated scripts are committed.

Continuous Integration (CI): Incorporate ShellCheck into your CI pipeline. This allows you to automatically check for issues whenever code is pushed or a pull request is made, ensuring that all scripts meet quality standards.

IDE Integration: Some Integrated Development Environments (IDEs) and text editors (like Visual Studio Code and Sublime Text) support ShellCheck plugins, providing real-time feedback as you write scripts.

8. Best Practices for Using ShellCheck

- **Run Regularly**: Make it a habit to run ShellCheck on your scripts regularly, especially before major changes or releases.
- **Review Warnings**: Pay attention to all warnings and suggestions provided by ShellCheck. Even if they don't seem critical, addressing them can prevent future issues.
- **Customize Configurations**: ShellCheck allows for configuration file customization to suppress specific warnings that may not apply to your scripts. This helps in maintaining focus on more critical issues.

9. Limitations of ShellCheck

While ShellCheck is a powerful tool, it has some limitations:

- **False Positives**: In some cases, ShellCheck may raise warnings that do not apply to your specific use case or script.
- **No Runtime Analysis**: ShellCheck does not execute scripts, so it cannot catch issues that only become apparent during execution (e.g., runtime errors due to external dependencies).

Static analysis with ShellCheck is a valuable practice for anyone writing Bash scripts. By identifying syntax errors, potential security vulnerabilities, and stylistic issues, ShellCheck helps developers create cleaner, more robust scripts. Integrating ShellCheck into your development workflow can enhance code quality, reduce bugs, and ultimately improve the reliability of your scripts. Embrace ShellCheck as an essential tool in your Bash scripting toolkit, and enjoy the benefits of writing safer, more maintainable code.

14. Version Control for Shell Scripts

In this chapter, you'll discover the importance of version control in managing your Bash scripts effectively. We'll introduce Git as a powerful tool for tracking changes, collaborating with others, and maintaining the integrity of your code. You'll learn how to set up a Git repository for your scripts, including essential commands for committing changes, branching, and merging code. We'll cover best practices for writing commit messages, organizing your repository, and using .gitignore to manage which files to track. Additionally, we'll explore how to use Git hooks to automate tasks, such as running tests or formatting scripts before committing. By the end of this chapter, you'll be equipped with the knowledge to implement version control in your Bash scripting workflow, ensuring that you can collaborate efficiently and maintain a history of changes with ease.

14.1 Introduction to Git for Version Control

Version control is an essential practice in modern software development, allowing developers to track changes, collaborate effectively, and manage code across different versions. Among various version control systems, Git has emerged as the most widely used tool, revered for its speed, flexibility, and powerful features. This section will introduce Git, explain its core concepts, and highlight its significance in the context of Bash scripting and shell programming.

1. What is Git?

Git is a distributed version control system (DVCS) designed to handle everything from small to very large projects with speed and efficiency. Unlike centralized version control systems (CVCS), where a single central server holds the repository, Git allows every developer to maintain a full copy of the repository on their local machine. This setup enhances collaboration, facilitates offline work, and provides robust mechanisms for branching and merging code changes.

2. Key Features of Git

Distributed Architecture: Every user has a complete local copy of the repository, including its history. This setup allows for rapid operations, as most actions can be performed locally without requiring network access.

Branching and Merging: Git makes it easy to create branches, enabling developers to work on new features or bug fixes independently. Merging branches back into the main codebase is straightforward, and Git intelligently resolves conflicts when they arise.

Commit History: Git records a detailed history of changes, making it easy to revert to previous versions, track modifications, and understand the evolution of the codebase.

Staging Area: Before committing changes, developers can use the staging area to prepare a set of changes. This allows for granular control over what gets included in a commit.

Collaboration: Git provides tools for collaboration, such as pull requests, which allow team members to review changes before merging them into the main branch.

3. Why Use Git for Bash Scripting?

Using Git for managing Bash scripts offers several advantages:

Version History: Keeping track of changes in scripts is crucial, especially for scripts that automate critical tasks or manage system configurations. Git's commit history allows developers to see who made changes, when they were made, and why.

Collaboration: When working in teams, Git simplifies collaboration. Multiple developers can work on different features simultaneously, merge their changes, and resolve conflicts in a structured manner.

Rollback Capability: If a new script introduces bugs or unintended consequences, Git allows you to revert to a previous version quickly.

Branching for Experimentation: Developers can create branches to experiment with new features or ideas without affecting the stable version of their scripts.

4. Core Concepts of Git

To effectively use Git, it's essential to understand some key concepts:

Repository (Repo): A repository is the fundamental unit of storage in Git. It contains all the project files, including the entire history of changes.

Commit: A commit is a snapshot of the project at a specific point in time. Each commit includes a unique identifier, a timestamp, and a message describing the changes.

Branch: A branch is a separate line of development. By default, every Git repository has a main branch (often called main or master). Developers can create additional branches for new features or bug fixes.

Merge: Merging combines changes from one branch into another. Git attempts to automatically resolve any conflicts that arise during the merge process.

Clone: Cloning creates a copy of a remote repository on your local machine, allowing you to work on the project offline.

5. Getting Started with Git

5.1 Installing Git

Installing Git is the first step toward version control. Here's how to install Git on different operating systems:

On Ubuntu/Debian:

sudo apt update
sudo apt install git

On macOS (using Homebrew):

brew install git

On Windows: Download the installer from the official Git website and follow the setup instructions.

5.2 Configuring Git

After installation, configure Git with your name and email. These details will be associated with your commits:

git config --global user.name "Your Name"
git config --global user.email "your.email@example.com"

5.3 Creating a Repository

To start using Git, create a new repository. Navigate to your project directory and run:

git init

This command initializes a new Git repository in that directory.

6. Basic Git Commands

Familiarizing yourself with basic Git commands is essential for effective version control:

git add: Stages changes for the next commit.

git add my_script.sh

git commit: Commits the staged changes to the repository.

git commit -m "Initial commit"

git status: Shows the status of changes in the working directory and staging area.

git status

git log: Displays the commit history.

git log

git branch: Lists all branches in the repository.

git branch

git checkout: Switches to a different branch.

git checkout my-feature-branch

git merge: Merges changes from one branch into the current branch.

git merge my-feature-branch

7. Best Practices for Using Git

Commit Often: Make small, frequent commits with clear messages. This practice helps track changes and makes it easier to identify issues.

Use Meaningful Commit Messages: Write concise and descriptive commit messages to clarify the purpose of each change.

Branch for Features: Use branches for new features or bug fixes, keeping the main branch stable.

Review Changes: Before merging branches, review changes carefully to catch any potential issues.

Back Up Your Repository: Regularly push your commits to a remote repository (like GitHub or GitLab) to ensure your work is backed up and accessible.

Git is an indispensable tool for version control in Bash scripting and software development in general. By understanding its core concepts, mastering basic commands, and adopting best practices, you can manage your scripts more effectively, collaborate with others seamlessly, and maintain a clean, organized codebase. Whether you're working on a personal project or collaborating with a team, integrating Git into your workflow will enhance your productivity and ensure the integrity of your code. As you progress in your Bash scripting journey, leveraging Git for version control will empower you to write, manage, and share your scripts with confidence.

14.2 Creating a Git Repository for Your Scripts

Creating a Git repository for your Bash scripts is a foundational step in implementing version control, allowing you to track changes, collaborate with others, and manage the evolution of your code over time. This section will guide you through the process of setting up a Git repository, including the various methods for both local and remote repositories, as well as best practices for organizing your scripts within the repository.

1. Understanding Git Repositories

A Git repository (or "repo") is a storage space where your project files are kept along with their entire history of changes. Git repositories can be local (on your computer) or remote (hosted on platforms like GitHub, GitLab, or Bitbucket). Local repositories are ideal for personal projects, while remote repositories facilitate collaboration with other developers.

2. Initializing a Local Repository

To create a Git repository for your scripts, follow these steps to initialize a local repository:

Step 1: Create a Project Directory

First, create a directory for your Bash scripts if you haven't already. Open your terminal and use the following command:

mkdir my-bash-scripts
cd my-bash-scripts

Step 2: Initialize the Repository

Once you are inside your project directory, run the following command to initialize a new Git repository:

git init

This command creates a hidden .git directory in your project folder, which Git uses to track changes.

Step 3: Add Your Scripts

You can now create or copy your Bash scripts into this directory. For example, create a simple Bash script:

echo -e '#!/bin/bash\necho "Hello, World!"' > hello.sh
chmod +x hello.sh

Step 4: Stage Your Scripts

Before you can commit your scripts, you need to stage them. Staging allows you to select which changes you want to include in your next commit. Use the following command to stage your script:

git add hello.sh

You can also stage all files in the directory with:

git add .

Step 5: Commit Your Changes

After staging your scripts, commit them to the repository with a descriptive message:

git commit -m "Initial commit: Add hello.sh script"

This command creates a new commit in the repository with the changes you staged.

3. Creating a Remote Repository

While a local repository is sufficient for personal projects, a remote repository is crucial for collaboration. Here's how to create a remote repository using GitHub as an example:

Step 1: Create an Account on GitHub

If you don't have an account, sign up for free at GitHub.

Step 2: Create a New Repository

- Once logged in, click the + icon in the top-right corner and select New repository.
- Give your repository a name, such as my-bash-scripts, and optionally add a description.
- Choose the repository visibility (public or private) according to your preference.
- You can skip the option to initialize with a README for now since you already have local scripts.
- Click Create repository.

Step 3: Link Local Repository to Remote Repository

Now, you need to connect your local repository to the newly created remote repository. In your terminal, run the following commands, replacing YOUR_USERNAME and REPO_NAME with your GitHub username and the name of your repository:

git remote add origin https://github.com/YOUR_USERNAME/my-bash-scripts.git

Step 4: Push Your Local Commits

After linking the local and remote repositories, you can push your local commits to the remote repository:

git push -u origin master

The -u flag sets the upstream reference, allowing you to use git push in the future without specifying the remote and branch.

4. Cloning an Existing Repository

If you want to start working on an existing repository, you can clone it. Cloning creates a local copy of the remote repository. Use the following command, replacing the URL with the repository you want to clone:

git clone https://github.com/YOUR_USERNAME/my-bash-scripts.git

This command creates a new directory named my-bash-scripts containing the entire repository history.

5. Organizing Your Scripts

As your collection of Bash scripts grows, it's essential to maintain a clear structure within your repository. Here are some best practices for organizing your scripts:

Subdirectories: Group related scripts into subdirectories based on functionality or purpose (e.g., utilities, data-processing, deployments).

Documentation: Include a README.md file at the root of your repository to provide an overview of your project, instructions on how to use the scripts, and any dependencies.

Versioning: Use version tags to mark significant milestones in your project (e.g., v1.0, v1.1). You can create a tag with the following command:

git tag -a v1.0 -m "Version 1.0: Initial release"
git push origin v1.0

6. Best Practices for Using Git with Bash Scripts

Commit Frequently: Make small, frequent commits with clear messages to maintain a detailed history of changes.

Branch for New Features: When developing new features or making significant changes, create a new branch to avoid disrupting the main codebase.

Use .gitignore: Create a .gitignore file to specify which files and directories Git should ignore. This is useful for excluding temporary files, logs, or sensitive information.

Review Before Merging: If you're collaborating with others, use pull requests to review and discuss changes before merging them into the main branch.

Creating a Git repository for your Bash scripts is a crucial step in implementing effective version control. By following the steps outlined in this section, you can set up a local repository, link it to a remote repository, and organize your scripts for efficient management. Utilizing Git not only enhances your development workflow but also allows for better collaboration and a clear record of your project's evolution. As you continue to develop your Bash scripting skills, mastering Git will empower you to write, manage, and share your scripts with confidence and professionalism.

14.3 Committing, Branching, and Merging Changes

Managing changes effectively is one of the core strengths of Git, and understanding how to commit, branch, and merge is essential for any developer working with Bash scripts. This section will delve into the fundamental concepts and practical steps involved in committing changes to your Git repository, creating and managing branches, and merging those branches to maintain an organized and efficient workflow.

1. Understanding Commits

A commit in Git is a snapshot of your repository at a specific point in time. Each commit records changes to the files, along with a unique identifier (hash), a timestamp, and an optional message that describes the changes made. Commits form the backbone of your project history, allowing you to track changes, revert to previous states, and collaborate with others.

1.1 Creating a Commit

To create a commit, follow these steps:

Stage Changes: Use the git add command to stage the changes you want to include in your commit. You can stage individual files or all modified files in your working directory.

git add my_script.sh

Commit the Changes: Once the changes are staged, commit them using the git commit command with a descriptive message.

git commit -m "Fix bug in my_script.sh: correct output formatting"

View Commit History: You can view the history of commits in your repository with the git log command. This will show a list of commits along with their hashes, authors, and messages.

git log

2. Understanding Branching

Branching is a powerful feature in Git that allows you to create a separate line of development. This is particularly useful for working on new features or bug fixes without affecting the main codebase (often called main or master). Each branch can evolve independently, enabling safer experimentation and development.

2.1 Creating a Branch

To create a new branch, use the git branch command followed by the name of the new branch. For example, to create a branch called feature/new-feature:

git branch feature/new-feature

2.2 Switching Branches

After creating a branch, you can switch to it using the git checkout command:

git checkout feature/new-feature

Alternatively, you can combine the branch creation and switch into one command with -b:

git checkout -b feature/new-feature

2.3 Viewing Branches

To view a list of all branches in your repository, run:

git branch

The current branch will be indicated with an asterisk (*).

3. Merging Changes

Once you have developed your new feature or made changes on your branch, you'll likely want to merge those changes back into the main branch. This is where merging comes into play.

3.1 Merging a Branch

To merge changes from one branch into another, first switch to the branch you want to merge into (usually main):

git checkout main

Then, use the git merge command followed by the name of the branch you want to merge:

git merge feature/new-feature

Git will attempt to automatically merge the changes. If there are no conflicts, your merge will be completed, and a new commit will be created.

3.2 Resolving Merge Conflicts

Sometimes, when merging, you may encounter merge conflicts if changes in the two branches overlap or conflict. Git will indicate which files have conflicts, and you'll need to resolve them manually. Here's how to do it:

Identify Conflicted Files: Use git status to see which files are in conflict.

Edit Conflicted Files: Open the conflicted files in a text editor. You will see conflict markers like <<<<<<<, =======, and >>>>>>>, which indicate the conflicting changes.

Resolve the Conflicts: Edit the file to resolve the conflicts by choosing which changes to keep.

Stage the Resolved Files: After resolving conflicts, stage the changes.

git add my_script.sh

Complete the Merge: Commit the merge using:

git commit -m "Resolve merge conflict in my_script.sh"

4. Best Practices for Committing, Branching, and Merging

Commit Often: Make frequent commits with descriptive messages to keep track of changes and make it easier to identify specific modifications in the history.

Use Meaningful Branch Names: Choose clear and descriptive names for branches that indicate their purpose (e.g., bugfix/fix-output-issue or feature/add-logging).

Keep Branches Short-lived: Aim to merge branches back into the main branch as soon as the feature or fix is complete. This reduces the chances of conflicts and keeps your codebase clean.

Review Before Merging: Before merging a branch, consider reviewing the changes to ensure they meet the project standards and do not introduce new issues.

Understanding how to commit, branch, and merge changes is crucial for effective version control with Git, especially when managing Bash scripts. By following the practices outlined in this section, you can maintain a well-organized and efficient development workflow. Utilizing Git's branching capabilities allows you to work on multiple features simultaneously, while committing and merging help keep your project history clear and manageable. As you continue to develop your Bash scripting skills, mastering these Git operations will empower you to collaborate effectively and ensure the integrity of your code.

14.4 Using Tags and Releases for Versioning Scripts

Versioning is an essential part of software development, allowing developers to track changes, manage releases, and ensure stability in their projects. Git provides a robust mechanism for versioning through the use of tags. Tags are markers that represent specific points in a repository's history and are often used to indicate releases. This section will explore how to create and manage tags in Git, as well as how to use them effectively for versioning your Bash scripts.

1. Understanding Tags

Tags in Git are similar to branches, but unlike branches, tags are static and do not change. They serve as a snapshot of a project at a specific point in time. Tags are primarily used to mark release versions of software, making it easier to reference and revert to those versions if needed. There are two types of tags in Git:

Lightweight Tags: These are simply pointers to a specific commit. They do not contain any extra information and are akin to bookmarks.

Annotated Tags: These are more robust and contain metadata such as the tagger's name, email, date, and an optional message. Annotated tags are stored as full objects in the Git database, making them suitable for marking releases.

2. Creating Tags

2.1 Creating a Lightweight Tag

To create a lightweight tag, use the following command, replacing v1.0 with your desired tag name:

git tag v1.0

2.2 Creating an Annotated Tag

To create an annotated tag, use the -a option and include a message with the -m option:

git tag -a v1.0 -m "Release version 1.0: Initial stable release"

3. Listing Tags

To view all the tags in your repository, you can use the following command:

git tag

If you want more detailed information about a specific tag, such as an annotated tag, use:

git show v1.0

This command will display the commit associated with the tag along with any associated message.

4. Pushing Tags to Remote Repositories

By default, tags are not pushed to remote repositories when you use the git push command. To push your tags, you can use one of the following commands:

4.1 Push a Specific Tag

To push a specific tag to a remote repository, use:

git push origin v1.0

4.2 Push All Tags

To push all tags at once, you can use the following command:

git push --tags

This command ensures that all of your local tags are uploaded to the remote repository.

5. Checking Out Tags

You may want to check out a specific tag to view or use the state of the code at that version. To do this, you can use the git checkout command:

git checkout v1.0

This will put your working directory in a "detached HEAD" state, meaning you are not on a branch but rather at a specific commit. You can still view the code and run scripts, but if you make any changes, you'll need to create a new branch from that state to preserve those changes.

6. Deleting Tags

If you need to delete a tag, you can do so with the following command:

6.1 Delete a Local Tag

To delete a local tag, use:

git tag -d v1.0

6.2 Delete a Remote Tag

To delete a tag from a remote repository, you can use the following command:

git push --delete origin v1.0

7. Using Tags for Releases

Tags are particularly useful for managing releases in your Bash scripting projects. Here are some best practices for using tags effectively:

7.1 Semantic Versioning

Consider adopting a semantic versioning strategy for your tags. Semantic versioning uses a three-part version number: MAJOR.MINOR.PATCH. For example, version 1.2.3 indicates:

- **MAJOR**: Incompatible API changes.
- **MINOR**: New functionality added in a backward-compatible manner.
- **PATCH**: Backward-compatible bug fixes.

7.2 Creating Release Notes

When you create a new tag for a release, it can be helpful to maintain a CHANGELOG or release notes that describe what changes were made in each version. This can help users understand the evolution of your scripts and the changes in functionality.

7.3 Utilizing GitHub Releases

If you are using GitHub, you can take advantage of the Releases feature. This feature allows you to create a release from a tag, including the ability to attach binary files, provide release notes, and communicate the new features or fixes in that version. To create a GitHub release from a tag:

- Navigate to your repository on GitHub.
- Click on the Releases section.
- Click the Draft a new release button.

Choose the tag you want to create a release for, and add any necessary notes or files.

Using tags and releases for versioning your Bash scripts is a powerful way to manage your project's history and stability. By leveraging Git's tagging features, you can mark significant milestones in your development process, maintain clear records of changes, and facilitate collaboration with other developers. Adopting a systematic approach to versioning will not only improve your workflow but also enhance the overall quality and reliability of your Bash scripting projects. As you progress in your development journey, mastering tags and releases will be invaluable in creating maintainable and well-organized scripts.

14.5 Automating Script Deployment with Git Hooks

Git hooks are powerful scripts that Git executes before or after events such as commits, merges, and pushes. They provide a way to automate various tasks associated with your workflow, such as code quality checks, notifications, and deployment processes. In this section, we will explore how to set up and utilize Git hooks for automating the deployment of your Bash scripts, ensuring that your deployment process is efficient and error-free.

1. Understanding Git Hooks

Git hooks are located in the hooks directory within your Git repository. Each hook is a script that executes automatically in response to specific events. Git provides several predefined hooks, including:

- **Pre-commit**: Runs before a commit is made. Useful for running tests or linters.
- **Post-commit**: Runs after a commit is completed. Can be used for notifications.
- **Pre-push**: Runs before pushing changes to a remote repository. Useful for final checks.
- **Post-merge**: Runs after a merge operation. Can be used to notify users or perform cleanup tasks.

You can create or modify these hooks to automate tasks related to your scripts.

2. Setting Up Git Hooks

To set up a Git hook, navigate to the .git/hooks directory in your repository. Inside this directory, you will find sample hook scripts (with a .sample extension) for various events. To create a custom hook, follow these steps:

Choose the Hook Type: Determine which hook you want to create (e.g., pre-commit, post-commit, pre-push).

Create the Script: Create a new file with the name of the hook (e.g., pre-commit) and remove the .sample extension.

Make the Script Executable: Ensure the script is executable by running:

chmod +x .git/hooks/pre-commit

Edit the Script: Open the file in your preferred text editor and add the necessary commands.

3. Example: Automating Deployment with a Post-Commit Hook

Let's create an example where we automate the deployment of a Bash script every time a new commit is made. In this scenario, we will use a post-commit hook to copy the latest version of our script to a deployment directory.

3.1 Create the Post-Commit Hook

Navigate to the .git/hooks directory in your repository:

cd /path/to/your/repo/.git/hooks

Create a new file named post-commit:

touch post-commit

Make it executable:

chmod +x post-commit

Open the post-commit file in a text editor:

nano post-commit

Add the following code to the file:

#!/bin/bash

 # Define the source script and the deployment directory
SOURCE_SCRIPT="/path/to/your/script.sh"
DEPLOY_DIR="/path/to/deployment/directory"

 # Copy the script to the deployment directory
cp "$SOURCE_SCRIPT" "$DEPLOY_DIR"

 # Notify of successful deployment
echo "Deployment completed successfully. Script has been copied to $DEPLOY_DIR."

3.2 Explanation of the Script

Defining Variables: The SOURCE_SCRIPT variable holds the path to the Bash script you want to deploy, and the DEPLOY_DIR variable holds the path to the directory where you want to deploy the script.

Copying the Script: The cp command copies the source script to the deployment directory. If the copy operation is successful, the script will output a success message.

4. Example: Using Pre-Push Hook for Pre-Deployment Checks

Before deploying, you might want to perform some checks to ensure that your scripts are functioning correctly. A pre-push hook can be used for this purpose. Here's how to set it up:

Navigate to the .git/hooks directory and create a file named pre-push:

touch pre-push
chmod +x pre-push

Open the pre-push file and add the following code:

#!/bin/bash

 # Run tests or checks on the script before pushing
if ! bash -n /path/to/your/script.sh; then
    echo "Script contains syntax errors. Push aborted."
    exit 1
fi

echo "Pre-push checks passed. Proceeding with the push."

4.1 Explanation of the Pre-Push Hook

Running Syntax Check: The bash -n command performs a syntax check on the specified Bash script. If there are syntax errors, the script will output an error message and prevent the push.

Exiting with an Error Code: If syntax errors are detected, the script exits with a non-zero status (exit 1), which indicates failure.

5. Best Practices for Using Git Hooks

Keep Hooks Simple: Avoid making hooks overly complex. The primary purpose is to automate simple tasks or checks, so keep them efficient and easy to understand.

Document Hooks: Add comments to your hook scripts to describe what they do and why. This will help you and others understand their purpose when revisiting the code later.

Test Hooks Thoroughly: Before relying on hooks in a production environment, test them thoroughly to ensure they work as intended and do not inadvertently disrupt your workflow.

Version Control Your Hooks: While Git does not automatically track the hooks in the .git/hooks directory, you can store them in a separate directory in your project and create a setup script to install them in the .git/hooks directory.

Git hooks provide a powerful mechanism for automating tasks related to your Bash scripts, including deployment processes. By leveraging hooks such as post-commit and pre-push, you can streamline your workflow, ensuring that your scripts are automatically deployed and thoroughly checked before changes are pushed to a remote repository. Implementing Git hooks not only enhances efficiency but also helps maintain code quality and reduces the risk of errors during deployment. As you continue to develop your Bash scripts, consider integrating Git hooks into your workflow to optimize your deployment processes and improve overall project management.

14.6 Collaborating on Scripts: Pull Requests and Code Reviews

Collaboration is a fundamental aspect of software development, especially when working on Bash scripts that may be part of larger projects or shared within a team. Two essential practices that facilitate effective collaboration are pull requests and code reviews. In this section, we will explore the processes involved in creating pull requests, conducting code reviews, and best practices for ensuring high-quality contributions to your Bash scripts.

1. Understanding Pull Requests

A pull request (PR) is a mechanism by which developers can propose changes to a codebase in a version control system, such as Git. When a developer has made changes in a branch of their repository, they can submit a pull request to merge those changes into another branch, typically the main branch of the project. The pull request serves as a request for the project maintainers to review and discuss the proposed changes before they are integrated into the main codebase.

2. Creating a Pull Request

To create a pull request, follow these steps:

2.1 Fork the Repository

If you are collaborating on a project that you do not own, the first step is to fork the repository. This creates a copy of the repository under your own GitHub account, allowing you to make changes without affecting the original project.

Go to the repository on GitHub and click the Fork button in the upper right corner.

2.2 Clone Your Forked Repository

Clone the forked repository to your local machine:

git clone https://github.com/yourusername/repo-name.git
cd repo-name

2.3 Create a New Branch

Before making changes, create a new branch from the main branch:

git checkout -b feature/new-script

2.4 Make Your Changes

Make the necessary changes to your Bash scripts. This could include adding new features, fixing bugs, or improving documentation.

2.5 Commit Your Changes

Once you are satisfied with your changes, stage and commit them:

git add script.sh

git commit -m "Add new script for data processing"

2.6 Push Changes to Your Fork

Push the changes to your forked repository:

git push origin feature/new-script

2.7 Create the Pull Request

- Navigate to your forked repository on GitHub.
- You will see an option to create a pull request for your recently pushed branch. Click on Compare & pull request.
- Provide a clear title and description for your pull request, outlining what changes you made and why they are important.
- Click on the Create pull request button to submit it for review.

3. The Code Review Process

Once a pull request is created, it enters the code review phase. This is an essential step that helps maintain code quality and promotes collaboration among team members.

3.1 Reviewers' Responsibilities

The reviewers (typically project maintainers or team members) will:

- **Examine the Code**: Review the changes made in the pull request for correctness, style, and adherence to project standards.
- **Test the Changes**: Run the modified scripts to verify that they work as intended and do not introduce new bugs.
- **Provide Feedback**: Leave comments on specific lines of code, suggesting improvements, highlighting issues, or asking for clarification.

3.2 Responding to Feedback

As the author of the pull request, it's crucial to engage with the feedback received:

- **Address Comments**: Make the necessary changes based on the reviewers' suggestions. You can do this by modifying the code in your local branch, committing the changes, and pushing them back to the same branch on your fork.
- **Discuss**: If there are disagreements or questions regarding feedback, engage in constructive discussions with the reviewers to reach a consensus.

4. Merging the Pull Request

Once all feedback has been addressed and the reviewers are satisfied with the changes, the pull request can be merged into the main branch. This is typically done by a project maintainer or the person who created the pull request.

4.1 Merge Options

There are different merge strategies in Git:

- **Merge Commit**: This creates a new commit that combines the changes from the pull request with the main branch.
- **Squash and Merge**: This combines all the changes from the pull request into a single commit. This is useful for keeping the commit history clean.
- **Rebase and Merge**: This replays the commits from the pull request onto the base branch, preserving a linear commit history.

Choose the merge strategy that aligns with the project's guidelines.

5. Best Practices for Pull Requests and Code Reviews

To ensure a smooth collaboration process, consider the following best practices:

5.1 Keep Pull Requests Small

Aim to create pull requests that are small and focused on a single feature or fix. This makes it easier for reviewers to understand the changes and provide feedback.

5.2 Write Clear Descriptions

When submitting a pull request, provide a detailed description explaining the purpose of the changes, how they work, and any relevant context. This helps reviewers understand your thought process and the rationale behind your modifications.

5.3 Follow Coding Standards

Adhere to established coding standards and conventions within your project. Consistent formatting and style make it easier for others to read and understand your code.

5.4 Be Open to Feedback

Approach code reviews with an open mind and a willingness to learn. Constructive criticism is a valuable part of the development process and can lead to improved code quality and collaboration.

5.5 Review Others' Code

Participate in reviewing other team members' pull requests. This fosters a culture of collaboration and knowledge sharing, and it also helps you learn from others' coding practices.

Collaborating on Bash scripts through pull requests and code reviews is an essential aspect of software development that enhances code quality, fosters teamwork, and promotes knowledge sharing. By effectively utilizing these practices, developers can streamline their workflows, maintain high coding standards, and ultimately produce better, more reliable scripts. Embracing pull requests and code reviews not only benefits individual contributors but also strengthens the overall development process within a team or organization. As you continue your journey in Bash scripting, leverage these collaboration tools to improve your scripts and contribute to a culture of excellence in coding.

15. Case Studies and Real-world Examples

In this chapter, you'll see the practical application of the skills and techniques covered throughout the book through a series of case studies and real-world examples. We'll start by examining common automation scenarios, such as setting up automated backups, monitoring system performance, and managing user accounts, showcasing how Bash scripts can simplify these tasks. Each case study will provide a step-by-step walkthrough of the script development process, highlighting key concepts and best practices along the way. You'll also learn how to adapt and customize scripts to fit your specific needs, empowering you to tackle unique challenges in your own environment. By the end of this chapter, you'll have a wealth of practical examples at your disposal, demonstrating how to leverage your Bash skills to enhance productivity and streamline operations in various real-world situations.

15.1 Automating File Backups and Restores

Automating file backups and restores is a critical aspect of maintaining data integrity and ensuring business continuity. Bash scripting provides an effective and efficient way to create, manage, and restore backups, allowing you to safeguard your important files with minimal manual intervention. In this section, we will discuss the importance of backups, explore methods for automating the backup process using Bash scripts, and demonstrate how to restore files from these backups.

1. Understanding the Importance of Backups

Backups are essential for several reasons:

- **Data Loss Prevention**: Hardware failures, accidental deletions, or data corruption can lead to significant data loss. Regular backups ensure you can recover lost data.
- **Version Control**: Keeping backups allows you to access previous versions of files, which is particularly useful for documents that undergo frequent changes.
- **Disaster Recovery**: In case of a catastrophic event, such as a system crash or a cyberattack, backups provide a lifeline for restoring operations.
- **Compliance**: Many industries have regulations requiring data retention and backup procedures, making backups essential for compliance.

2. Backup Strategies

Before automating backups, it's crucial to choose a backup strategy that suits your needs. Common strategies include:

- **Full Backups**: A complete copy of all files and data. While thorough, full backups can be time-consuming and require significant storage space.
- **Incremental Backups**: Only the files that have changed since the last backup are copied. This method saves time and storage space.
- **Differential Backups**: Similar to incremental backups, but they copy all changes since the last full backup. While this method requires more space than incremental backups, it simplifies the restore process.

3. Automating Backups with Bash Scripts

Here, we will create a simple Bash script to automate the backup process. This script will use the tar command to create a compressed archive of specified directories or files.

3.1 Sample Backup Script

Create a Backup Directory: Start by creating a directory where backups will be stored.

mkdir -p ~/backups

Create the Backup Script: Open your favorite text editor and create a new script file named backup.sh.

nano ~/backup.sh

Add the Following Code:

```
#!/bin/bash

# Define variables
BACKUP_DIR=~/backups
SOURCE_DIR=~/important_files  # Directory you want to backup
DATE=$(date +"%Y-%m-%d_%H-%M-%S")
BACKUP_FILE="$BACKUP_DIR/backup_$DATE.tar.gz"

# Create a backup
```

```
tar -czf "$BACKUP_FILE" -C "$SOURCE_DIR" .

# Print success message
echo "Backup created at $BACKUP_FILE"
```

3.2 Explanation of the Script

Defining Variables:

- **BACKUP_DIR**: The directory where backups will be stored.
- **SOURCE_DIR**: The directory containing files you want to back up.
- **DATE**: A timestamp to differentiate backups.
- **BACKUP_FILE**: The complete path for the backup file.

Creating a Backup: The tar command creates a compressed archive of the specified directory, saving it in the designated backup directory. The -C option changes to the source directory before performing the backup, ensuring the file paths are correct.

Success Message: After the backup is created, a message is displayed to inform the user of the backup location.

3.3 Make the Script Executable

Before running the script, ensure it is executable:

```
chmod +x ~/backup.sh
```

4. Scheduling Backups with Cron Jobs

To automate the execution of the backup script, you can use a cron job. Cron is a time-based job scheduler in Unix-like operating systems that allows you to run scripts or commands at specified intervals.

4.1 Setting Up a Cron Job

Open the Crontab: Open the cron table for editing:

```
crontab -e
```

Add a New Cron Job: Add a line to schedule your backup script. For example, to run the backup every day at 2 AM, add the following line:

*0 2 * * * /bin/bash ~/backup.sh*

4.2 Explanation of the Cron Job

Schedule: The first five fields define the schedule:

- 0: Minute (0)
- 2: Hour (2 AM)
- *: Day of the month (every day)
- *: Month (every month)
- *: Day of the week (every day of the week)

Command: The command to execute, which in this case is the backup script.

5. Restoring Files from Backups

In case you need to restore files from a backup, you can create a restore script. Here's how to do it:

5.1 Create the Restore Script

Create a New Script File:

nano ~/restore.sh

Add the Following Code:

#!/bin/bash

 # Define variables
BACKUP_FILE=~/backups/backup_*.tar.gz # Use the most recent backup file
RESTORE_DIR=~/restored_files

 # Create restore directory
mkdir -p "$RESTORE_DIR"

 # Extract the latest backup

```
tar -xzf "$BACKUP_FILE" -C "$RESTORE_DIR"

# Print success message
echo "Files restored to $RESTORE_DIR"
```

5.2 Explanation of the Restore Script

BACKUP_FILE: This variable uses a wildcard (*) to identify the most recent backup file in the backups directory.

Creating the Restore Directory: The script creates a directory to store restored files.

Extracting the Backup: The tar command extracts the contents of the backup archive into the specified restore directory.

Automating file backups and restores using Bash scripts is a practical approach to ensuring data safety and availability. By leveraging Bash's scripting capabilities, you can create robust backup solutions that require minimal manual intervention. Implementing scheduled backups with cron jobs further enhances this automation, allowing you to safeguard your important files effortlessly. By creating a straightforward restore process, you can ensure that recovering lost data is as efficient as creating the backups themselves. As you continue to develop your Bash scripting skills, consider integrating these automation techniques to enhance your data management practices.

15.2 Writing System Monitoring and Health Check Scripts

Maintaining the health and performance of a system is crucial in any IT environment, whether it's a personal computer, a server, or an entire network of devices. Bash scripting provides an efficient way to automate system monitoring and health checks, allowing administrators to gather important metrics, identify issues, and take proactive measures to ensure optimal performance. In this section, we will explore how to write Bash scripts for system monitoring and health checks, covering essential metrics, common monitoring tasks, and tips for effective implementation.

1. Importance of System Monitoring

System monitoring involves continuously assessing the performance and health of your systems. The benefits of implementing system monitoring scripts include:

- **Proactive Issue Detection**: Early detection of issues such as high CPU usage, low disk space, or network connectivity problems can prevent system failures and downtime.
- **Performance Optimization**: Regular monitoring helps identify resource bottlenecks, allowing for optimization and better resource allocation.
- **Capacity Planning**: Understanding resource usage trends over time aids in planning for future needs and scaling infrastructure effectively.
- **Compliance and Reporting**: Monitoring scripts can help maintain compliance with internal and external regulations by providing logs and reports of system performance.

2. Key Metrics to Monitor

When writing system monitoring scripts, there are several key metrics to consider:

- **CPU Usage**: Monitor CPU load to identify processes that may be consuming excessive resources.
- **Memory Usage**: Track memory utilization to ensure sufficient free memory is available for applications.
- **Disk Space**: Check available disk space to prevent applications from crashing due to insufficient storage.
- **Network Usage**: Monitor incoming and outgoing network traffic to identify potential bottlenecks or unauthorized access.
- **Service Status**: Verify that essential services (e.g., web server, database) are running as expected.

3. Writing Basic Monitoring Scripts

Let's explore how to create a simple system monitoring script that checks CPU usage, memory usage, and available disk space.

3.1 Creating a Monitoring Script

Create a New Script File:

nano ~/system_monitor.sh

Add the Following Code:

#!/bin/bash

```
# Define thresholds
CPU_THRESHOLD=80
MEMORY_THRESHOLD=80
DISK_THRESHOLD=80

# Check CPU Usage
CPU_USAGE=$(top -bn1 | grep "Cpu(s)" | sed "s/.*, *\([0-9.]*\)%* id.*/\1/" | awk '{print 100 - $1}')
if (( $(echo "$CPU_USAGE > $CPU_THRESHOLD" | bc -l) )); then
    echo "Warning: High CPU Usage detected: $CPU_USAGE%"
else
    echo "CPU Usage is normal: $CPU_USAGE%"
fi

# Check Memory Usage
MEMORY_USAGE=$(free | grep Mem | awk '{print $3/$2 * 100.0}')
if (( $(echo "$MEMORY_USAGE > $MEMORY_THRESHOLD" | bc -l) )); then
    echo "Warning: High Memory Usage detected: $MEMORY_USAGE%"
else
    echo "Memory Usage is normal: $MEMORY_USAGE%"
fi

# Check Disk Usage
DISK_USAGE=$(df / | grep / | awk '{ print $5 }' | sed 's/%//g')
if [ "$DISK_USAGE" -gt "$DISK_THRESHOLD" ]; then
    echo "Warning: High Disk Usage detected: $DISK_USAGE%"
else
    echo "Disk Usage is normal: $DISK_USAGE%"
fi
```

3.2 Explanation of the Script

Defining Thresholds: We set thresholds for CPU, memory, and disk usage. If usage exceeds these thresholds, a warning will be displayed.

Checking CPU Usage:

- The top command is used to retrieve CPU usage.

- The output is parsed using grep and awk to calculate the CPU usage percentage.

Checking Memory Usage:

- The free command retrieves memory usage.
- Similar parsing is performed to compute memory usage as a percentage.

Checking Disk Usage:

- The df command checks disk space usage for the root filesystem (/).
- The output is parsed to extract the usage percentage.

Displaying Results: Based on the calculated metrics, the script displays whether the system is operating normally or if there are warnings.

3.3 Make the Script Executable

Ensure the script is executable:

chmod +x ~/system_monitor.sh

4. Scheduling Monitoring with Cron Jobs

To keep tabs on your system's health continuously, you can schedule your monitoring script to run at regular intervals using cron jobs.

4.1 Setting Up a Cron Job

Open the Crontab:

crontab -e

Add a New Cron Job: For example, to run the monitoring script every hour, add the following line:

*0 * * * * /bin/bash ~/system_monitor.sh >> ~/system_monitor.log 2>&1*

4.2 Explanation of the Cron Job

- **Schedule**: The first five fields define the schedule to run the script every hour on the hour.
- **Logging Output**: The >> ~/system_monitor.log 2>&1 part redirects both standard output and standard error to a log file for later review.

5. Advanced Monitoring Techniques

As you become more comfortable with Bash scripting, you can enhance your monitoring scripts with more advanced features:

5.1 Sending Notifications

Implement email or messaging notifications to alert you when a threshold is breached. You can use tools like mail or sendmail to send alerts.

Example of sending an email notification:

echo "Warning: High CPU Usage detected: $CPU_USAGE%" | mail -s "CPU Alert" you@example.com

5.2 Logging and Historical Data

Maintain a historical log of system metrics to analyze trends over time. You can append metrics to a CSV file for easier data analysis.

Example:

echo "$(date),$CPU_USAGE,$MEMORY_USAGE,$DISK_USAGE" >> ~/system_metrics.csv

5.3 Monitoring Specific Services

Expand your monitoring to check specific services (e.g., Apache, MySQL) to ensure they are running correctly.

Example of checking service status:

if systemctl is-active --quiet apache2; then
   echo "Apache is running."
else

```
    echo "Warning: Apache is not running!"
fi
```

Writing system monitoring and health check scripts in Bash is a powerful way to automate the assessment of your system's performance and health. By continuously monitoring key metrics such as CPU usage, memory usage, disk space, and service status, you can proactively identify and address potential issues before they escalate into critical problems. Leveraging cron jobs for scheduling and implementing advanced features like notifications and historical logging enhances the effectiveness of your monitoring scripts. As you gain experience with Bash scripting, consider expanding your monitoring capabilities to cover a broader range of metrics and services, ensuring a robust and responsive IT environment.

15.3 Data Processing: Parsing Logs and Analyzing CSV/JSON

Data processing is an essential part of system administration, where logs and structured data formats like CSV (Comma-Separated Values) and JSON (JavaScript Object Notation) are commonly used for storing and exchanging information. Bash scripting provides powerful tools for parsing these data formats, allowing system administrators and developers to automate analysis tasks, extract meaningful insights, and make informed decisions. In this section, we will explore how to effectively use Bash for data processing, focusing on parsing log files, analyzing CSV files, and working with JSON data.

1. Importance of Data Processing

Data processing is critical in various domains, including system administration, application monitoring, and data analysis. The benefits of effective data processing include:

- **Automated Reporting**: Automating the extraction of relevant information from logs and structured data formats reduces manual effort and minimizes human error.
- **Performance Monitoring**: Analyzing logs can help identify performance bottlenecks, error patterns, and system health metrics, leading to timely remediation.
- **Decision Making**: Extracting insights from data enables informed decision-making, whether for capacity planning, debugging, or operational efficiency.

2. Parsing Log Files

Log files are crucial for monitoring the behavior of applications and systems. They contain records of events, errors, and transactions that can be analyzed for various purposes.

2.1 Common Log File Formats

Log files typically consist of lines of text that may include timestamps, severity levels, messages, and other information. Common log file formats include:

- **Apache/Nginx Access Logs**: Records of web server requests, including IP addresses, requested URLs, and response codes.
- **System Logs**: Logs generated by operating systems, such as /var/log/syslog or /var/log/messages, containing system events and errors.
- **Application Logs**: Logs generated by applications, which can vary significantly in format and content.

2.2 Basic Log Parsing with Bash

Let's explore how to parse a sample Apache access log using Bash to extract useful information like the top requested URLs and the number of requests by IP address.

Sample Apache Log File: Here's an example of a line from an Apache log file:

192.168.1.1 - - [17/Oct/2024:15:30:15 +0000] "GET /index.html HTTP/1.1" 200 2326

Create a Log Parsing Script:

nano ~/parse_log.sh

Add the Following Code:

#!/bin/bash

# Define the log file path
LOG_FILE="/var/log/apache2/access.log"

Extract requested URLs and count occurrences

```
echo "Top Requested URLs:"
awk '{print $7}' $LOG_FILE | sort | uniq -c | sort -nr | head -n 10

# Count requests by IP address
echo -e "\nRequests by IP Address:"
awk '{print $1}' $LOG_FILE | sort | uniq -c | sort -nr | head -n 10
```

Explanation of the Script:

awk Command: This command is used for pattern scanning and processing. In this script:

awk '{print $7}' extracts the requested URLs (the 7th field in the log line).
awk '{print $1}' extracts the IP addresses (the 1st field).

sort and uniq Commands: These commands are used to sort and count unique occurrences.

sort sorts the output, while uniq -c counts occurrences.

The output is sorted numerically in descending order with sort -nr.

Output: The script prints the top requested URLs and the number of requests by IP address.

2.3 Make the Script Executable

Ensure the script is executable:

chmod +x ~/parse_log.sh

3. Analyzing CSV Files

CSV files are a popular format for storing tabular data. Analyzing CSV files using Bash can be straightforward, especially when you only need basic operations.

3.1 Structure of CSV Files

CSV files consist of rows of data where each row is separated by a newline and each field within a row is separated by a comma. Here's an example of a CSV file:

Name,Age,Department
Alice,30,Engineering
Bob,25,Marketing
Charlie,35,Sales

3.2 Basic CSV Analysis with Bash

Let's create a script to analyze a sample CSV file to calculate the average age of employees.

Create a Sample CSV File:

nano ~/employees.csv

Add Sample Data:

Name,Age,Department
Alice,30,Engineering
Bob,25,Marketing
Charlie,35,Sales

Create a CSV Analysis Script:

nano ~/analyze_csv.sh

Add the Following Code:

```
#!/bin/bash

# Define the CSV file path
CSV_FILE="~/employees.csv"

# Calculate the average age
total_age=0
count=0

while IFS=, read -r name age department; do
    if [[ $name != "Name" ]]; then # Skip the header line
        total_age=$((total_age + age))
```

```
        count=$((count + 1))
    fi
done < "$CSV_FILE"

if [ $count -gt 0 ]; then
    average_age=$(echo "scale=2; $total_age / $count" | bc)
    echo "Average Age: $average_age"
else
    echo "No data to analyze."
fi
```

Explanation of the Script:

Reading the CSV File: The while loop reads each line of the CSV file. The IFS=, sets the internal field separator to a comma, allowing for easy splitting of fields.

Calculating Average Age: The script skips the header line and accumulates the ages in total_age, incrementing the count for each valid entry.

Computing the Average: If there are valid entries, the average age is computed using the bc command for floating-point division.

3.3 Make the Script Executable

Ensure the script is executable:

```
chmod +x ~/analyze_csv.sh
```

4. Working with JSON Data

JSON is a lightweight data interchange format that is easy for humans to read and write and easy for machines to parse and generate. It's commonly used in web applications and APIs.

4.1 JSON Structure

JSON data is structured in key-value pairs, often nested. Here's a sample JSON object representing employee data:

```
{
```

```
  "employees": [
    {"name": "Alice", "age": 30, "department": "Engineering"},
    {"name": "Bob", "age": 25, "department": "Marketing"},
    {"name": "Charlie", "age": 35, "department": "Sales"}
  ]
}
```

4.2 Parsing JSON with jq

To analyze JSON data in Bash, you can use jq, a command-line tool for parsing and processing JSON.

Install jq (if not already installed):

sudo apt-get install jq

Create a Sample JSON File:

nano ~/employees.json

Add Sample Data:

```
{
  "employees": [
    {"name": "Alice", "age": 30, "department": "Engineering"},
    {"name": "Bob", "age": 25, "department": "Marketing"},
    {"name": "Charlie", "age": 35, "department": "Sales"}
  ]
}
```

Create a JSON Analysis Script:

nano ~/analyze_json.sh

Add the Following Code:

#!/bin/bash

 # Define the JSON file path
JSON_FILE="~/employees.json"

```
# Calculate the average age using jq
average_age=$(jq '[.employees[].age] | add / length' "$JSON_FILE")

echo "Average Age: $average_age"
```

Explanation of the Script:

Using jq: The jq command reads the JSON file, extracts the ages of employees, sums them up, and divides by the number of employees to calculate the average age.

Output: The script prints the average age of employees based on the JSON data.

4.3 Make the Script Executable

Ensure the script is executable:

```
chmod +x ~/analyze_json.sh
```

Parsing logs, analyzing CSV files, and processing JSON data are vital skills for system administrators and developers working with Bash scripting. By automating these tasks, you can efficiently extract insights from logs and structured data formats, improving decision-making and system performance. Whether you are monitoring server behavior, analyzing employee data, or integrating with APIs, mastering data processing in Bash will enhance your scripting capabilities and streamline your workflows. As you continue to explore these techniques, consider expanding your scripts with advanced features like data visualization or integrating them with other tools for comprehensive data analysis.

15.4 Web Scraping and Data Collection with Bash

Web scraping is the automated process of extracting data from websites. As data continues to grow exponentially across the internet, the ability to scrape and collect this information has become increasingly valuable for tasks such as market research, competitive analysis, and data mining. Bash, while not as commonly used for web scraping as Python or Ruby, offers several powerful tools that can be effectively utilized for this purpose. In this section, we'll explore how to perform web scraping and data collection using Bash, focusing on practical examples and tools.

1. Importance of Web Scraping

Web scraping provides numerous benefits, including:

- **Data Collection**: Automatically gathering data from various sources, making it easier to compile information for analysis.
- **Market Research**: Understanding competitor pricing, product availability, and customer reviews by collecting data from multiple e-commerce platforms.
- **Real-time Monitoring**: Tracking changes in web content, such as news articles or stock prices, to inform decision-making.
- **Aggregating Information**: Compiling data from various websites into a single dataset for easier analysis.

2. Basic Tools for Web Scraping in Bash

Several command-line tools can assist with web scraping in Bash:

2.1 curl

curl is a versatile tool for transferring data with URLs. It can send HTTP requests and retrieve data from web pages.

Example Usage:

curl -O http://example.com/data.csv

This command downloads a file named data.csv from example.com.

2.2 wget

wget is another command-line tool that retrieves files from the web using HTTP, HTTPS, and FTP protocols. It is particularly useful for downloading entire websites or directories.

Example Usage:

wget -r -l 1 -p -k http://example.com

This command recursively downloads a website while converting links to make them suitable for local viewing.

2.3 grep, awk, and sed

These text processing tools can be used to filter, format, and manipulate the data obtained from web pages.

- **grep**: Searches for specific patterns in text.
- **awk**: Processes and analyzes text files, suitable for structured data.
- **sed**: Performs text transformations on an input stream (i.e., text).

3. Example: Scraping Data from a Web Page

Let's consider a practical example of web scraping using Bash. We will scrape weather data from a publicly available API, and then format and extract useful information from the response.

3.1 Using curl to Retrieve Weather Data

Assuming we want to get the current weather data for a specific city, we can use an open API like OpenWeatherMap. First, you will need to sign up for an API key if required.

Retrieve Weather Data:

curl -s
"http://api.openweathermap.org/data/2.5/weather?q=London&appid=YOUR_API_KEY&units=metric"

Explanation:

The -s option makes curl run in silent mode, preventing progress and error messages from being displayed.

Replace YOUR_API_KEY with your actual API key.

3.2 Parsing JSON Data with jq

To extract specific fields (like temperature, weather conditions, etc.) from the JSON response, we can use jq.

Install jq:

If you haven't installed jq, you can do so with:

sudo apt-get install jq

Combine curl and jq:

We can combine the curl command with jq to extract the relevant information:

curl -s "http://api.openweathermap.org/data/2.5/weather?q=London&appid=YOUR_API_KEY&units=metric" | jq '.main.temp, .weather[0].description'

Output Example:

12.34
"clear sky"

Explanation:

- .main.temp extracts the temperature from the main object.
- .weather[0].description retrieves the description of the weather from the weather array.

4. Example: Scraping a Simple HTML Page

In some cases, you may want to scrape data from a simple HTML page directly. Let's look at how to extract specific information, such as product prices, from a hypothetical e-commerce page.

4.1 Retrieving the HTML Page

Use curl to Download the HTML:

curl -s http://example.com/products > products.html

4.2 Extracting Data with grep and sed

Assuming the HTML has prices formatted like this:

`<span class="price">$19.99</span>`

You can extract the prices using a combination of grep and sed.

Extract Prices:

grep 'class="price"' products.html | sed 's/.>\(.*\)<.*/\1/'*

Explanation:

grep 'class="price"' filters the lines containing product prices.
sed 's/.>\(.*\)<.*/\1/'* uses a regular expression to capture the price between the > and < tags.

4.3 Saving the Extracted Data

To save the extracted prices into a new file, you can redirect the output:

grep 'class="price"' products.html | sed 's/.>\(.*\)<.*/\1/' > prices.txt*

5. Scheduling Web Scraping Tasks with Cron

Once you have a working web scraping script, you may want to automate its execution using cron jobs.

5.1 Creating a Bash Script

Let's put together a complete scraping script that retrieves and saves weather data:

Create a Script:

nano ~/scrape_weather.sh

Add the Following Code:

#!/bin/bash

 # Define variables
CITY="London"

```
API_KEY="YOUR_API_KEY"
OUTPUT_FILE="weather_data.txt"

# Retrieve and parse weather data
curl -s "http://api.openweathermap.org/data/2.5/weather?q=$CITY&appid=$API_KEY&units=metric" | jq '.main.temp, .weather[0].description' > $OUTPUT_FILE

echo "Weather data saved to $OUTPUT_FILE"
```

Make the Script Executable:

```
chmod +x ~/scrape_weather.sh
```

5.2 Setting Up a Cron Job

To run the script every hour, you can set up a cron job:

Edit Crontab:

```
crontab -e
```

Add the Following Line:

```
0 * * * * /bin/bash ~/scrape_weather.sh
```

This cron job runs the scrape_weather.sh script at the start of every hour.

Web scraping with Bash is a powerful approach for automating the collection of data from the web. While there are more advanced languages and tools available for complex web scraping tasks, Bash provides sufficient capabilities for straightforward data extraction tasks. By utilizing command-line tools such as curl, wget, jq, grep, awk, and sed, you can create effective scripts for data collection and automate the scraping process with cron jobs.

As you dive deeper into web scraping, remember to respect the website's robots.txt file and terms of service to avoid violating any usage policies. Additionally, consider implementing error handling and data validation in your scripts to ensure robustness and reliability. With these skills, you can leverage the vast amounts of information available online to gain valuable insights and drive decision-making in your projects.

15.5 Building Deployment Pipelines for Applications

In today's fast-paced software development environment, delivering applications efficiently and reliably is paramount. Continuous Integration (CI) and Continuous Deployment (CD) are key practices that enable teams to automate the process of building, testing, and deploying applications. In this section, we will explore how to create deployment pipelines using Bash scripts, discuss best practices, and provide practical examples for setting up CI/CD pipelines for various types of applications.

1. Understanding Deployment Pipelines

A deployment pipeline is a series of automated processes that allow developers to build, test, and deploy their code to production environments seamlessly. This pipeline typically consists of several stages:

- **Source Stage**: Code is pushed to a version control system (e.g., Git).
- **Build Stage**: The application is compiled and packaged.
- **Test Stage**: Automated tests are executed to ensure code quality.
- **Deploy Stage**: The application is deployed to a staging or production environment.

2. Why Use Bash for Deployment Pipelines?

Bash is a powerful scripting language that can automate many aspects of the deployment process. Some reasons to use Bash for building deployment pipelines include:

- **Simplicity**: Bash scripts are easy to write and maintain.
- **Availability**: Bash is typically pre-installed on Unix-based systems, making it accessible.
- **Integration**: Bash can easily interact with other command-line tools and external services.

3. Setting Up a Basic Deployment Pipeline

Let's create a simple deployment pipeline for a web application using Bash. We will outline the essential steps, including pulling code from a repository, building the application, running tests, and deploying to a server.

3.1 Prerequisites

Before we begin, ensure that you have the following tools installed:

- **Git**: For version control.
- **Docker (optional):** For containerizing applications.
- **A Web Server**: For hosting the application (e.g., Apache, Nginx).

3.2 Example Project Structure

Assume you have a basic web application structured as follows:

```
/my-app
│
├── src/
│   └── main.py
│
├── tests/
│   └── test_main.py
│
└── Dockerfile
```

4. Creating the Deployment Script

Let's create a Bash script that will automate the deployment pipeline for our application.

Create a Deployment Script:

nano deploy.sh

Add the Following Code:

```bash
#!/bin/bash

# Define variables
REPO_URL="https://github.com/user/my-app.git"
APP_DIR="/var/www/my-app"
BRANCH="main"
```

```bash
# Function to log messages
log() {
  echo "[INFO] $(date +'%Y-%m-%d %H:%M:%S') - $1"
}

# Step 1: Clone the repository
log "Cloning repository..."
if [ ! -d "$APP_DIR" ]; then
  git clone $REPO_URL $APP_DIR
else
  cd $APP_DIR
  git pull origin $BRANCH
fi

# Step 2: Build the application (if applicable)
log "Building the application..."
cd $APP_DIR
docker build -t my-app .

# Step 3: Run tests
log "Running tests..."
if ! python3 -m unittest discover -s tests; then
  log "Tests failed. Aborting deployment."
  exit 1
fi

# Step 4: Deploy the application
log "Deploying the application..."
# Example command to start a Docker container (adjust based on your setup)
docker run -d -p 80:80 my-app

log "Deployment completed successfully!"
```

4.1 Breakdown of the Script

- **Logging Function**: The log function helps to output timestamped messages for better tracking.
- **Cloning the Repository**: The script checks if the application directory exists. If not, it clones the repository; otherwise, it pulls the latest changes.

- **Building the Application**: In this example, we use Docker to build the application. You can adjust this step based on your project's requirements.
- **Running Tests**: The script runs unit tests using Python's unittest framework. If tests fail, it aborts the deployment.
- **Deploying the Application**: This example deploys the application by running a Docker container.

5. Automating the Deployment Pipeline with CI/CD Tools

To take your deployment pipeline to the next level, you can integrate it with CI/CD tools such as Jenkins, GitLab CI, or GitHub Actions. These tools can trigger your Bash script automatically based on code changes, making your deployment process even more efficient.

5.1 Example with GitHub Actions

You can create a GitHub Actions workflow to automate the deployment process whenever you push code to the main branch.

Create a Workflow File:

Create a new file in your repository: .github/workflows/deploy.yml.

Add the Following Configuration:

name: CI/CD Pipeline

on:
 push:
  branches:
   - main

jobs:
 deploy:
  runs-on: ubuntu-latest
  steps:
   - name: Checkout code
    uses: actions/checkout@v2

   - name: Set up Docker Buildx

```
    uses: docker/setup-buildx-action@v1

- name: Build and Push
  run: |
    echo ${{ secrets.DOCKER_PASSWORD }} | docker login -u ${{ secrets.DOCKER_USERNAME }} --password-stdin
    docker build -t my-app .
    docker push my-app

- name: Deploy
  run: |
    ssh user@your-server "bash -s" < deploy.sh
```

5.2 Explanation of the Workflow

- **Triggers on Push**: The pipeline is triggered whenever code is pushed to the main branch.
- **Checkout Step**: It checks out the code from the repository.
- **Docker Setup**: Prepares the environment for building Docker images.
- **Build and Push**: Builds the Docker image and pushes it to a Docker registry.
- **Deploy Step**: It connects to your server via SSH and executes the deploy.sh script.

6. Best Practices for Building Deployment Pipelines

To ensure your deployment pipeline is efficient and reliable, consider the following best practices:

- **Version Control**: Keep your deployment scripts in version control alongside your application code.
- **Testing**: Implement automated tests for your application and ensure they are run in the pipeline.
- **Error Handling**: Make sure your scripts handle errors gracefully and provide meaningful feedback.
- **Environment Configuration**: Separate environment-specific configurations (e.g., production, staging) to avoid deployment issues.
- **Documentation**: Maintain documentation for your deployment process to help onboard new team members.

Building deployment pipelines using Bash scripts can significantly enhance your development workflow. By automating the processes of building, testing, and deploying applications, you can reduce the time and effort required to deliver high-quality software. Whether you use standalone scripts or integrate them into CI/CD tools like GitHub Actions or Jenkins, a well-defined deployment pipeline will streamline your software delivery process and ensure consistent results.

As you gain experience, you can expand your deployment pipelines with more advanced features, such as multi-environment support, notifications, or rollback strategies, to create a robust system tailored to your development team's needs.

15.6 Managing Cloud Infrastructure with Bash Scripts

In the era of cloud computing, organizations are increasingly relying on automated solutions to manage their infrastructure. Bash scripting plays a crucial role in automating tasks related to cloud resources, enabling efficient management and deployment of services across various cloud platforms. This section will explore how Bash scripts can be utilized to manage cloud infrastructure, discuss best practices, and provide practical examples for using Bash in popular cloud environments such as AWS, Google Cloud Platform (GCP), and Microsoft Azure.

1. Understanding Cloud Infrastructure Management

Cloud infrastructure management involves overseeing cloud resources such as virtual machines (VMs), databases, storage, and networking components. Effective management ensures that resources are provisioned, monitored, and scaled efficiently. Key tasks include:

- **Provisioning resources**: Creating and configuring cloud resources as needed.
- **Monitoring and reporting**: Keeping track of resource utilization, performance, and costs.
- **Scaling**: Adjusting resource capacity based on demand.
- **Automation**: Using scripts to automate repetitive tasks and workflows.

2. Why Use Bash for Cloud Management?

Bash is a powerful scripting language that provides a straightforward way to automate cloud management tasks. Some advantages of using Bash scripts for cloud infrastructure management include:

- **Simplicity and Familiarity**: Many developers and system administrators are already familiar with Bash, making it easy to adopt.
- **Integration**: Bash scripts can easily interact with cloud provider command-line interfaces (CLIs), APIs, and other command-line tools.
- **Portability**: Bash scripts can be executed on various operating systems, ensuring compatibility across different environments.

3. Setting Up Your Environment for Cloud Management

Before diving into cloud infrastructure management with Bash scripts, you need to set up your environment. Here are the steps to get started:

3.1 Installing Cloud Provider CLIs

Most cloud providers offer command-line interfaces that allow you to interact with their services directly from your terminal. Below are installation instructions for popular cloud providers:

AWS CLI:

Install the AWS Command Line Interface (CLI) by following the instructions here.

pip install awscli

Google Cloud SDK:

Install the Google Cloud SDK, which includes the gcloud command-line tool, by following the instructions here.

curl https://sdk.cloud.google.com | bash

Azure CLI:

Install the Azure CLI by following the instructions here.

curl -sL https://aka.ms/InstallAzureCLIDeb | sudo bash

3.2 Configuring Authentication

After installing the CLI tools, you need to authenticate with your cloud provider:

AWS: Run the following command to configure AWS credentials:

aws configure

Google Cloud: Authenticate using the following command:

gcloud auth login

Azure: Sign in to your Azure account with the command:

az login

4. Automating Cloud Resource Management with Bash

Once your environment is set up, you can start automating cloud management tasks using Bash scripts. Below are examples of common tasks that can be automated using Bash:

4.1 Provisioning EC2 Instances on AWS

You can use the AWS CLI to automate the creation of EC2 instances with a Bash script. Below is an example script:

```bash
#!/bin/bash

# Variables
INSTANCE_TYPE="t2.micro"
AMI_ID="ami-12345678"  # Replace with a valid AMI ID
KEY_NAME="my-key-pair"
SECURITY_GROUP="my-security-group"

# Launch an EC2 instance
aws ec2 run-instances --image-id $AMI_ID --count 1 --instance-type $INSTANCE_TYPE \
   --key-name $KEY_NAME --security-groups $SECURITY_GROUP

echo "EC2 instance launched!"
```

4.2 Creating a Google Cloud VM Instance

For GCP, you can automate the creation of VM instances with a similar script:

```bash
#!/bin/bash

# Variables
INSTANCE_NAME="my-vm"
ZONE="us-central1-a"
MACHINE_TYPE="f1-micro"
IMAGE_FAMILY="debian-10"
IMAGE_PROJECT="debian-cloud"

# Create a VM instance
gcloud compute instances create $INSTANCE_NAME --zone=$ZONE \
  --machine-type=$MACHINE_TYPE --image-family=$IMAGE_FAMILY --image-project=$IMAGE_PROJECT

echo "Google Cloud VM instance created!"
```

4.3 Managing Azure Virtual Machines

For Microsoft Azure, you can automate VM management using the Azure CLI:

```bash
#!/bin/bash

# Variables
RESOURCE_GROUP="myResourceGroup"
VM_NAME="myVM"
LOCATION="eastus"

# Create a resource group
az group create --name $RESOURCE_GROUP --location $LOCATION

# Create a virtual machine
az vm create --resource-group $RESOURCE_GROUP --name $VM_NAME \
  --image UbuntuLTS --admin-username azureuser --generate-ssh-keys

echo "Azure VM created!"
```

5. Monitoring Cloud Resources

Monitoring cloud resources is crucial for maintaining performance and cost efficiency. You can automate the monitoring process using Bash scripts combined with cloud provider CLI commands.

5.1 AWS EC2 Instance Status Check

You can use the following script to check the status of your EC2 instances:

```bash
#!/bin/bash

# Get the status of all EC2 instances
aws ec2 describe-instances --query "Reservations[*].Instances[*].{ID:InstanceId,State:State.Name}" --output table
```

5.2 GCP VM Status Check

For GCP, you can check the status of your VM instances using this script:

```bash
#!/bin/bash

# Get the status of all VM instances
gcloud compute instances list --format="table(name,status)"
```

5.3 Azure VM Status Check

For Azure, use the following command to list the status of your VMs:

```bash
#!/bin/bash

# Get the status of all VMs
az vm list --output table --query "[].{Name:name, Status:powerState}"
```

6. Best Practices for Managing Cloud Infrastructure with Bash

To ensure effective cloud infrastructure management with Bash scripts, follow these best practices:

Use Variables: Store frequently used values, such as resource IDs and regions, in variables to avoid duplication and improve readability.

Error Handling: Implement error handling in your scripts to catch and respond to failures. Use conditional statements to check the success of commands.

if ! aws ec2 describe-instances; then
  echo "Failed to describe instances."
  exit 1
fi

Modularity: Break down complex scripts into smaller functions to improve maintainability and readability.

Logging: Implement logging to track script execution and errors. This can help troubleshoot issues and understand script behavior over time.

Version Control: Store your scripts in a version control system (e.g., Git) to manage changes and collaborate with others.

Documentation: Comment your scripts thoroughly and maintain documentation to help other team members understand the scripts' purpose and usage.

Managing cloud infrastructure with Bash scripts offers a powerful way to automate repetitive tasks and streamline operations. By leveraging cloud provider CLIs, you can provision resources, monitor status, and manage configurations efficiently. As cloud environments continue to evolve, mastering Bash scripting will provide you with the tools to handle complex infrastructure challenges, ensuring that you can deliver scalable, reliable, and cost-effective solutions.

Whether you are managing AWS, GCP, or Azure resources, the principles and practices outlined in this section will serve as a solid foundation for automating cloud management tasks, enabling you to focus on building and improving your applications while ensuring that your infrastructure runs smoothly. As you gain experience, consider expanding your scripts to include more advanced features, such as integrating with cloud-native tools, using infrastructure as code (IaC) frameworks, or implementing automated scaling and deployment strategies.

16. Appendix: Useful Bash Shortcuts and Resources

In this appendix, you'll find a curated collection of useful Bash shortcuts, commands, and resources to enhance your scripting experience. We'll provide a handy cheat sheet featuring commonly used Bash commands, syntax tips, and one-liners that can save you time and improve efficiency. You'll also discover best practices for writing clean, maintainable scripts, including naming conventions and commenting strategies. Additionally, we'll compile a list of valuable resources for further learning, including books, online courses, and community forums where you can connect with other Bash enthusiasts. This chapter serves as a quick reference to reinforce your learning and help you navigate the world of Bash scripting with confidence, ensuring that you have the tools and knowledge to continue improving your skills long after finishing the book.

16.1 Bash One-liners for Everyday Tasks

Bash one-liners are compact and efficient commands that can accomplish a variety of tasks quickly, often in a single line of code. These one-liners are particularly useful for system administrators, developers, and anyone who frequently interacts with the command line. In this section, we'll explore several practical Bash one-liners that can streamline your daily tasks, enhance productivity, and showcase the power of the shell.

1. File and Directory Operations

1.1 Creating a Directory and Navigating into It

mkdir my_project && cd $_

This command creates a directory named my_project and immediately navigates into it. The $_ variable refers to the last argument of the previous command.

1.2 Listing Files with Details

ls -lh

This command lists all files and directories in the current directory with human-readable sizes. The -l option displays details, while -h formats the sizes in a more readable way.

1.3 Searching for Files

find . -name ".txt"*

This command searches the current directory (and its subdirectories) for all .txt files. The . indicates the current directory, and the -name option allows pattern matching.

1.4 Deleting Empty Directories

find . -type d -empty -delete

This one-liner finds and deletes all empty directories in the current directory and its subdirectories.

1.5 Copying Files with Progress

cp --progress source.txt destination.txt

This command copies source.txt to destination.txt while showing the progress of the copy operation.

2. Text Processing

2.1 Displaying the First 10 Lines of a File

head -n 10 file.txt

This command displays the first ten lines of file.txt, which is helpful for quickly previewing its contents.

2.2 Displaying the Last 10 Lines of a File

tail -n 10 file.txt

Conversely, this command displays the last ten lines of file.txt.

2.3 Searching for a Pattern in a File

grep "pattern" file.txt

This command searches for the specified pattern within file.txt and outputs matching lines.

2.4 Replacing Text in a File

sed -i 's/old_text/new_text/g' file.txt

This one-liner uses sed to replace all occurrences of old_text with new_text in file.txt. The -i option edits the file in place.

2.5 Counting the Number of Lines in a File

wc -l < file.txt

This command counts and outputs the number of lines in file.txt.

3. System Monitoring and Management

3.1 Checking Disk Usage

*du -sh **

This command displays the disk usage of all files and directories in the current directory, summarizing the output in a human-readable format (-h).

3.2 Monitoring System Resource Usage

top -b -n 1 | head -n 20

This command runs top in batch mode (-b) for one iteration (-n 1), showing the top 20 processes by CPU usage.

3.3 Displaying System Uptime

uptime

This simple command shows how long the system has been running, including the current time, how many users are logged in, and the load averages.

3.4 Checking Memory Usage

free -h

This command displays the system's memory usage in a human-readable format, showing total, used, and free memory.

4. Networking

4.1 Checking Connectivity to a Host

ping -c 4 google.com

This command sends four ping requests to google.com to check network connectivity.

4.2 Downloading a File

curl -O https://example.com/file.zip

This command uses curl to download a file from a specified URL, saving it with the same name as on the server.

4.3 Checking Open Ports

netstat -tuln

This command lists all open TCP and UDP ports, providing insight into active network services.

4.4 Tracing the Route to a Host

traceroute google.com

This command traces the route packets take to reach google.com, which can help diagnose network issues.

5. Process Management

5.1 Killing a Process by Name

pkill -f process_name

This command terminates all processes matching the specified process_name.

5.2 Finding and Killing a Process

kill $(pgrep process_name)

This one-liner finds the process ID(s) of process_name using pgrep and then kills it.

5.3 Checking Running Processes

ps aux | grep process_name

This command lists all running processes and filters the output to show only those related to process_name.

6. File Compression and Archiving

6.1 Compressing Files with gzip

gzip file.txt

This command compresses file.txt, creating file.txt.gz.

6.2 Extracting a .tar.gz File

tar -xzvf archive.tar.gz

This command extracts the contents of archive.tar.gz while displaying the file names being extracted.

6.3 Creating a .tar Archive

tar -cvf archive.tar directory/

This command creates a .tar archive of the specified directory.

7. Custom Aliases

7.1 Creating a Quick Access Alias

alias ll='ls -lah'

This command creates an alias ll for ls -lah, allowing you to list files with detailed information quickly.

Bash one-liners are invaluable tools for streamlining everyday tasks and enhancing productivity in the command line. By mastering these one-liners, you can automate repetitive tasks, manipulate files, manage processes, and monitor system performance efficiently. As you become more familiar with Bash, consider customizing your one-liners and creating aliases to further optimize your workflow. Whether you're a beginner or an experienced user, integrating these techniques into your daily routine can significantly improve your efficiency and effectiveness in working with the shell.

16.2 Creating Your Own Bash Shortcuts and Aliases

Bash shortcuts and aliases are powerful features that allow users to create custom commands, streamline workflows, and improve efficiency when working in the command line. By defining shortcuts for frequently used commands or complex command sequences, you can save time and reduce typing effort. In this section, we will explore how to create and manage your own Bash shortcuts and aliases, making your shell environment more tailored to your needs.

What are Bash Aliases?

Aliases are essentially shortcuts that allow you to define a new name for an existing command. When you type the alias name, the shell interprets it as the associated command. This feature is particularly useful for simplifying lengthy commands or making them easier to remember.

Creating Aliases

To create an alias, you can use the alias command followed by the desired shortcut name and the command you want to associate with it. The syntax is as follows:

alias shortcut_name='command'

Example 1: Simple Alias

For example, if you frequently use the ls -l command to list files in long format, you can create an alias:

alias ll='ls -l'

Now, typing ll in the terminal will execute ls -l, providing a quick way to view file details.

Example 2: Complex Command Alias

You can also create aliases for more complex commands. For instance, if you often need to navigate to a specific directory and list its contents, you can define:

alias docs='cd ~/Documents && ls -l'

With this alias, typing docs will take you to your Documents folder and list the files inside it in long format.

Making Aliases Persistent

By default, aliases created in the terminal are temporary and will disappear once you close the terminal session. To make your aliases persistent, you need to add them to your Bash configuration file, typically located at ~/.bashrc or ~/.bash_profile. Here's how to do it:

Open your .bashrc or .bash_profile file in a text editor. For example:

nano ~/.bashrc

Add your aliases at the end of the file:

alias ll='ls -l'
alias docs='cd ~/Documents && ls -l'

Save the changes and exit the editor (in nano, press CTRL + X, then Y, and Enter).

To apply the changes to your current terminal session, run:

source ~/.bashrc

Viewing Your Aliases

To view all currently defined aliases in your terminal session, you can simply type:

alias

This command will list all the aliases that have been created, allowing you to verify that your new aliases are set up correctly.

Removing Aliases

If you need to remove an alias, you can use the unalias command followed by the alias name:

unalias shortcut_name

For example, if you want to remove the ll alias, you would run:

unalias ll

To make the removal permanent, also remove the corresponding line from your ~/.bashrc or ~/.bash_profile.

Creating Functions for More Complex Shortcuts

For more complex sequences of commands that cannot be effectively handled with simple aliases, you can create functions. Functions allow you to define a series of commands that can be executed with a single command name.

Defining a Bash Function

Here's the syntax to define a function:

function_name() {
  command1
  command2
   ...
}

Example: Custom Backup Function

Suppose you frequently back up a specific directory. You can create a function for this:

```
backup() {
  cp -r ~/Documents/my_project ~/Backups/my_project_$(date +%F)
}
```

With this function, you can quickly back up the my_project directory to your Backups folder, appending the current date to the backup folder name.

To make this function persistent, add it to your ~/.bashrc or ~/.bash_profile, and remember to run source ~/.bashrc after editing.

Tips for Creating Effective Aliases and Shortcuts

Keep It Short and Memorable: Choose names that are easy to remember and quick to type. For example, gs for git status is much faster than typing the full command.

Use Descriptive Names: When possible, use names that describe the action they perform. For example, update_packages for a command that updates system packages.

Avoid Overwriting Important Commands: Be careful not to create aliases that conflict with existing commands. For instance, don't alias ls to something else, as this is a fundamental command.

Comment Your Aliases: Adding comments in your .bashrc file helps you remember why you created each alias. For example:

```
# Alias for listing files in long format
alias ll='ls -l'
```

Test New Aliases: Before adding an alias to your configuration file, test it in the terminal to ensure it works as intended.

Creating your own Bash shortcuts and aliases is a powerful way to streamline your workflow and increase productivity in the command line environment. By defining aliases for frequently used commands and creating functions for more complex operations, you can customize your shell to fit your specific needs. This section has provided the tools and examples needed to start building your personalized Bash environment, allowing you to work more efficiently and effectively. As you continue to use Bash, you'll find even more opportunities to create shortcuts that save time and effort in your daily tasks.

16.3 Common Gotchas and Pitfalls in Bash Scripting

Bash scripting is a powerful tool that allows users to automate tasks, streamline workflows, and manage system configurations. However, as with any programming or scripting language, there are common pitfalls and gotchas that can lead to unexpected behavior, errors, or inefficiencies. This section will explore some of the most prevalent issues that beginners and even experienced users might encounter when writing Bash scripts, along with tips on how to avoid or mitigate them.

1. Not Quoting Variables

One of the most common mistakes in Bash scripting is failing to quote variables. When variables contain spaces, special characters, or are empty, omitting quotes can lead to unexpected results or script failures.

Example of a Gotcha:

```
my_var="Hello World"
echo $my_var   # Outputs: Hello World
echo $my_var > file.txt  # Redirects 'Hello' to file.txt, ignores 'World'
```

Solution: Always quote your variables.

```
echo "$my_var"   # Outputs: Hello World
```

2. Misusing Conditionals

When using if statements, a common error is to forget to use double brackets or single brackets correctly. Additionally, users often confuse the equality operators between strings and integers.

Example of a Gotcha:

```
num=10
if [ $num = 10 ]; then   # Incorrect for integer comparison
    echo "Ten"
```

fi

Solution: Use the appropriate operators for comparison.

if ["$num" -eq 10]; then   # Correct for integer comparison
   echo "Ten"
fi

3. Unintended Word Splitting

Bash automatically splits words based on spaces, which can lead to unexpected behavior if you're not careful.

Example of a Gotcha:

my_array=("one" "two three" "four")
for item in "${my_array[@]}"; do
   echo $item
done

Output:

one
two
three
four

Solution: Always quote your variable expansions when iterating over arrays.

for item in "${my_array[@]}"; do
   echo "$item"
done

4. Forgetting to Declare Arrays

When working with arrays, forgetting to declare them properly can lead to confusion and errors.

Example of a Gotcha:

```
my_array[0]="one"
my_array[1]="two"
my_array[2]="three"

echo ${my_array[*]}  # Outputs: one two three
```

Mistake: Accessing non-declared indices can lead to unexpected results or errors.

Solution: Always initialize your arrays explicitly and check their indices.

```
my_array=()  # Declare the array
my_array=("one" "two" "three")  # Initialize
```

5. Exit Status Misinterpretation

Every command in Bash returns an exit status (0 for success, non-zero for failure). Failing to check the exit status of commands can lead to scripts that appear to work but silently fail.

Example of a Gotcha:

```
cp non_existent_file.txt destination_folder
if [ $? -eq 0 ]; then
    echo "File copied successfully."
fi
```

Solution: Use the set -e option at the beginning of your script to exit immediately on error, or use more explicit error handling.

```
set -e  # Exit on error
cp non_existent_file.txt destination_folder
echo "File copied successfully."
```

6. Incorrect Use of * in Patterns

Using the * wildcard incorrectly can lead to unintended matches or failures.

Example of a Gotcha:

```
for file in *; do
```

```
    echo "Processing $file"
done
```

This will include all files in the current directory, including unintended files like . and ...

Solution: Be specific in your patterns or add conditions to filter results.

```
for file in *.txt; do  # Only process .txt files
    echo "Processing $file"
done
```

7. Assuming Variables are Set

In scripts, it's easy to assume that a variable has been set, especially when passing values between functions or subshells. If a variable isn't set, it can lead to confusion.

Example of a Gotcha:

```
my_function() {
    echo "$my_var"  # Assume my_var is set
}

my_function
```

Solution: Use default values or check if a variable is set.

```
my_var="${my_var:-default_value}"  # Set default if not already set
my_function() {
    echo "$my_var"
}
```

8. Using = Instead of == in String Comparisons

In Bash, using a single equals sign = is valid for string comparisons, but using == is also valid within double brackets. Using = in double brackets can sometimes lead to unexpected results.

Example of a Gotcha:

```
if [[ $string = "test" ]]; then   # Works, but it's better to use '=='
```

```
    echo "Matched"
fi
```

Solution: Use == when using double brackets.

```
if [[ $string == "test" ]]; then
    echo "Matched"
fi
```

9. Neglecting Shell Compatibility

Scripts that work in Bash may not work in other shells (like Dash or Sh). Neglecting to specify the correct shebang line or using Bash-specific features in other shells can lead to script failures.

Example of a Gotcha:

```
#!/bin/sh
array=("one" "two" "three")  # Bash-specific syntax
```

Solution: Use the appropriate shebang and test scripts in the intended environment.

```
#!/bin/bash
array=("one" "two" "three")
```

10. Ignoring Safety Practices

Many users neglect to implement safety practices in their scripts, which can lead to unintended data loss or damage.

Example of a Gotcha:

```
rm -rf /some/important/directory
```

Solution: Implement safety checks and confirmation prompts.

```
read -p "Are you sure you want to delete this directory? (y/n) " choice
if [[ "$choice" == "y" ]]; then
    rm -rf /some/important/directory
fi
```

Bash scripting can be a highly effective way to automate tasks and manage system operations. However, being aware of common pitfalls and gotchas is crucial for writing efficient and error-free scripts. By paying attention to quoting, variable handling, conditionals, and shell compatibility, you can avoid many of the pitfalls that lead to frustration and unexpected behavior. As you develop your Bash scripting skills, keep these common issues in mind, and you'll be well on your way to creating robust and efficient scripts that improve your productivity and system management capabilities.

16.4 Best Bash Practices and Coding Style Guide

Bash scripting is a powerful tool for automating tasks and managing system configurations, but writing clear, maintainable, and efficient scripts requires adherence to certain best practices and coding standards. A consistent coding style not only improves readability but also helps prevent errors and facilitates collaboration with other developers. This section outlines essential best practices and a coding style guide that can help you write better Bash scripts.

1. Use Meaningful Names

Choosing clear and descriptive names for variables, functions, and scripts is crucial for readability and maintainability. Avoid cryptic abbreviations and opt for names that reflect the purpose of the entity.

Example:

```
# Poor naming
f1() { echo "Hello"; }

# Better naming
greet_user() { echo "Hello"; }
```

2. Comment Your Code

Comments help explain the purpose and functionality of your code, making it easier for others (and yourself) to understand it later. Use comments generously, especially for complex logic or non-obvious decisions.

Example:

```bash
# Check if the directory exists before creating it
if [ ! -d "$DIR" ]; then
    mkdir "$DIR"  # Create the directory
fi
```

3. Follow a Consistent Indentation Style

Consistent indentation helps improve readability. Choose a style (e.g., 2 spaces, 4 spaces, or tabs) and stick with it throughout your script. Most Bash scripts prefer spaces over tabs.

Example:

```bash
if [ "$condition" ]; then
    echo "Condition is true"
else
    echo "Condition is false"
fi
```

4. Quote Variables Properly

Always quote your variables to prevent word splitting and globbing. This is especially important when dealing with user input or filenames.

Example:

```bash
echo "$my_variable"  # Correct
echo $my_variable    # Incorrect if $my_variable contains spaces
```

5. Use set -e and set -u

Using set -e ensures that your script exits immediately if any command returns a non-zero exit status, which helps catch errors early. set -u will cause the script to exit if you try to use an uninitialized variable.

Example:

```bash
set -e  # Exit on error
set -u  # Exit on uninitialized variable
```

6. Use Functions to Organize Code

Break your script into smaller, reusable functions to improve modularity and readability. Each function should perform a specific task, making it easier to test and maintain.

Example:

```
function backup_files() {
   # Function to back up files
   cp -r "$1" "$2"
}

backup_files "/path/to/source" "/path/to/destination"
```

7. Handle Errors Gracefully

Implement error handling to provide informative messages and avoid silent failures. Use exit codes to indicate the success or failure of operations.

Example:

```
if ! cp "$source" "$destination"; then
   echo "Error: Failed to copy $source to $destination" >&2
   exit 1
fi
```

8. Avoid Hardcoding Values

Avoid hardcoding values like paths, filenames, or configuration settings directly in your script. Instead, use variables or configuration files to make your scripts more flexible and easier to modify.

Example:

```
# Poor practice
backup_dir="/backup/$(date +%Y-%m-%d)"

# Better practice
backup_dir="${BACKUP_DIR:-/default/backup}/$(date +%Y-%m-%d)"
```

9. Keep Your Scripts Portable

When writing Bash scripts, aim for portability by avoiding Bash-specific features if you expect your script to run in other shells. Use POSIX-compliant syntax wherever possible.

Example:

```
# Avoid using Bash-specific arrays if portability is a concern
# Use a simple string manipulation or external tools instead
```

10. Use Arrays for List Management

When dealing with lists of items, use arrays instead of space-separated strings. This prevents issues with word splitting and makes it easier to manage the list.

Example:

```
# Using an array
my_array=("item1" "item2" "item3")
for item in "${my_array[@]}"; do
    echo "$item"
done
```

11. Validate User Input

When accepting user input, validate it to ensure it meets expected formats or criteria. This helps prevent errors and enhances security.

Example:

```
read -p "Enter your age: " age
if ! [[ "$age" =~ ^[0-9]+$ ]]; then
    echo "Error: Please enter a valid number." >&2
    exit 1
fi
```

12. Structure Your Scripts with a Header

Include a header comment in your scripts to provide metadata such as the script name, author, date, purpose, and usage instructions. This helps others understand the context and intent of the script quickly.

Example:

#!/bin/bash
Script Name: backup.sh
Author: Your Name
Date: 2024-10-17
Purpose: Back up specified files to a designated directory
Usage: ./backup.sh /path/to/source /path/to/destination

13. Use trap for Cleanup

When dealing with temporary files or processes, use the trap command to ensure that resources are cleaned up, even if your script exits unexpectedly.

Example:

trap 'rm -f /tmp/tempfile' EXIT
Create a temporary file
touch /tmp/tempfile

14. Regularly Test and Debug Your Scripts

Test your scripts in a controlled environment before deploying them. Use debugging options like set -x to trace command execution and identify issues.

Example:

set -x # Enable debugging
Your script here
set +x # Disable debugging

15. Document Your Code

In addition to inline comments, consider maintaining external documentation that outlines the script's functionality, usage examples, and any dependencies or environment requirements.

By following these best practices and coding style guidelines, you can create Bash scripts that are not only functional but also maintainable, readable, and efficient. Good coding practices lead to fewer errors, easier debugging, and improved collaboration with other developers. As you gain experience in Bash scripting, remember that clarity and maintainability are just as important as functionality. Embrace these practices, and you'll set yourself up for success in your scripting endeavors.

16.5 Essential Bash Resources and Documentation

Bash scripting is a powerful skill that can greatly enhance your productivity and efficiency in managing tasks on Unix-like systems. However, to become proficient, it's essential to have access to quality resources and documentation. This section provides a curated list of essential Bash resources that can help you learn, reference, and troubleshoot Bash scripting effectively.

1. Official Bash Documentation

The most authoritative resource for Bash is its official documentation, which includes the Bash manual and reference material.

Bash Reference Manual: This comprehensive guide covers all aspects of Bash, including syntax, built-in commands, and programming constructs. You can find it here.

Bash FAQ: The FAQ provides answers to common questions about Bash and its features. It's a great starting point for troubleshooting and understanding specific topics. Available here.

2. Online Tutorials and Guides

Numerous online resources offer tutorials ranging from beginner to advanced levels. These can be extremely helpful for self-paced learning.

The Linux Documentation Project: This site hosts several guides on Bash scripting, including "Bash Guide for Beginners" and "Bash Guide for Advanced Users." Check it out here.

Bash Academy: An educational platform that provides free interactive Bash scripting tutorials for beginners. The content is user-friendly and well-structured. Visit the Bash Academy here.

Shell Scripting Tutorial: This comprehensive tutorial covers the basics of shell scripting, with clear examples and explanations. You can access it here.

3. Books on Bash Scripting

Books provide in-depth knowledge and structured learning paths. Here are some highly recommended titles:

"Learning the bash Shell" by Cameron Newham: This book is an excellent resource for beginners, covering both basic and advanced concepts in Bash scripting.

"Bash Cookbook" by Carl Albing, Joe Baker, and Mike Gnu: This book offers practical recipes for common scripting tasks, ideal for those looking to expand their skills through hands-on examples.

"Pro Bash Programming" by Chris F.A. Johnson: Aimed at experienced programmers, this book delves into advanced scripting techniques and best practices.

4. Online Forums and Communities

Engaging with communities can provide support and insights from experienced Bash users.

Stack Overflow: A popular Q&A platform where you can ask questions and find answers related to Bash scripting. Make sure to search for existing questions before posting. Visit Stack Overflow.

Reddit: Subreddits like r/bash and r/linux offer discussions, tips, and shared experiences related to Bash and Linux scripting.

Unix & Linux Stack Exchange: This is another great resource for asking technical questions about Bash and Unix systems. You can visit it here.

5. Online Course Platforms

If you prefer structured learning, consider enrolling in online courses that focus on Bash scripting.

Coursera: Offers courses such as "Linux Shell Scripting: A Project-Based Approach to Learning" which covers the basics and advanced topics in Bash scripting.

edX: The platform has courses from various universities that include Bash scripting as part of broader programming or Linux system administration topics.

Udemy: Numerous courses on Bash scripting can be found here, covering a range of topics from beginner to advanced. Look for courses with high ratings and reviews for the best experience.

6. Cheat Sheets and Quick Reference Guides

Cheat sheets can serve as handy references for common commands and scripting syntax.

Bash Cheat Sheet: Websites like Cheatography provide downloadable cheat sheets that summarize essential commands and constructs.

GitHub Repositories: Many GitHub repositories offer curated cheat sheets and quick reference guides for Bash scripting.

7. Tools for Bash Development

Using the right tools can streamline your Bash scripting workflow.

Text Editors: Editors like Visual Studio Code, Atom, and Sublime Text have plugins and extensions that enhance Bash scripting, such as syntax highlighting, code completion, and debugging tools.

ShellCheck: This is a static analysis tool for shell scripts that helps you identify and correct common scripting mistakes. You can use it online or install it on your system. Visit ShellCheck.

8. Videos and Tutorials on YouTube

YouTube hosts countless tutorials and videos on Bash scripting, providing visual demonstrations that can aid learning.

Search for channels that specialize in programming and Linux tutorials, such as "The Net Ninja" and "ProgrammingKnowledge," which frequently upload quality content related to Bash scripting.

In the realm of Bash scripting, a wealth of resources exists to aid your learning and mastery of the subject. By utilizing official documentation, online tutorials, books, community forums, online courses, cheat sheets, and development tools, you can cultivate a deep understanding of Bash scripting. Continuous practice and engagement with the community will enhance your skills and ensure you stay up-to-date with the latest practices in the field. Whether you're a novice looking to learn the basics or an experienced programmer seeking advanced techniques, these resources will support your journey into the world of Bash scripting.

16.6 Popular Bash Scripting Libraries and Tools

Bash scripting is a versatile skill that allows you to automate tasks and manage system operations efficiently. To enhance the capabilities of your Bash scripts, several libraries and tools can help streamline your workflows, add functionality, and improve script readability. This section highlights popular Bash scripting libraries and tools that can elevate your scripting game.

1. ShellCheck

Description: ShellCheck is a static analysis tool designed to identify issues in shell scripts. It helps you catch common mistakes, such as syntax errors, improper use of variables, and potential bugs.

Key Features:

- Provides warnings and suggestions to improve script quality.
- Offers explanations for each warning to help you learn.
- Can be used as a command-line tool or integrated into text editors.

Installation: ShellCheck can be installed using package managers like apt, brew, or downloaded from its GitHub repository.

2. Bash-completion

Description: Bash-completion is a library that adds programmable completion to Bash commands. It allows you to use tab completion for various commands, making it easier to work with options, files, and arguments.

Key Features:

- Supports completion for many command-line tools, improving productivity.
- Customizable for user-defined scripts and commands.
- Reduces the chances of typing errors by suggesting available options.

Installation: Many Linux distributions come with bash-completion pre-installed. If not, it can usually be installed via the package manager (e.g., apt install bash-completion).

3. jq

Description: jq is a lightweight and flexible command-line JSON processor. It allows you to easily parse, filter, and manipulate JSON data directly from your Bash scripts.

Key Features:

- Supports complex queries to extract specific data from JSON.
- Can convert JSON to various formats, including CSV.
- Ideal for working with APIs that return JSON responses.

Installation: jq can be installed using package managers like apt, brew, or downloaded from the jq website.

4. curl

Description: curl is a command-line tool for transferring data with URLs. It supports various protocols, including HTTP, HTTPS, FTP, and more, making it a powerful tool for web-related tasks.

Key Features:

- Allows sending and receiving data in a variety of formats.
- Supports authentication, file uploads, and more.
- Can be used to interact with REST APIs directly from your scripts.

Installation: curl is typically pre-installed on most Linux distributions and macOS. If not, it can be installed via the package manager (e.g., apt install curl).

5. GNU Parallel

Description: GNU Parallel is a shell tool for executing jobs in parallel using one or more computers. It allows you to speed up tasks by running multiple processes simultaneously.

Key Features:

- Supports executing commands with multiple input sources, improving efficiency.
- Can be used to distribute workloads across multiple CPU cores or machines.
- Offers advanced features for job management and output handling.

Installation: GNU Parallel can be installed using package managers (e.g., apt install parallel) or downloaded from its website.

6. Ansible

Description: Ansible is an open-source automation tool that simplifies configuration management, application deployment, and task automation. While it's not solely a Bash tool, it allows for writing Bash scripts as part of its playbooks.

Key Features:

- Uses YAML syntax for defining automation tasks, making it easy to read and write.
- Supports a wide range of modules for different tasks, including system administration.
- Facilitates orchestration of complex multi-server deployments.

Installation: Ansible can be installed via pip, apt, or brew. More information is available on the Ansible website.

7. Docker

Description: Docker is a platform for developing, shipping, and running applications in containers. While Docker itself is not a Bash scripting library, it allows you to automate the deployment of applications using Bash scripts.

Key Features:

- Enables consistent environment setup across different machines.
- Facilitates continuous integration and deployment workflows.
- Can be integrated into Bash scripts for container management.

Installation: Docker can be installed following the instructions on the Docker website.

8. Fig

Description: Fig is a tool that enhances your command-line experience by adding autocomplete and snippets for Bash, Zsh, and Fish. It improves efficiency by providing suggestions as you type.

Key Features:

- Offers contextual suggestions based on commands.
- Allows you to create custom snippets and workflows.
- Improves productivity by reducing the need to remember commands.

Installation: Fig can be installed from its official website.

9. Netcat (nc)

Description: Netcat is a versatile networking utility that can read and write data across network connections using TCP or UDP. It's often referred to as the "Swiss Army knife" of networking.

Key Features:

- Can be used for network debugging, data transfer, and port scanning.
- Useful for creating simple server-client setups.
- Supports various protocols and options for customization.

Installation: Netcat is typically included in most Linux distributions. If not, it can be installed via the package manager (e.g., apt install netcat).

10. Fzf

Description: fzf is a command-line fuzzy finder that allows you to search and filter through lists quickly. It can be integrated into your Bash scripts to improve interactivity.

Key Features:

- Provides a fast and efficient way to search through command history, files, and directories.
- Supports custom actions and integrations with other tools.
- Enhances productivity by reducing the time spent searching.

Installation: fzf can be installed via package managers, GitHub, or through its installation instructions.

11. Bash-it

Description: Bash-it is a collection of community Bash commands and scripts that enhance your command-line experience. It includes themes, plugins, and aliases for everyday tasks.

Key Features:

- Provides pre-defined commands, aliases, and functions.
- Offers customizable themes to change your shell prompt.
- Helps streamline your command-line workflow.

Installation: Follow the instructions on the Bash-it GitHub repository.

Incorporating libraries and tools into your Bash scripting can significantly enhance your productivity and efficiency. From static analysis with ShellCheck to parallel processing with GNU Parallel and network management with Netcat, these resources will provide you with a wealth of options to expand your Bash scripting capabilities. By leveraging these tools, you can automate complex tasks, streamline workflows, and create more robust scripts that improve your overall efficiency in managing system tasks. Whether you're a beginner or an experienced scripter, exploring these libraries and tools will enhance your Bash scripting journey.

The Bash Programmer's Guide: Writing Efficient Shell Scripts is your definitive resource for mastering the art of Bash scripting. Whether you're a system administrator, DevOps engineer, or simply someone who works in a Linux or Unix environment, this guide provides a comprehensive, step-by-step approach to writing powerful and efficient shell scripts.

Starting from the basics, the book introduces you to the foundational elements of Bash scripting, including syntax, file operations, and process management. As you progress, you'll dive deeper into advanced topics such as error handling, performance optimization, and integrating Bash with external tools and APIs. Real-world examples and case studies show how to automate everyday tasks, manage systems, and enhance productivity through well-crafted scripts.

Key concepts covered include:

1. Writing and running scripts from scratch
2. Using conditionals, loops, and functions for modular design
3. Handling command-line arguments and user inputs
4. Optimizing script performance and resource usage
5. Debugging, error handling, and writing secure scripts
6. Working with external tools, cloud services, and APIs
7. Version controlling scripts with Git and collaborating effectively

With practical examples, best practices, and clear explanations, this guide is perfect for both beginners and experienced scripters looking to enhance their skills. By the end of this book, you'll have the knowledge and confidence to write efficient, maintainable, and scalable Bash scripts for any project.

Let The Bash Programmer's Guide be your go-to reference for taking full advantage of the power of Bash!

www.ingramcontent.com/pod-product-compliance
Lightning Source LLC
Chambersburg PA
CBHW082243220526
45469CB00009B/2858